Hiking the Dream

A family's four-month trek along the Trans Canada Trail

Kathy (Belmore) Didkowsky

NIMBUS
PUBLISHING LTD

This book is dedicated to ...

my children, Nora, Maria, and Nicholas, for the countless hours they walked beside me on the trail and for sharing this incredible journey.

my husband, John, who listens to my dreams and whose love, and moral and financial support gave us strength along the way.

my brother Rod and my niece Julie, who crossed the biggest mountain of all.

all those heroes who worked on the Canadian Railway.

Copyright © Kathy Didkowsky, 2002

www.spiritadventure.com

All rights reserved. No part of this book may be reproduced, stored in a retrieval system or transmitted in any form or by any means without the prior written permission from the publisher, or, in the case of photocopying or other reprographic copying, permission from CANCOPY (Canadian Copyright Licensing Agency), 1 Yonge Street, Suite 1900, Toronto, Ontario M5E 1E5.

Nimbus Publishing Limited
PO Box 9166, Halifax, NS   B3K 5M8
(902) 455-4286

Printed and bound in Canada
Design: Kathy Kaulbach, Paragon Design Group

National Library of Canada Cataloguing in Publication Data

> Didkowsky, Kathy Belmore, 1950-
> Hiking the dream : a family's four-month trek along the Trans Canada Trail

Includes bibliographical references.
ISBN 1-55109-396-0

1. Trans Canada Trail—Description and travel. 2. Didkowsky, Kathy Belmore, 1950- —Journeys—Canada. 3. Didkowsky family. I. Title.

FC75.D52 2002   917.104'648   C2002-900615-5
F1017.D52 2002

Canadä   The Canada Council | Le Conseil des Arts
          for the Arts | du Canada

We acknowledge the financial support of the Government of Canada through the Book Publishing Industry Development Program (BPIDP) and the Canada Council for our publishing activities.

Table of Contents

Acknowledgements vi
Foreword v
Personality profiles ix

Newfoundland 1
May 6   St John's to Topsail Pond
May 7   Brigus Junction to Whitbourne
May 8   Arnold's Cove to Come By Chance
May 9   Kitty's Brook to Pond Crossing
May 10 Woody Point
May 11 Western Brook, Gros Morne
May 12 Corner Brook
May 13 Black Duck Siding to St. George's
May 14 Robinsons to Codroy Pond
May 15 MacDougall's Gulch to Port aux Basques
May 16 Port aux Basques, Rest day
May 17 Ferry to Nova Scotia

Nova Scotia 31
May 18 Shenacadie to Grand Narrows
May 19 Grand Narrows to Ottawa Brook
May 20 Mabou to Port Hood
May 21 Long Point to Judique
May 22 Judique to Creignish
May 23 Guysborough
May 24 Tidnish
May 25 Wallace to Tatamagouche
May 26 Tatamagouche to River John
May 27 Meadowville to Pictou

Prince Edward Island 55
May 28 Wood Islands to Murray River
May 29 Montague to Georgetown
May 30 Souris to Elmira
May 31 Selkirk to Morell
June 1 Bethel to Glenroy
June 2 Bedford to Charlottetown
June 3 Winsloe to Hunter River
June 4 Cavendish
June 5 Alma to Tignish
June 6 Wellington to Summerside
June 7 P.E.I. to New Brunswick

New Brunswick 85
June 8   Waterfowl Park, Sackville
June 9   Oromocto to Fredericton
June 10 Durham Bridge, Rest day
June 11 Fredericton to Keswick
June 12 Grafton to Hartland
June 13 Hartland to Florenceville
June 14 Florenceville to Upper Kent
June 15 Upper Kent to Perth Andover
June 16 Perth Andover to Brooks Bridge
June 17 Mulherin to Grand Falls

Quebec 119
June 18 St. Jacques to Dégelis
June 19 Dégelis to Notre-Dame-du-Lac
June 20 Cabano to St-Honoré
June 21 St-Simeon
June 22 Chute Fraser to La Malbaie
June 23 St. Irene to Les Emboulements (Quebec City)
June 24 Victoriaville to Warwick
June 25 Kingsey Falls to Danville
June 26 Magog to Eastman
June 27 Eastman to Waterloo
June 28 Montreal

Ontario 149
June 29 Hull to Ottawa
June 30 Ottawa River to Bells Corners
July 1   Ottawa, Rest day
July 2   Magnetawan
July 3   North Bay
July 4   North Bay to Goulais River (drive day)
July 5   Goulais River
July 6   Tremblay to Michipicoten Harbor
July 7   Neys, Thunder Bay
July 8   Ignace
July 9   Dinorwic and Kenora

Manitoba 181
July 10 West Hawk Lake to Falcon Lake
July 11 Birds Hill Park
July 12 Winnipeg, Rest day
July 13 Spirit Sands Desert
July 14 Carberry to Wellwood
July 15 Wellwood to Neepawa
July 16 Neepawa to Clanwilliam

Table of Contents

July 17   Erikson to Sandy Lake
July 18   Sandy Lake to Elphinstone
July 19   Elphinstone to Oakburn
July 20   Vista to Birdtail
July 21   Russell to Lake of the Prairies

Saskatchewan 209
July 22   Good Spirit Lake
July 23   Melville
July 24   Crooked Lake
July 25   Katepwa, Labret
July 26   Lumsden
July 27   Buffalo Pound Provincial Park
July 28   Shamrock Regional Park
July 29   Shamrock Regional Park to Gravelbourg
July 30   Thompson Lake Regional Park

Alberta 237
July 31   Elkwater, Cypress Hills
August 1   Medicine Hat
August 2   Medicine Hat
August 3   Enchant
August 4   Arrowwood to Carseland
August 5   Glenmore Park, Calgary
August 6   Elbow River Trail
August 7   Calgary
August 8   Canmore
August 9   Canmore to Banff
August 10 Lake Louise to Nelson, British Columbia (drive day)

British Columbia 259
August 11 Nelson to South Slocan
August 12 Castlegar, Paulson Bridge
August 13 Greenwood to Midway
August 14 Rhone to Coyote Creek to Beaverdell
August 15 Myra Canyon
August 16 Naramata
August 17 Kaledon to Okanagan Falls
August 18 Coalmont to Tulameen
August 19 Hope
August 20 Victoria
August 21 Victoria

List of Contributors to the HIKE 2000 Auction 291
Bibliography 292

Acknowledgements

I have many people to thank:

First, my mother, Eleanor (Dolly) Belmore, for instilling in me a fighting spirit, strong family values, determination and a love of music. Her sincere interest in people is one we all aspire to. And my deceased father, Bernie Belmore, who gave to me compassion for humble, honest people, an ability to see humour in just about everything and a loose foot.

My sisters, Bonnie, Shirley-Dale, Dianne, Glenda and Betty, for the extended periods of time they spent with us on the trail and the encouragement they gave us when they couldn't be there.

My nieces and nephews who traveled great distances to be with us, if only for a day.

Bruce Graves, for being brave or adventurous enough to drive our support vehicle in Newfoundland. His continual care of our first muscle aches was the best!

Billy Redden, for driving the van from Nova Scotia to British Columbia. We thank him for his kindness and patience from the bottom of our hearts.

To Mark Hingley for all his help with photographs, scanning, etc.

Maurice Anthony, for the use of his great trailer.

Those who made donations to the Hike 2000 auction (listed at the back of the book).

Our Hike 2000 sponsors: Valhalla Pure Outfitters for the tent, camping gear and excellent rain gear; Pharmasave for sunscreen and first aid supplies; Rogers AT&T Wireless for the cell phone; Radio Shack for the recording equipment; Olympus for the digital camera; Carsand Mosher for film; Atlantic Photo Supply Ltd. for photofinishing; and Go for Green for the laptop computer.

To all who shared their photographs used in the making of this book, thank you.

To all of you who fed us and opened your homes and halls to us, a heartfelt thank you.

And last, but definitely not least, thank you to all who shared your stories, songs and lives with us. Without you, it would only have been a walk.

Foreword

The tremendous size of Canada escapes you when you step on a plane on one coast and arrive on the opposite coast five hours later, or when you whisk through the countryside on the Trans Canada highway, mesmerized by the flashing scenes. To cross Canada on foot is a different experience. You smell the rich earth after a spring rain, feel the wind sweeping off the barrens, hear the songbirds and the people chatting on their backyard swings. In essence, you experience the heart of Canadians at a pace that allows you to reach out, take a hand, hear a story, and sing a song with the people who are willing to share a moment of their lives with you. It is such an experience that I longed for when I had the idea to hike across Canada on what would become the Trans Canada Trail. On the way home from a Rails to Greenways Conference in Ontario in 1992, I said it out loud for the first time. At the time, the idea to create the longest trail in the world, linking Canadians from coast to coast, was only a scratch on paper and a room full of enthusiastic trails people. Many projects had been developed to celebrate Canada's 125th birthday, and this idea had to be one of the greatest. I became a member of that driving force to oversee the construction of such a trail by joining the Nova Scotia Trans Canada Trails Council. With a handful of others who believed in the dream, I have remained on the council since that time.

On November 7, 1885, the last spike was driven in the trans-continental railway line linking the Atlantic to the Pacific. The national dream of building a railway from coast to coast had been realized. The passage of the line, like an artery supplying blood, created a unifying strength for the small communities. The trains, in fact, were the pulse of the country. Not in their wildest dreams would those brave railroaders have believed that, 115 years later, the very lines that tied them together would be torn and fragmented, leaving the communities with a sense of loss. Of the many theories surrounding the demise of the Canadian railway in these remote areas, most point to a decline in economic profit from these sections of rail line. With the increase in other modes of transportation and transport, many rail services just couldn't compete and the lifelines to these small communities began shutting down one by one. That certain familiar way of life in these small railway towns is now gone and the bond that linked them to the rest of Canada is shattered. The emotional ties that these people had to the trains run deep—a sentiment I sought to capture as I passed these small communities on Canada's abandoned rail lines.

I have always been drawn to trains, the melancholy sound of its whistle consistently brings a lump to my throat. Perhaps it comes from my father who would trap me as I tried to avoid the repeated stories of the dirty thirties and how he, like many other men, would 'ride the rails' to northern Ontario in search of work in the mines. Now, as an adult, I would give anything for him to be here with us to tell me of these unbelievably heroic acts of climbing beneath the trains and clinging to the rods as they rolled from town to town. How dangerous it was and how desperate these men, like my father, must have been to try to find work in a time of severe economic depression. And it was people just like my father—who was compassionate and could tell a great story—that I wanted to find across the country.

The Trans Canada Trail traverses much of our country on these abandoned rail lines. Lying idle, covered in wildflowers and crowded with alders, these lines would provide the perfect baseline for much of the trail linking Canada. Thus, the process began, to adopt the corridors where once the great iron steel carved its way through the wilderness. It is on these lines that I planned much of my journey. Contacting both the local trails people in each province and the Brotherhood of Locomotive Engineers, I was able to plan a mixed route that would not only give me varied terrain, but would allow me to mingle with the people in these small railway villages and talk to them about what the trains meant to them and how they are coping with their loss. I have thought many times along the route how walking through these small railway communities is like walking through the hallway of a senior citizens' home. The frail bodies hold stories dear to their hearts, undisturbed, until some passerby stops. Then, like the dam on a flood plain opening, stories of a past that pulsed with activity come flowing out, rich and clear. Now quiet, these small railway villages hold only the memories in the folks whose lives were shaped by this past.

To many, the transformation of the rail line into a multi-use trail is intrusive and unwanted. Private land owners have adopted part of this abandoned line as their own and feel the trail is an invasion of their privacy. Yet, the enthusiasm of the trail builders is contagious, and communities have rallied to become part of the great movement.

Foreword

To plan a 4-month hike across Canada isn't easy. You don't just strap on a pair of hiking boots and start walking. There were many things I had to consider. How far can I walk in a day, every day for four months? Where will I walk? How will I carry all of the supplies? Who will join me? Where will I get funding to undertake such a project? Where will I sleep? How will I manage to walk all day, then cook food each night? Where will I get first aid supplies? What about illness on the trail? What about the changing weather? What clothing will I need? What threats are there on the trail in Canada's wilderness that I have to be aware of? Where could I get a support vehicle? Who would give up their time to drive such a vehicle? Where will I put all the supplies such as camping gear and extra clothing? How will I keep all of my bills paid while I am on the trail?

I have to admit that I am a bit of a gambler to start with. When I believe in something, I am determined to see it through. There were many obstacles in the preparation of this trek that would have discouraged the more faint of heart. To say the least, each aspect of planning had its barriers. I tried to receive funding for my project with the many millennium grants that were handed out in the year 2000. This quest for financial aid and sponsorship was unsuccessful, but after making a list of all of the tangible items that I needed, I basically went door-to-door searching for companies who might sponsor us. I was successful to some degree; the sponsors are listed in my acknowledgements. The transportation puzzle was not solved until one week before our departure when I, in desperation, bought a second-hand, 15-passenger van. In retrospect, it was the best move I could have made. This van became our home in the following months and caused us no grief along the way. As for food and transportation costs, my sisters helped me plan an auction at the Thirsty Duck pub in Halifax with many donations from supportive companies and tour operators. In March, many friends and curious people braved the cold and the freezing rain to support us. The money from this auction would be used for gas and oil. As for food money, my husband, John, who had been working in Moscow, Russia, brought home a queen-sized handmade quilt which we sold raffle tickets for across Canada.

So, step-by-step, the plan was put in place. My children, Nora, Maria and Nicholas, would join me for the trip. Other family members would join us when they could. Nora's German professor, Heike Ortscheid, expressed a desire to join us and see Canada before returning to her home in Germany. We welcomed her on board. Bruce Graves, an outdoor enthusiast and a wilderness tripping guide, agreed to drive our support van in Newfoundland and Billy Redden, my cousin, agreed to take over in Nova Scotia and continue to the west coast. As for the threats on the trail, we would have to deal with the unknown as we went. The plan was to hike 20 kilometers a day for ten days in each province to reach a goal of 2000 kilometers by the time we reached the Pacific Coast. It was a reasonable distance given the conditions of the trail and the fact that I also intended to interview railroaders along the way. We also would have to set up camp and cook our meals at night and, of course, rest time would be needed so that we would be able to repeat the exercise each day for almost four months. It was important that we keep our pace so as not to create a backlog of needed kilometers as we neared the end. With all details in place, our journey would begin on the second of May. As the day came close, the excitement rose in all of us. We were really going to do it after all this time.

I have been asked many times, "Would you do it over?" My answer has always been the same, not because it wasn't an incredible journey, but because I have other dreams to fulfill and I feel that to repeat one is to cheapen the first. In 1923, Ernest Hemmingway said it simply:

> We can't ever go back to old things or try and get the old kick out of something or find things the way we remembered them. We have them as we remember them and they are fine and wonderful and we have to go on and have other things because the old things are nowhere except in our minds now.

So now, as I become tired of writing, lean back in my chair and close my eyes, I can see the long dusty trail stretch out before me to the horizon in a blur. It has been a passage I will never forget and a bonding with those who shared it with me that will exist forever.

Personality Profiles

Kathy Didkowsky was born to Eleanor (Dolly) and Bernie Belmore, the sixth child in a family of six girls and one boy. She grew up in the tiny Nova Scotia mining village of Caribou Gold Mines. She obtained her Physical Education and Health Education degrees at Dalhousie University, and was goalkeeper for both the Nova Scotian and Canadian women's field hockey teams, leading to her induction into the Sports Hall of Fame in 1995. She married John Didkowsky in 1974. In 1979 the couple's first child, Nora, was born, followed by Maria in 1981 and Nicholas in 1987.

In 1986, Kathy struck upon the idea of living with her family in a foreign country for a year, and in 1990 they lived in Kandersteg, Switzerland. In 1994 the family lived in Moscow, Russia, where John worked and Kathy homeschooled the children and volunteered at a sick children's hospital. To raise funds to purchase medicine for these sick children, Kathy arranged for a group of Russian musicians to perform a series of concerts in Canada. When she's not teaching at Hants North Rural High, Kathy runs a small adventure company, Spirit Adventure Tours, and guides hiking excursions in the Swiss Alps.

Nora Didkowsky is a 21-year-old student in her fourth year at Acadia University in Wolfville, Nova Scotia. She has a keen interest in music; she plays the guitar and fiddle, and sings. Nora was invaluable to the development of the Hike 2000 website as the group progressed across the country.

Maria Didkowsky is a 19-year-old student in her second year of animal science at the Nova Scotia Agricultural College in Truro, Nova Scotia. Maria plays the guitar, sings and is athletic. Her passion for horses brought several moments of pause along the trail as she stopped to share an apple with a horse in a pasture. Maria took charge of many duties on the trail—from setting up camp and cooking supper to trimming Billy's hair.

Nicholas Didkowsky is 13 years old and would be the first to say that he made the journey for his mom. He plays guitar and loves music; when not drawing or reading, he spent his free time on the trail listening to music on his headphones. Nicholas was always willing to help out with setting up camp, making meals or cleaning up. His love of animals and their attraction to him brought out many a stray dog. Nicholas' favorite pastime along the trail was to see how many consecutive times he could rally the ball with his foot—his final best was over two hundred!

Heike [Hai'ka] **Ortscheid** was Nora's German professor at Acadia University. As an exchange teacher, she was in Canada on a one-year term and had a desire to see the country before returning to Germany. Heike's quick wit kept us entertained around many evening campfires. She plays the flute and spent a lot of time practicing harmonies with Nora and Maria. With her love of drawing and reading, she had an automatic friendship with Nicholas. In the long days spent on the trail, we discussed many views of life and grew to appreciate our differences. Her courage for making this journey, in a foreign country with people she barely knew, is admirable.

Bruce Graves, a wilderness guide and canoe expert, was our support driver in Newfoundland. Bruce is easygoing and accommodating. We enjoyed his navy stories and his massages to our aching muscles. Sometimes, at the end of the day, we would sit on the floor of some remote hall in Newfoundland and share the best stories and jokes with Bruce. We were sure he couldn't do without us when he left us in Nova Scotia.

Billy Redden, also from Caribou Gold Mines, is Kathy's first cousin. Patient and good-natured, he woke each morning and asked, "Do we know where we're going today or is it too early to ask?" Of course, it was always too early to ask! Each day, Billy would drop the group at the trailhead, then drive to the end and wait. Often, he would meet the local people and make sleeping arrangements. Other times, we would drive to a campground and Billy would make a campfire, also his first task in the morning. We don't know how we would have survived without Billy.

Newfoundland

May 2 - May 17

The rugged coast of Wreckhouse.

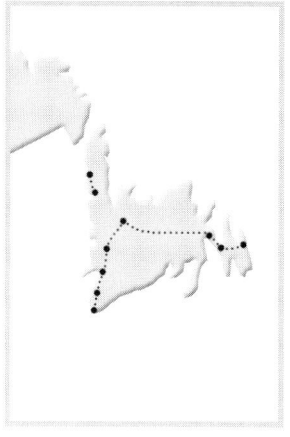

I am awake. It is 5:00 A.M., May 2, pouring rain and cold. We are leaving today for Newfoundland. I steal one last minute tucked against John's warm body, then jump out of bed, committed to my deadline to leave at 6:00 A.M. As we scurry to pack our last minute things in the Hike 2000 van, I feel anxious. This dream of mine is about to become a reality.

Behind our shiny, blue, 15-passenger van is the trailer that has been kindly lent to us by Maurice Anthony, from the nearby village of Kennetcook. Each of us has our belongings stowed in a personally marked, 18x28-inch storage bin. Anything that does not fit in that bin must simply be left at home. Basically, the bins contain our hiking clothes and boots, lots of wool socks, warm fleece, long johns, rain gear, sleeping bag, and one good outfit not to be worn on the trail. All personal items, like journals and souvenirs collected on the trail, must also be stored in our own bins, which will be our only personal space for the next four months. Needless to say, our very characters are reflected in their organization and contents.

Rain dripping from our faces, we establish an order for packing the trailer in the most efficient way possible. First, the tents and cooking utensils are pushed to the back of the trailer. Next, the bins are placed one on top of the other on either side. Our three guitars, fiddle, mandolin, banjo and percussion instruments fit neatly between these two rows. The food cooler and first aid supplies are kept close to the door

Bruce Graves. From driving the van to massaging our tired muscles, Bruce was attentive to our needs in Newfoundland.

for emergencies. The trailer will be strategically packed this way each day, twice a day, for the following four months.

The van wheels shift the gravel on the driveway as we ease away from our eighteenth-century farmhouse. John is standing on the verandah, watching us go. Why am I leaving this quiet little community, tucked down over the ridge from the Rawdon Hills in central Nova Scotia? This question will be asked of us many times. My reply is always the same: There are some dreams that need to be followed.

So, on this cold, wet morning in early May, the five of us who crawl into the van for the first time are the same five who will journey from coast to coast. My children, Nora, Maria, and Nicholas, our German traveling companion, Heike Ortscheid, and I feel light-headed with excitement as we bump over the potholes and frost heaves on Highway 14 on our way to meet Bruce Graves, our support driver for Newfoundland. In Elmsdale, just a half-hour drive away, we meet Bruce and his wife Laura, my mother, my sisters Dianne, Glenda and Betty, and my cousin Billy Redden. Billy will take over as support driver when we reach Nova Scotia and stay with us until the end. Today, our destination is Port aux Basques en route to St. John's, where our trek will begin. We warm ourselves with hot chocolate and literally brace ourselves for what lies ahead.

As we reach Cape Breton, snow is in the air and the wind is turning the water into a roller coaster. Upon seeing this, I force everyone (except Bruce) to take a Gravol to prevent motion sickness on our ferry ride to Port aux Basques. On boarding, I am comforted by the fact that the name of the ferry is "Caribou," the name of my childhood home. We rush to find extended seats, as the effect of the Gravol is upon us. In minutes, we are next to comatose, our bodies twisted and contorted in the small, uncomfortable seats. When I awaken, I am lying face down and drooling, my face flattened on the slippery vinyl bench. I feel as if someone has smacked me over the head with a board.

Port aux Basques. Russell Penny strums a tune on his guitar. Lorna Penny welcomed us like family into her home.

Russell Penny is waiting on the shores of Newfoundland and soon welcomes us to his home in Port aux Basques with hearty bowls of soup and homemade wine. Lorna and Russell Penny, parents of our friend Karen Penny, will be our hosts for the night. They have never met us but have agreed to open their home to us while we are in Port aux Basques. We crowd into their kitchen, feeling as though we've known them for years.

The hour is late, but not too late for music. Russell's friends Ron Keeping and Joe Jeans drop in on their way home from a meeting. Soon, a keyboard and banjo arrive. We sing and play until 3:00 A.M. We are soon to find out that the generous and outgoing nature of the Pennys is not unique in Newfoundland, but typifies the warm people we are to meet before we return to Port aux Basques to celebrate the first leg of our journey.

Port aux Basques is banked in fog as we drag ourselves from our warm beds and into the raw air. As we make our way toward Deer Lake, the wind howls and snow swirls in front of us. Bruce and I, the only ones awake in the van, marvel at the barren landscape, now covered in snow. It is 7:00 P.M. when we reach St. John's. Kirk Newhook, a friend of my nephew Rob Easley, has offered us full use of his home in the days preceding our hike. We are greeted by Llazlo, his dog, who will become one of us in the days that follow.

On the day before our hike begins, we visit Cape Spear, the most easterly point in North America, and the site of Newfoundland's oldest standing lighthouse. This is where "Relay 2000," a millennium project of the Trans Canada Trail Foundation, is conducting its official speeches nestled in the shelter from the wind. Tomorrow, water drawn from the Atlantic will begin its journey, passing from hand to hand, through communities across Newfoundland on its way to Ottawa. There, it will join waters from the Pacific and the Arctic in celebration of the opening of the Trans Canada Trail, the longest trail in the world. Our expedition will also mark the trail's beginning. Our spirits are high as we laugh and dance around the boulders on the cliff.

Back at Kirk Newhook's, a 'send-off' party is in full swing. Local characters pile in with instruments, food and wishes for a safe and successful journey. We are happy to finally meet Wade Kearley, author of *The People's Road* (1995), an account of his solo trek across Newfoundland on the abandoned railway line. Amid the festivities, we pepper him with questions about the trail, the animals, his fears and thoughts. He reads from his book as we sit on the floor in front of the roaring fireplace. We are mesmerized by his every word.

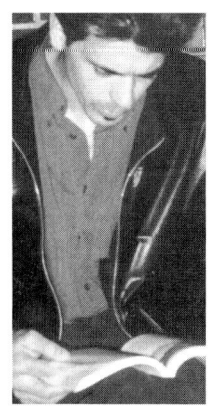

Wade Kearley - "The strange thing about walking is that you start thinking about distances and places in terms of the time it takes to walk, instead of how many miles it is. Another thing I found was that I'd go through sections of the day where I would just come to, not knowing how long I'd been walking or anything else. You just kind of go into yourself, especially when you walk by yourself. I was either doing that or blanking out or singing songs. I don't know how many songs I wore out on the way. Thank God there was no one there to hear me! But anyway, about halfway through my walk from Bishops Falls I cross the Exploits trestle. It is mile 266 (from St. John's). When the railway was marked and the rail line was built in the 1880s, we already had the 'east of the overpass' mentality, naming everything in terms of distance from St. John's, even though there was no overpass.

[Reading.] Around the first bend is a long stretch through the forest with another turn at the far end. Entering this straight section I am stopped in my tracks by the sound of a train approaching from beyond the far turn. The earth shakes under me, the bushes swish. The wind from the ghost train sweeps back my hair, blows right through me. Frozen for a moment, I shake my head to dislodge the sensation. It is as if this place is imbued with the spirit of the train. For a few moments I grapple with the experience, make a few notes in my journal, but there is nothing more to be done, so I hike on over the abandoned rail bed, away from the Exploits River."

You can hear a pin drop as we collect our own thoughts about our passage through this area in just a few days. We sit in utter silence as Wade relates his exhaustion and loneliness on the trail—one that would soon be our own. Glen Collins, a friend of Kirk's, tells us that his father, Vince, loaded steel from the boats to the train in Port aux Basques. Every night, the lights would go out and all of the power would shut down. A ghost ship would arrive in the harbour. How strange!

May 6

Place: St. John's to Topsail Pond
Distance: 21 km
Wildlife: Mallard ducks, "serpentine" rocks, bog of wild irises not yet in bloom.

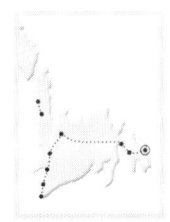

Finally, the day has arrived. I look around me on the floor of the bedroom and see the bodies of the people who have trustingly come here with me...my sisters, Betty and Glenda, my children and Heike. Something about this scene strikes me as hilariously funny. I laugh uncontrollably—a laugh straight from the gut. Tears pour from the corners of my eyes onto my pillow. I can't stop. I stuff my blankets in my mouth and gasp for breath in between my hysterical laughing. "Oh my God," Glenda moans, "our leader has gone insane. It's going to be another Franklin Expedition!"

We scramble to begin our first day of hiking. What will we need in our packs? Will we need long johns? Will it be snowing? Who will carry what food? What about extra socks? Who has the sun protection? It is a procedure that will become automatic in the weeks that follow. We reach the main train station in downtown St. John's. This station, now a bus terminal, was first occupied in January 1903 and was built with granite from the Gaff Topsails. Our journey begins here.

School children are arriving by the busload and lining up to be part of the water relay. Shivering and shaking in the cold, they proudly sport their Relay 2000 T-shirts, which are theirs for the moments the Atlantic water will pass through their hands.

While I am having a quick interview with the local TV station, Llazlo, Kirk's dog, catches the scent of a nearby bitch in heat, and in full view of the camera begins madly pumping the air. As we scramble to hide this embarrassing display, Relay 2000 officials continue with their speeches, oblivious to the ruckus going on behind them. As if this spectacle isn't enough, with our train whistles blowing, we head out of town in the wrong direction. Realizing our mistake, we are mortified and quickly backtrack. We need not worry; Relay 2000 speeches continue unaware.

Out on the trail, we frantically race to ensure we are ahead of the water relay. As we pass the Relay 2000 pit stops, we are kindly given water and are cheered on by the relay workers. The trail is on a well-graded surface leading through the city's suburbs, stretching into the parks and through the forest. An elderly couple calls to us from their porch, "Come in for tea—it is too cold to be out walking." Later, we regret our decision to decline this generous offer. By noon, the weather is turning cold and we don every layer in our packs. Snow whirls around us as we reach Paradise. Heike amusingly remarks, "Can this really be Paradise?"

The rail bed turns to rough, loose gravel. Llazlo skirts on and off the trail ahead of us while we continue on to Topsail Pond. A healthy winter glow shines on our faces as we return to Kirk's warm fireplace for just one more night of comfort before heading out into the unknown. We pull the instruments from their cases and sing with Kirk well into the night.

May 7

Place: Brigus Junction to Whitbourne
Distance: 22.2 km
Wildlife: 1 rabbit, 1 loon, 4 butterflies, red ants, pitcher plants, moose tracks

Newfoundland

It is Sunday morning, 7:00 A.M. Under a cloudless sky, with a warm sun on our backs, we wind our way from Brigus Junction. This small railway community had its beginnings in 1901, with its population reaching its height around 1935 with more than a hundred people. In 1969, passenger trains ceased travelling on the Brigus Junction line connecting to the Harbor Grace line.

The trail bed is easy going and we make good time, passing bogs with brilliant blue ponds and marshy areas layered with scrub trees. Along the route, we notice several cottages, their owners whizzing up and down the line on their ATVs. This seems to be the Sunday morning entertainment. We hurry past a wasted ghost of a school bus that sends shivers up my spine. As a teacher, I can imagine the ruckus of the children on board as they pile on and off this now empty shell. We reach Ocean Pond and spread our lunch on the warm grassy clearing. Kirk has brought along leftover black and red Thai rice, which we pile between hunks of bread.

As we approach Whitbourne station, we can hear the far off ringing of the station bell. The bell's once familiar tones have not been heard by this community since the last train came through in the mid 1980s. A lump forms in my throat, and despite my efforts at self-control, tears well in my eyes. The folks at Whitbourne know we are coming and give us this most moving welcome. Whitbourne was once Harbor Grace Junction, Newfoundland's first inland town. The station was built in 1883 and is now the local museum and heritage center. John Gosse greets us with Mayor Max Reid, the mayor's two sons, Deputy Mayor Norma Dawe, Secretary to the Mayor and Museum Coordinator Wanda Lynch, and Ralph Peddle, the former station agent. Exploring the station, we notice old menus on the wall...

Sirloin Steak dinner .80	Plain or Sultana cake .20
Ham & Tongue .75	A pot of Coffee .20
No order served for less than 30 cents.	

John Gosse tells me how he misses the sound of the train. It had been so important in his life growing up. He shares with me one of the poems he has written about the railway.

Ghosts of Railway Builders

Alone he wearily walks his Section
With bucket and shovel on his back
with an eye out for smoldering cinders
Along the winding railroad track

In scorching sun he rests, then looks
At the fifty-eight, there's smoke and flame
His steel-like frame alertly moves
This fiery threat he soon must tame.

Patrol man John Mercer by strength of arm
Pumps upgrade in his velocipede,
This three-wheeled machine to ease his work
At his command to move with speed.

The sounds of wheel upon iron rails
Challenges all his power and strength
Grimy sweat and strain of aching toil
To douse the flames, his sole intent.

Power pumps and speeders came at last
New machines for man's heavy load
And diesels created by brawn and brain
Great changes on the old railroad.

Such scenes of labor no longer linger
Nor bell nor whistle, smoke nor steam
Nor shunting, braking or rolling stock
Memories of a distant dream.

Today we "trike" the naked roadbed
A "narrow gauge" park across this land
Voices echo from pioneer builders
Plaintive cries of the railroad man!

John Gosse

We are invited to stay in Whitbourne for some hot pea soup, but have to decline as we are meeting Kirk's mother, Gloria, for supper in

Don and Gloria Newhook welcome us to their summer home in Bellevue Beach.

Bellevue Beach overlooking Trinity Bay. Upon reaching Bellevue Beach, we sort our storage bins on the side of the road. A local fisherman, calling himself "Ivan the Terrible" offers us one of the brown trout he has caught this afternoon. We will save it for our breakfast tomorrow. Gloria and her good friend Joan have a hearty meal of chicken, pork chops, corn on the cob, and rice waiting for us. As the evening hours pull us closer to this family, we already lament tomorrow's parting.

May 8

Place: Arnold's Cove to Come By Chance
Distance: 8.3 km
Wildlife: 6 caribou, 1 fox, 3 ducks

With heavy hearts, we say our tearful good-byes to Kirk and Llazlo. They have become part of us and to leave them behind now seems wrong. "Such warm, genuine people ...it was like we always knew them" (from Glenda's diary). Our breakfast of sea-run brown trout and eggs give us strength as the snow and hail whip around us on the trail from Arnold's Cove. We pull ourselves deep inside our windbreakers, our bodies bent into the wind that reaches 70 kilometres/hour. The wet snow lands on the coarse stones, then trickles off, turning the stones a brilliant red and green. Old telegraph poles, once the only form of communication with the rest of the island, border the rail line.

(from Glenda's diary)
As we approach the overpass, a lonely figure appears before us. It is Bruce, our ever-faithful driver, checking to see that we are all right and that we are on the right trail. What a support driver. Under the overpass, on the wall, is a painted sign

saying, 'Good-bye Nan and Pop—We will miss you." On the other side it says, "Wade, don't go past this line...You'll be sorry." The messages are just another sad reminder of days gone by.

We arrive in Come By Chance amidst a fierce winter blizzard. Ice gathers on our eyelashes and frost outlines every hair on our faces. We strike up a conversation with Fred George, the local mail carrier. He tells us that his daughter is married to John Gosse's son. Funny how we know the local connections already. In Sunnyside, we scan the water for whales tumbling in the bay. By now, the wind is even stronger and we vote to call it a day. Our plans to hike from Millertown Junction in the morning are curtailed, as the snow up there is just too deep. We can not take our support vehicle to the summit, and to carry all of our gear in waist deep snow for 35 kilometres in this wind just does not make sense. Upset by the fact that our trip over the Gaff Topsails is not to be, we climb into the van and drive in silence to Deer Lake.

The Gaff Topsails, once a small community of railway workers and their families, was the highest point of the Newfoundland railway. It supported a school in the late 1930s and the early 1940s for less than 20 children, with its teacher making less than $35 per month. The station, used until 1956, no longer stands at the summit.

Feeling our disappointment, Bruce makes arrangements for us to stay at the Trappers Lounge in Howley. The Corner Brook hiking club has decided to hike with us in the morning to the summit on the Gaff

Bundled against the cold, Maria and Nicholas make their way along the old railbed from Arnold's Cove to Come By Chance.

Topsails and back down to Howley. We are elated! Reaching the small village of Howley is like coming home. There is a wild bareness that resembles Caribou Gold Mines, our family home in Nova Scotia. The road is rough and smoke filters from the chimneys of the few houses. The setting sun sends a crimson glow across the snow. A caribou crosses our path just before we enter the village.

Trappers Lounge, our home for the night, is run by Rod Kelly Jr., whose father, Ron, runs the Howley Shopping Center and is a former railway man. As we talk about the railway, I sense a sadness in Ron's tone. He pokes fun at his railway days, but behind this joking is a sentiment that I am sure only men like him know; men who have worked on the Gaff in snow higher than the trains. Ron rode the "peedy," following the trains to put out fires started by the sparks on the rails. In winter, he drove the snowplow, breaking trail in front of the train. Ron tells me about those days on the Gaff.

Ron Kelly - "It was wicked up there (on the Gaff Topsails) in the wintertime. The train would be waiting a week and a half, just hung up waitin' for the main line to get through. The people would just sit aboard the train, day and night, just sleep, eat and whatever. They got stuck up there one day in the Gaff Topsails. There was nothing up there to buy. They were stuck in a snowbank and they were there a couple of days. And the conductor, Cyril Daniels, wired the superintendent in St. John's and he said, 'Send grub today, or it will be coffins tomorrow.' The conductor was kind of a comical lad...

We were on the plows. We'd go out on the tracks and there would be snowbanks. The train would be waiting for us to clean up the hill and then the train would come on behind. The road on the Gaff Topsails is four feet, probably higher in places. They tried to get clear of the snow so it would blow off. They spent two to three years and thousands of dollars trying to raise the tracks so that the snow would blow off. But they couldn't raise it, so what they used to do was park tractors there after a storm, blow 'er all off, and get ready for another storm. In later years, they'd run the plow special, just with the caboose. But when we were running, it could be a 70- or 80-car train and we'd be stuck in the front, and that was it. And this is going down the hill. There's nothing going to bring that up, you know? If you are off, you are off in the woods. So, it was scary at times. I went off the track many times! Never hurt, though. One time we went off in Port aux Basques and we were hanging over a cliff. The ocean was right down there below us. And

The snowplow train that pushed the snow in front of the famous "Newfie Bullet" over the Gaff Topsails.

the only thing that was holdin' the plow from goin' down was where it was coupled up to the diesel. We had to call people in the middle of the night to come out with a crane to hook into her. I was sleepin' in her, so the helper opened the door and he said, 'If anyone's in there, you better get out or you will die!' I said, 'I'm dyin' for sleep, so I'm part way gone anyway!"

May 9

Place: Kitty's Brook to Pond Crossing
Distance: 23.5 km
Wildlife: 7 caribou, 1 great horned owl, 1 fox, ducks, 1 "four eared" squirrel (spring must be in the air)

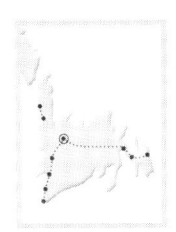

Weather and trail conditions dictate that our original plans to hike to the summit of the Gaff Topsails today have to be scaled down. Joining us on the trail are Corner Brook hiking club members Bob Day, Bob Diamond, Perry Young, Jan Grebneff, Judy May and Vicky Pike. Driving to our trailhead this morning, we spot a lone caribou in the tall scrub. The wind is strong, but with clouds drifting over a blue sky, there is no threat of storm, as on previous days. A great horned owl peers nervously from her nest as we approach. She has been returning to this same nest for eight years. This is her neighborhood and we are her intruders. We move on, feeling her uneasiness. The rail bed twists and climbs up the valley, passing points with names such as Tender Curve, Blue Rock and Kitty's Sidehill. The bed then raises onto a windswept barren of sub arctic tundra. Blues, purples, fast moving streams…I can only imagine the wild beauty of this place in autumn. Snow sweeps over part of the trail and we trudge on, the wind turning to a biting cold.

We huddle behind a cabin with the Corner Brook hiking club members at Pond Crossing.

Moose tracks and fresh scat remind us that we are not on these barrens alone.

At Pond Crossing, we huddle together behind a small cabin owned by Ford Morley. He is happy at the arrival of unexpected guests and offers us toilet paper and the use of his outdoor facility with Styrofoam seats. We are grateful for the private luxury on this treeless, windswept landscape. A handful of cabin owners, like Morley, come to the Gaff for berry picking and hunting in the fall. In the early railway days, twenty or more cabins existed in the area.

Bracing ourselves against a strong wind and occasional flurry, we retreat back down toward Kitty's Brook. Ron Kelly told me a story this morning about a woman who had a baby while aboard the "Newfie Bullet" at Kitty's Brook Trestle. He said she wasn't even pregnant when she got on the train in Port aux Basques. This is just one of the many jokes about the famous train, sarcastically dubbed 'Newfie Bullet,' which slowly wound its way over the Gaff Topsails. Ron also told of a conductor who was commenting on the number of years he had worked on the railway. The conductor said, "I've been on twenty years." "Oh," another replied, "You must have got on in St. John's!"

As we descend, I can almost hear the grinding of the trains as they wound their way up the steep grades to the summit. I walk at a comfortable pace with Bob Day, a quiet, gentle man, enjoying the stretches of wilderness that lie around us. We stop at a high ridge and look over the meeting of two waterways, which pour into a large lake far below. On the far side, a caribou, oblivious to our presence, nibbles on the new growth of the bushes. We continue on in appreciative silence.

Back at Trappers Lounge, we listen to Perry Young talk about the Beothuk, Newfoundland's native people. According to Perry, initial trade relations between the Beothuk and French Europeans were good, but as more Europeans began arriving, misunderstandings arose and relations deteriorated. The increase in settlement along the coast created problems for the Beothuk in accessing their traditional food sources—salmon and hawk eggs, for example—so they withdrew to the interior to hunt caribou and trap small animals such as beaver. When the Europeans also moved inland and started trapping, many Beothuk were killed for stealing from traps or stealing the traps themselves for iron to make tools. As the Beothuk became more and more scarce, a reward went out for the capture of a live Beothuk. Demasduit, who the Europeans called Mary March, was captured and taken to St. John's. She fell ill and died of tuberculosis en route to Red Indian Lake, where she was buried by her husband, Chief Nonosabawsut. The last known surviving Beothuk was Shanawdithit, the chief's niece, who also died of tuberculosis.

Finally, it is time for Bob Day, Bob Diamond and Perry Young to return to Corner Brook. Betty, Glenda and I drop into Trappers Lounge, where Rod Kelly Jr., his girlfriend and a couple of local men are having a few drinks and playing darts. Soon, we join in, pairing up in teams. Rod brings out pictures portraying his life in Howley—his sons, Christmas, and the opening of the lounge.

It is time to sing. We pull ourselves up to the bar. Rod Jr. entertains us from behind the bar with songs from Newfoundland, which he interrupts only to get up and pour double rum and cokes for his father, which he takes with a chaser of beer. We take our turns singing railroad tunes and pleading Rod for more songs. Just before it is time to call it a night, Rod goes to the juke box and puts on an old Willy Nelson favourite. Ron sweeps me onto the dance floor. His wide grin masks his hard life and his sense of loss, his love of the railroad. We leave the lounge feeling warmth from a family we have barely met.

Back in our cozy room, in the middle of the night, I awaken with a start. "Maria, Maria! IT'S A TRAIN!!" My fears subside, as I realize the sound of the train in my dream is only Betty's soft snoring filtrating from the mattress on the floor below.

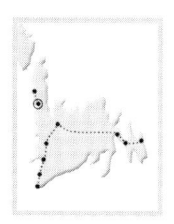

May 10

Place: Woody Point
Distance: 3.8 km
Wildlife: 1 moose

Rod Kelly Jr. and I are bumping along in his half-ton truck on the old rail bed leading to the lift bridge and the dam with eight gates that supplies water to Deer Lake. This is an enormous structure which caused extensive flooding of the rail bed and subsequent rerouting at the time it was built. Rod relates the story of a family called the Pierceys who lived right alongside the tracks out here next to the barren. They all died of food poisoning after eating a moose that was struck by a train. "Guess they didn't clean it soon enough," Rod remarks, nonchalantly. We stop occasionally while a caribou lumbers up the track, head high in the air, body loping along with legs that seem to be connected with loose, revolving joints.

(from Nora's diary)
We scramble once more to pack our bins into the back of the van. Rod Jr. comes and says good-bye to us. Every time we leave some place it feels like we are saying good-bye to family. On the highway, the van is silent for a long time as we watch a couple in a pick up truck. An older woman and man sit close, his arm around her shoulder, her head tucked into his neck. A sad love song plays on the radio. It is an absolutely amazing drive. Mountains appear out of the barrens, touching a crisp, blue sky, and sloping into water of dark blue. White rests between the layers of rock on the cliffs. I never imagined that Newfoundland would have such varied terrain.

Just before Woody Point, we pull off onto the shoulder of the road and turn up the radio. There, on CBC radio, Bill Richardson (Sad Goat) is reading Betty's letter about our trip across Canada. Afterward, "Hobo's Lullaby," by Betty Belmore and The Mighty Oaks, drifts sadly through the air. We really are hobos, roaming from place to place, following the rails, hoping, but never knowing if and where we will have a place to sleep. It is almost surreal, listening to Betty's voice coming from the radio as she sits behind me in the van. It is very touching. I don't dare look at anyone, I feel so emotional.

Woody Point is a friendly little village nestled between the Tablelands and Gros Morne. We will spend the night at the hostel here, right above the medical clinic. The sun is already low in the sky as we trek up the Discovery Trail, which lies behind the new Discovery Centre. The trail is straight up through evergreen shrubs. Quickly, the wet trail turns to a winding, snow-covered path. Maria breaks the trail as we clamber along behind her in single file, lifting and sinking our now heavy boots into the snow. The snow becomes deeper and heavier, causing us to lift our legs, which are now sinking to our hips, out of each deep hole and down into another. Heike, who has had little experience with snow, let alone trekking uphill in the wet, heavy accumulation, trudges on without complaint. Bruce leads the way as we reach the top. We have insisted he come with us today as our protector from moose should they charge. Stopping to contemplate if it makes sense to go on, Glenda spots our first moose. It is huge, and after giving us a lingering glance, it moves off deeper into the woods. This sighting starts a myriad of questions. Do moose charge? Would they come here? Can they smell us? The sightings of moose dung and antler scrapings on the trees soon answer some of our questions.

At the top, the snow resembles the snowfields of a ski hill, packed with the wind into ripples, like a petrified grain field. Far below us, the sun is glistening on the dark blue waters of Bonne Bay. This is truly a magnificent spot and well worth the climb. We slide our way back down the trail to the van and return to the hostel. Betty and Glenda are making filet gumbo and enjoying a little pre-dinner drink. We bring out the mandolin and banjo to entertain ourselves as my biscuits cook in the oven. What a treat to have an oven! Nora, Maria, Heike and Nicholas are lying on their chosen cots, reading, having a snooze and doing some journal writing. Bruce has joined us in the kitchen. Suddenly, Glenda, Betty and I get an idea.

When we were young, our father taught us how to call a moose by rolling up a piece of tar paper and letting out guttural grunts and howls until a moose answers. Then you wait a bit, answer him and continue until you've got him convinced that you are interested in making his acquaintance ... that is, if you were a female moose. So, out into the cold air we go. The moon is bright in the sky as Glenda, Betty and I, heads circling, howl through our rolled up magazines. Bruce, peeling with laughter, has to be locked in the hostel, so as not to break our spell. We wait. "It's not like calling the dog," Betty says, "they don't come right away." The next morning, a moose is spotted next to our hostel.

Inside the hostel, the idea of having a stage in our bedroom is just too much of a temptation. First, Betty jumps up on the stage, dancing and singing a piercingly high vaudeville tune.

(from Nora's diary)
That starts the ball rolling, as one after the other, we perform the craziest skits and songs we can think of. Mom starts off her rendition in a bright orange hat that someone has left at the hostel, and gives a little tap dance with her hiking stick. She replaces the hiking stick with a broom stick, which she smacks over and behind her head with a piece of wood as I play the fiddle. Scenes come and go. Nicholas' Robberblues skit, mine and Maria's manure song, the "Hags" dance (the cousins' term of endearment for our mothers and aunts), Glenda's Elvis song, Mum's interpretive dance of the arrival of the Vikings...Not to be outdone, Betty gets up with an ice cream tub on her head covered with a dishcloth. A curtain rod, with the curtain still attached and flowing, runs through her sleeves across her back, forcing her arms into a fixed straight position as she dances for us, her captive audience. Heike, our friend from Germany, watches in...well...I'll just say, amazement. Even after everyone else is in bed, Glenda can't tear herself away from the stage, and she dances around, singing 'Nighty Night' in her underwear. In bed, we get a giggling fit on...Where will we be tomorrow? What kind of props will we have there? And wouldn't it be great to have a dinner theater with beds? Or even a stage in your own bedroom all of the time?

May 11

Western Brook, Gros Morne National Park
Distance: 11.4 km
Wildlife: 24 moose, 3 spruce partridge, 1 snowshoe hare, 1 arctic hare, 1 squirrel, many sheep

Betty has made some hot scones for breakfast. They are delicious with the partridge berry jam we acquired in Howley. Before leaving Woody Point, Glenda and I cannot resist the temptation to visit the school that is next to the hostel. We sit in the computer class and tell them of our journey. They look at our website and pump us with questions. Today, Bob Day is meeting us at Wiltondale to direct us up the west coast of Gros Morne Park. The banks on the sides of the highway are sprouting with fresh greenery and several moose are just finishing their morning meal. Bob explains the geography of the area as we pull on our hiking boots. A boardwalk winds into the barren. The sun is shining on the snow drizzled mountains and the promising waters of the fiord.

(from Maria's diary)
The fiords in the background and the marshy plain in front of us seem like the perfect setting for a medieval movie, with knights, princesses, goblins, and wizards. We take the longer way through the forest, where the trees are twisted and warped and not much taller than us. Nora, Nicholas and I pretend we were on a mission to take a potion to the king. I am the mighty warrior, Nicholas is the wizard, and Nora, the healer. We come to a lookout where the boats are launched and have our lunch of cheese, sardine and pickle sandwiches. Mmm, mmm. That definitely has to go in our "best sandwiches ever" book! We walk down a boardwalk for a long time, our bodies following one after the other, resembling the cars of a train. The sides are muddy and, farther off, the trees look almost dead, so twisted because of the wind and almost silver in colour. The colour scheme around us is brilliant…red mosses, dark black mud, soft sand, long tan grasses, deep blue water, and, rising from behind, rocky cliffs spotted with snow. There are caribou or moose hoofprints on the bridge where they have come from the thicket for a drink at the beach. We stop at the beach and skip stones, collect a few, then continue until the trail ends.

Bob Day has arranged our stay at the Lions Club. On our return from Western Brook, we are invited to his home to change before meeting the Corner Brook hiking club for supper. The contents of our bins spew onto his front lawn as we hurry to prepare for the evening. At the Environmental Center, we share songs and homemade wine. Benny Cooper entertains us with his Newfoundland songs, accompanying himself with his guitar and mouth organ. The others join in, sharing good ole' songs and stories from this rich corner of the earth. Returning to the Lions Club, Nicholas is elated with the fact that there is a gymnastics club upstairs. He pleads with me to join him as he tumbles and springs over the mats. I am too pooped. What a shame!

May 12

Place: Corner Brook
Distance: 15 km

It is pouring rain and cold. We are informed that the Lions Club is not available for us tonight. We are waiting for Bob Day, who has courageously gone next door to inquire about the possibility of us spending the night at the local funeral parlor. In his absence, we conjure up the scenes for tonight's episode. To our chagrin, it is fully occupied. Bob Day and his wife, Evelyn, kindly offer us a place to stay in their home for the night. We pile into Tim Horton's for some hot soup before facing the driving rain. Tromping along the 'outer ring' road, which circumnavigates Corner Brook, rain drenches our faces as truckers honk their sympathy.

(from Nicholas' diary)
I decide not to go on the hike with everyone else and it is a good decision. I am very happy that I chose not to walk. It is wet and miserable outside, and nobody is looking forward to it. So, Bob Day and I get in his car and drive to his house. He keeps the heat on full blast in his car, and I have all of my layers on. Bob Day is a very kind person, so he turns the heat down when I ask if I can open the window. I listen to the same weather channel broadcast every ten minutes on his TV. I still can't get that music out of my head. Bob gives me a place to lie down. This is where the day ends for me, basically. I sleep for the rest of the time.

    Meanwhile, the others are hiking on the highway in the cold. When they get home, they tell me exactly how wet the hike was. When I get up, I have a drink of Coke, then go to sleep again. Later, I get up and have some of Evelyn's homemade soup. By that time it is bedtime. What an interesting day. Newfoundland is a pretty good place when you are awake to see it.

Evelyn has the supper table ready as we hurry into the warmth of their kitchen. We are cold and wet and the smell of the homemade soup is inviting us to the table. Evelyn's neighbour, Greta Newhook, has also brought some food for us to share. After supper, she tells stories of her life growing

Bob Day and Evelyn Parrot become our guardian angels in Corner Brook, Newfoundland.

up near Gros Morne. Nora and I return to the Environmental Center, where we work on the website until midnight. We have no luck and return to Bob and Evelyn's and crawl into our sleeping bags in the comfort of their living room.

May 13

Place: Black Duck Siding to St. George's
Distance: 22.4 km
Wildlife: hawks, osprey and pipers

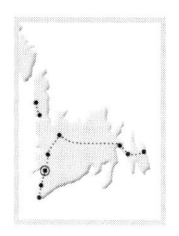

Evelyn prepares a hearty breakfast for us before we leave Corner Brook. The comfortable manner of Bob and Evelyn puts us at ease in their home and we linger on parting.

Today, Glenda returns to Nova Scotia. First, she must take the long bus ride from Corner Brook to St. John's, stay all night at Kirk's, then fly back to Nova Scotia. It has been so much fun to have Glenda with us on the trail and with another empty seat in the van heading to Black Duck Siding, we feel incomplete.

As I crawl from the van at 4:20 in the afternoon, the cold air penetrates my clothes. We have worked all day on our website and I imagine the comfort of sliding my body under a warm duvet for an endless sleep. The cold wind sweeps across the barrens and I pull myself deep into my layers. So many times while planning this trip I wrote the name "Black Duck Siding." And now, as I stand on this lonely meeting spot between the road and gravel bed, I am reminded of the loss of the railway. The rail bed resembles a pebbled beach and as we try to warm up for the trek ahead, our ankles wobble and roll around the stones, as if they're not firmly attached to our stiff legs. This stretch of trail runs along St. George's Bay to St. George's, which was first settled by the Mi'kmaq. In 1896, when the railway first went through, almost five hundred people lived here. To our right are windswept sand dunes and long, brown tufts of grass. Far in the distance, a rise in the hills suggests what the next few days' hiking will bring. We stop to watch two hawks carrying long sticks to build their nest.

At Stephenville Crossing, the rail line comes to a junction where a small handmade stop sign stands. Across the road, a group of faces appears in the window of a bungalow, fingers pointing and gesturing. Surely, these people must know which is the right way to St. George's. I approach the door and hear a heated debate about who will answer. Finally, the door squeaks open and standing before me is a small, older woman by the name of Evelyn. Her hair is long and tangled, her smile opens wide, and her eyes dance. Her bed is strategically situated in front of the living room window where she can watch passersby. She apologizes for the state of her house but insists we come in for tea. Peering over her shoulder are three men, all in different styles of sweat suits. Two are her sons and the third is a friend. They proceed to show us their treasured possessions, including pins, nametags, pictures and tickets to various events. They are delightful and when we leave, our day is brighter.

Stephenville Crossing is located on the flood plain of St. George's Bay. The railway came through in 1896. As we stroll through the village, four wheelers whiz by us in both directions. Windows are lined with faces, dogs bark and tires squeal until we are out of sight. A small graveyard of wooden crosses at the end of the village speaks of family tragedies in this Newfoundland town.

We cross Main Gut Bridge, just one kilometre out of town. This leaning trestle spans an inlet of water. Some of the trestle's planks are rotten, and others are missing altogether. With water flowing swiftly under the graying ties, we watch our feet intently, not to miss a step. The sun is setting as we reach a high beach cliff. Birds of prey are diving for their evening meal. It is 7:00 P.M.—the favorite meal time for the moose. How comforting!

We reach St. George's Bay and Finny's Take Out and Restaurant.

We stumble in and plunk ourselves down to plate loads of food. Later in the parish hall, which Bruce has secured, Betty and I pour a sink full of hot water. Sharing a measuring cup of Bruce's rum, we soak our aching feet. Meanwhile, Bruce kindly massages the taut muscles of the rest of the gang.

May 14, Mother's Day

Place: Robinsons to Codroy Pond
Distance: 32.4 km
Wildlife: many signs of bear and moose

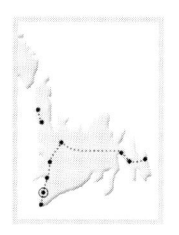

(from Betty's diary)
A beautiful Sunday morning. After a good night's sleep at St. George's Parish Hall, we all get up early and pack up. We call Mom in Caribou and wish her a happy Mother's Day. I call home so that Taylor can do the same for me. The church bells are ringing as we leave the parish hall and drive to Finny's Restaurant. Jorma Torkkeli, known as Finny in St. George's, has breakfast ready for us, as per last night's plan. Jorma is from Finland. He decided to see the world and ended up in Corner Brook where he met Marie, his wife. They have operated Finny's Restaurant for six years. Jorma keeps us entertained, regaling us with stories, all the while serving a delicious breakfast of eggs, bacon, sausage, homefries, toast, and a lot of coffee. Nora and Maria treat Kathy and me, the two mothers.

We drive to Robinsons and set out. It is T-shirt weather for the first time. Soon, we even roll up our pant legs, the first time this season for me. My legs look like two freshly peeled spruce logs. (Toward the end of the hike that's exactly how they feel.) The landscape is, for the most part, quite pastoral: open fields, barns and sheds. Our first trestle bridge gives us pause. It is quite shaky with a serious list to port. We pick our way across, not looking ahead or down at the rushing water far below, but only at our feet. We stop for a water break high above flat lands that stretch for miles. The view is incredible. We cross two more trestle bridges before reaching St. Fintan's. I buy film at a little store there while Kathy tends to her feet, then we are off again. Nicholas opts to stay behind. For ninety per cent of the walk, the trail bed is large, loose, crushed stone. It is very hard to walk on and it slows us down considerably. Just a note to communities upgrading their hiking trails—get rid of the large crushed stone. It is very hard on hikers' feet. Also a cautionary note to ATV users: Please slow down when approaching hikers. Flying stones are potential lethal missiles. Maria is having trouble with her Achilles tendon, and the walk is especially hard for her. We stop for lunch beside the trail in late afternoon. It suddenly strikes us that we are in the middle of God knows where, chatting away as if in a coffee shop. I realize that I have been sitting all this time on an ant hill. I do a quick screaming strip tease, much to the hilarity of everyone else. After lunch, an ominous feeling hovers around us. We pass a place cordoned off with police tape. All kinds of horrible thoughts go through our minds. We discover later that a boy was killed there in a car accident. It is evening when we come to our last trestle bridge. There was a washout and a sign says that the trail is closed. We are too far along to turn back. Someone has fashioned a makeshift ladder of spruce poles up to the bridge itself. We crawl up the ladder and over the bridge. Here, everything changes abruptly. The trail becomes much narrower, overgrown with grass and bushes. There are no signs of ATVs. We know we are completely on our own. We trudge along, buoying each other up. We come across bones...animal bones, some lying on the trail, some in garbage bags, making us feel uneasy, especially since we really don't know how far we have yet to walk or what might lay ahead.

We stop at the Side Wall, a great wall straight up on our right. On our left is a steep embankment and far below are the rushing waters of River Brook. The trail is littered with huge stones that have tumbled down the mountain. The place is very beautiful and yet foreboding. We spot bear tracks. All along we have seen signs of moose, but now we know we are in bear country. There are lots of tracks, fresh sign, and rotten stumps where they have been clawing for grubs. We sing boisterously. Heike picks up railway spikes and clinks them together in time. I never thought I'd live to see the day when a rusted car seat would be a welcome sight—it means civilization must be close by. Soon, traffic from the Trans Canada becomes audible. Around 8:30 P.M. we spot Bruce walking toward us. I could cry with relief. We have walked thirty-two kilometres over harsh stones and through deep wilderness. We decided on the trail that if it got dark we would still keep walking, and if Bruce was not at the highway, we were not walking any further.

At a service station down the road, Kathy calls Martin's Cabins in Upper Ferry. We roll in there around 9:30, unload what we need for the night and settle in. Seven in one cabin. I make spaghetti. We drink the heels of bottles from our cooler. I have a gin and tonic while Bruce massages my feet. Some things are worth walking toward. The cabin is very cozy and we all sit around enjoying laughs and good conversation before turning in. We walked so far over such rough terrain but I feel good. Every day I am surprised at how fast one's body can recover and strengthen. This is my last entry for Newfoundland. I am sad to go. I am in awe of this province. The beauty, ruggedness and diversity are truly amazing. If humankind is looking for something to aspire to in terms of grace and humility, we need look no further than to the people of Newfoundland. I am so glad I came.

As we recount the day, I recall feeling as if our tired bodies were separating themselves from our minds as we plodded and stumbled over the uneven stones on this endless trackage. The pain in my Achilles felt like someone had shoved hot coals down in the heels of my boots. I vaguely remember telling Heike where all of my files are in case I should die of fatigue in the night. Late into the night, as we sit recalling the day and listening to Bruce's stories of his navy days, Maria, who by now is delirious with exhaustion, appears in the doorway with her sleeping bag pulled up around her to her chin. Her temperature has soared and she has gone to bed before us to get some rest and ease the pains in her stomach. "What do you call the first?" she mumbles. We look at her with curious amusement. She repeats the question, but this time impatiently. "What do you call the first?" she demands. Finally, Betty replies, "Number one!" Disgusted, Maria falls back onto the bed into a deeper sleep, as we let out a peal of unsympathetic laughter.

May 15

Place: McDougall's Gulch to Port aux Basques
Distance: 25.4 km
Wildlife: seagulls, mayflowers, whales

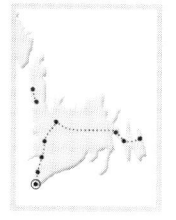

Our breakfast of porridge and baked apples gives us strength for our morning hike with Russell Penny and Harry Anderson into Port aux Basques. Embracing Russell Penny again, we realize that we are approaching the last leg of our first province. We did it! And now we know that we have the heart and courage to continue across Canada. As Harry struggles into his yellow oilskins, we pile on the layers for our trek through Wreckhouse. The locals claim that this is the windiest spot in Newfoundland, with winds reaching over 120 miles/hour. Harry finally ditches the oilskins, as they just won't fit over the other layers. Maria has pinched a nerve in her back while lifting the bins which are now becoming increasingly heavy, laden with favorite stones and railway spikes that we have picked up along the trail.

The rest of us head out, soon becoming separated into small groups...Harry and Betty, Russell and I, Nora and Nicholas and Heike trooping on out front. The wind funneling through the passes of the Table Mountains forces us to lean straight forward in order to continue. This is where Lauchie MacDougall, his wife and twelve children lived. Dubbed "the human wind gauge," he would inform the train dispatcher when the wind was too strong for the trains. Watching the long, brown grass being swept by the wind, he could tell its velocity. The trains relied on him, only proceeding past Wreckhouse when he deemed it safe. Everyone knew of Lauchie. They talk of how he was strong and could run like the wind. One story related to me told of how Lauchie went out to catch his sheep. Before he caught his sheep, it died of exhaustion and Lauchie was still going strong. Lauchie's oldest daughter, Kay (MacDougall) Carter, tells me about her life in Wreckhouse. When she was young, there were no roads—only trains. They had a path to their house for the horse and buggy. When she first moved to Port aux Basques, she missed the sound of the train whistle blowing as it did when it passed close to her home in Wreckhouse. The sound of the fog horn just wasn't the same for her.

Weary from the previous day's hike, the walk to Port aux Basques seems endless. We create word games to keep ourselves distracted from the agony of blistered feet and depleted energy. Russell names a place in Newfoundland, and with the last letter of that name we think of a new place in Newfoundland

Kaye (MacDougall) Carter, daughter of Lauchie (the human wind gauge) tells of her life in Wreckhouse, the windiest spot in Newfoundland.

Emily and Lauchie MacDougall raised their family of twelve in Wreckhouse. They informed the trains when it was safe to pass.

that begins with that same letter. Russell obviously chooses this game to his advantage, being a native of Newfoundland.

(from Heike's diary)
A major washout, which renders the trestle at Red Rocks impassable, gains us a scenic tour along some cabins and through a dense, low forest. The trail turns into a roofless tunnel, and the best part is that there are no bears to worry about. I watch the mist settle onto Port aux Basques as I approach my final port of call in this province, feeling both relieved and sad at the same time.

We are welcomed with an amazing turkey supper at the Pennys'. It is comforting to be back in this familiar home with people who treat us like family. David Davis, a train engineer, entertains me with stories after supper. He is a quiet man with a terrific smile and an obvious love of the railway.

David Davis - "In 1960 I went railroading. I spent a lot of my time in the yard in Port aux Basques loading and unloading the railcars. It was kind of exciting times. I started engineering in '84. We had a freight train break apart one time and the locomotive just left the train completely. We had to keep the brakes off and keep ahead of the train.

There was an accident on the Gaff Topsails between Kitties East and Kitties West. They had brake trouble...heavy train. Probably didn't have enough air pressure. Coming around the curve, the engine went off...she was 100 ton. It takes somethin' to upset an engine, right? When they had that wreck up on south branch, one of those green terra transport containers was over on its side and there was a rail gone right through the car. There'd be a lot of washouts in the spring of the year and they would happen fast. And in the summertime, there'd be sun kinks. On a hot day, the rails would heat up and when the rails heat up they expand, right? And there is nowhere for them to go when they spring, so they'd just buckle. If you'd see it ahead of you quick enough, you'd stop. The section crew would come out and cut a piece out of the rail, then put it all back and join them up again. If you didn't see it, you would go off of the track and you'd have to call the section crew. In a rainstorm, you would watch for washouts and in the wintertime, you'd watch for heavy snow."

I mention that the country we were in yesterday was definitely bear country. Dave agrees.

"It's bear country there, going down to Riverbrook. Don't believe all these tales they tell you about bears, like if a bear chases you, run down hill, because the bear's hind legs are higher than the front legs, so they'll tip over. Never heard that one before? I've seen bears run down drains and up the other side of the ditch. I've seen them run more than 35 miles an hour. That's how fast we were going over the bog on the Gaff—you can't outrun them. From Millertown Junction, we counted 57 moose one night. Moose are usually a night animal, caribou you see in the day. I struck two moose one day. They were side by side. Didn't jar the train.

The names of train sections get their names in the most interesting ways. In one place when they laid the track, a section man got food poisoning, so call that piece of track 'Scutter Straight.' There was a straight out here called 'Never Been Laid.' There's another place on the other side of the Gaff called 'Mary March,' where the Beothuk woman was captured. Where you came through today was called Crooked Brook, right down there by Riverbrook. Imagine a river being called a river and a brook at the same time. Riverbrook. Stuck for names, eh?"

Dave Davis, Betty and I discuss the legends of the ghost train. Some said that they could hear the train coming over the Mary March Bridge, and some people saw the light of it coming. Others have even said that they saw it go by and that they could see the engineer and then the train just disappears. Legend has it that dispatchers have called ahead to say that the train is coming through early. However, despite this sighting, there was no train. Dave has had his own haunting visions on the Gaff.

"I fell asleep going down the Gaff once and saw a fella jump on the front of the engine. He came up the runnerboard then reached for the door. When he opened the door, I woke up.

There is still a boxcar down over the bank at Horseshoe Curve. I almost upset a train there, around on the big downgrade. When they had me trainin', I reached for the brake and Charley said, " No, no! Let 'er go! Let 'er go! Let 'er go!" So I hit the points—the west points at Fishhooks at 35 miles an hour—just like we were on a roller coaster. I'm sweatin' now just thinking about it! I looked back at the regular engineer, Ozzy Bennet, and John Park, the conductor...two of them with their faces right up in the window. They wondered why I didn't have the brake on. I said to Charley, 'You better pick up the train now, I'm new at this.' He said, 'No. Go on!'

The old engineers were pretty skilled. They knew where every curve was. Every grade they had to know, because in the wintertime they couldn't see. They had to concentrate on counting the curves. The speed chart tells you that if you go 44 poles in 12 minutes you are doing 5 miles an hour. If you went 44 poles in 40 seconds, you are doing 90 miles an hour. You can count poles if you want to spot check. You'd say that engineer is driving a bit fast and you'd count and phone him up and say, 'Now boys, slow down.' I still dream about the trains. I'd go back tomorrow."

May 16
Place: Port aux Basques, rest day

It is a day of well-needed rest as we prepare for our next province. We have forgotten Nicholas' hat in Corner Brook and Bob Day is kindly sending along the hat, as well as a huge block of cheese for our lunches on the bus...thus begins the cheese saga.

(from Nora's diary)
How do you go about finding out if someone you've never met before is carrying cheese, without sounding like a nut? Nobody, even the people working at the bus terminal, seem to know when or where the bus from Corner Brook will come in. After an hour, a lady got off of a bus with a small bag in her hand. Small enough to hold a hat and cheese. No luck. If someone did have our cheese, wouldn't they be looking for us too? We begin walking around, talking about cheese, hoping someone will pick up on our cues. Mom goes right up to one woman and asks, "Do you have my hat?" The lady scuttles away, scared. By this time we are confused and giddy. Finally, a tall, blond girl, about to go out the door, turns around and she's holding a small package. It is a weird coincidence, but this girl, Danielle Boutlier, chosen at random by Bob at the Corner Brook bus terminal, was in one of my first-year courses at Acadia University. Isn't it a small world?

After that, Mom and I start walking back to Russell's. We are stopped by a traffic director, who tells us we are going up the wrong ramp. He points out the exit we should take. He has sent us onto the Trans Canada Highway. It is dark and foggy and we cling to the guard rails as the transfer trucks zip by. It is a scary and dangerous place to be walking. We are inching our way along the rail, holding onto each another, when a car pulls up beside us. Alarmed, we turn around. It is the police. 'Out for a walk, ladies?' the officer asks suspiciously, 'Didn't see anyone else walking out here tonight, did you?' he questions. We ask if he is looking for someone. He says that he is looking for someone from the hospital. 'Are they sick?' we ask. Not physically sick, we learn and then we decide to accept his offer of a drive back to the Penny's. Albert Lomond, Russell's friend, is already there, picking up a storm on the mandolin, as Russell plays the guitar and Betty sings. We join in, me on the fiddle and Mom on the banjo, until 3:30 A.M. Crawling into bed, I think about this being our last day in Newfoundland. I'm sad to leave. The landscape has everything—mountains, barrens, the ocean. But it is the people we have met who have started Hike 2000 out in the best way possible. There is no one we have met who hasn't made us feel completely at home. People here just seem to put all of themselves into everything that I value—music, friends, family, love, and life. The prospect of going back to Nova Scotia and seeing what lies ahead is exciting, but for some reason I can't get rid of this pit of sadness that the first leg of our journey is over.

May 17

Place: Ferry from Port aux Basques to North Sydney, Nova Scotia
Distance: hiked the remaining distance to make 202.2 km

(from Maria's diary)
Russell, Mom and I go for a walk, putting all of our warm clothes on. It is beautiful and sunny out, but the wind is chilling. We leave the house, walking down the road, over the bridge, into sea grass, and eventually onto the beach. Two horses are tethered, eating the dried strands of grass left from the year before, which are whipping in the wind. We walk on a small path of sand, pebbles and broken shells dropped by gulls. We walk over the sand, close to the beach, picking up and inspecting shells and stones. We jump over small streams which flow to the sea, leaving footprints deep in the water-soaked sand. The sand soon turns to pebbles,

then rocks, as we head up and over boulders that scatter the beach. We walk between and over tiny footprints, possibly left by caribou calves. I sit down on a boulder which has trapped water in a small bowl. Small animals scuttle and swim through the water; some look similar to miniature crayfish. We turn around and head back to the beach, where I walk down by the water, letting the waves just lap against my soles.

I look out over the water. I am no longer a hiker. I am a sailor, looking out over the sea, checking for high waves that'll cause me to change my course for the day's journey. I am a geologist, looking carefully at the combinations of minerals left on the beach. I am a bird, soaring in the wind looking for fish. I am a wild horse, breathing in air laden with saltwater.

I continue on my way, catching up with Mom and Russell. We finish our hike and pack our bins, then have a wonderful brunch of corned beef and potato cakes. Sadly we leave for the ferry, leaving Newfoundland and completing our first province. The ferry ride is quiet, all of us remembering so many new friends, so many experiences. I have taken a Gravol, and after my last experience, you'd think I'd have learned. I quickly pass out on a chair, unable to even open my eyes to respond to the small boy who is standing by my head, waving his arms and exclaiming over the water outside. Heike has a gift of shells tied with string, used as a necklace to signify the bond which we have grown.

I watch the tiny, brightly painted houses grow smaller as we move farther out onto the cold Atlantic. We are leaving Newfoundland and now, looking back, I think how it truly is 'the rock'. What impresses me are the reds and purples of the barrens, that unforgiving landscape that rolls across the rock like a loose carpet. The animals that make this vast sub arctic tundra their home are not always seen, but are forever in our presence. I think of the moose peering back at us as we crawled up through the snow on the way to the summit of the Discovery Trail by Woody Point. There is the vision of the caribou, loping along the old rail bed in Howley, frightened by our intrusion. These animals are the real inhabitants here in this sometimes cruel environment.

A moon, low in the sky, sends a pinkish-purple tinge across the wide span of water that will separate us from this wildly beautiful, rugged island and its humble, gracious people.

Nova Scotia

Heike, Betty, Nora, Maria, Kathy, and Nicholas.

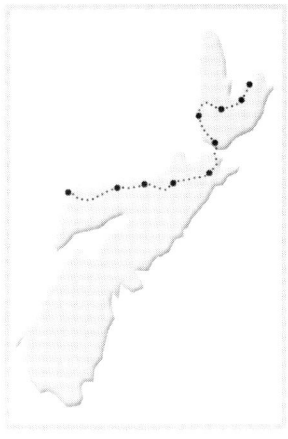

May 18

Shenacadie to Grand Narrows
Distance: 22.14 km
Wildlife: violets, loons, eagles, ducks

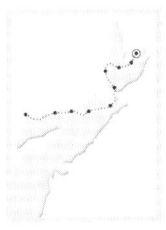

The sun streams through the window onto the brightly coloured spread of my double bed. I can hardly believe I have slept this long. Outside, white and pink blossoms appear on the cherry trees and there is a hint of green in the fields. We have sailed from a cold winter into the freshness of spring overnight. We are in Glace Bay, Cape Breton, at the home of Karen Morrison, a long-time friend of my sister Glenda. Despite her early departure to school, Karen has prepared for our stay with a refrigerator full of food. Her home is warm, spacious and comfortable and we linger over our morning breakfast, enjoying this luxury.

Jim Redden, a Cape Breton trail representative, has agreed to meet us in Shenacadie with East Link Cable for an interview. The trailhead today is situated right below an operating train track, our first on this venture. As East Link begins its interview, a small working train chugs by. The timely appearance of this train is the first of many as we make our way across the country. With the passenger trains now gone from this area and an employment base in decline, many residents have to seek work elsewhere or resort to employment insurance. Glenn McInnis, my niece Julie's boyfriend, grew up in Glace Bay. His "Train Song" is about the trains leaving Cape Breton and the plight of the people: "The time is long and your tolerance is short/When you've got yourself a family to support/Now, pretty soon, I'll have to go away/Because…We thought we saw a light at the end of the tunnel/Lord, and then they took away the train."

The trail, which is obstructed with thick growing bushes, curls along a winding river. It is wet underfoot and in some places, impassable. We cling to alders on the side of the trail, trying to balance ourselves so as not to land head first in the water. This unmarked trail is confusing, linking to cross roads and logging roads. We stop often, disputing our instructions. Finally, we meet a man who is doing some work on one of the trails. He informs us we have passed the meeting spot for the highway and we have to backtrack. We are annoyed by this constant confusion with directions. Bruce has marked the trail with marking tape, realizing that we may have difficulty. He backtracks to find us and we hike together to Jim's property for lunch. Jim owns an expanse of woodland that offers amazing views and rich forest.

Meeting up with Jim, we pull some rotting logs from a pile he has cut and squat for lunch. And a disappointing lunch it is. The rolls we had purchased the day before are so dry they could have been breathed down. We choke our lunch down with gulps of water amid the newly arrived mosquitoes. The sun brings added warmth and we strip some layers for the afternoon hike. Jim has done an extensive amount of work on trail development in the area and kindly shows us a look-off point on his property with a view right out to the Bras d'Or lakes. The green of the forest and the bright blue of the water in the distance is such a contrast to the low shrub and windswept barrens that we were accustomed to seeing in Newfoundland.

We listen intently to the directions for the afternoon hike. We don't need more back-tracking on an already long trek. Heike decides it is a day to rest her aching muscles, so she stays behind. We continue on the road that cuts through Jim's property. It is wide and hard-packed with wet mud. The road climbs up over a high ridge where we are greeted with a motley array of greens. The fields are sprouting with fresh growth and the pale green of the hardwoods contrasts with the deep evergreens. If only a picture could capture the freshness of this new spring growth. The muddy road passes the occasional farm, with family names written in Gaelic on little signposts, then snakes back into the wooded area. After coming upon many unmentioned "Ts" in the road, and traveling more than five kilometres in the wrong direction, we finally reach the main road leading to Christmas Island. We have stopped often, rehearsing the directions outlined to us, and still they are unclear. Fortunately, this confusion isn't an everyday occurrence.

Our trek is brightened occasionally with a visit by local dogs: first Hughie, then Misty, another larger dog that just wants to tag along, then a puppy that has to be retrieved by its owner. The last stretch is along a winding highway bordered by the deep blue waters of the bay. Passing Christmas Island, we stop for a few photos at the legendary post office. This post office is busiest, as one might expect, during the Christmas season, with people sending their cards from all over the world to be postmarked here. We finally sight Bruce and Heike coming to meet us in our van. It is the last day for Bruce to be with us and as we drive to Boisdale, the mood is glum.

It is a relief to reach the summer home of Jim Morrison in Boisdale. He is the father of my friend Kirk Morrison, and he has kindly offered us a place to stay for two nights. Jim is standing in the yard waiting for us. I am sure he is apprehensive as we are complete strangers and Kirk has not yet arrived. He watches as the new arrivals pile out of the van and meet their new hosts with grateful enthusiasm. Laura, Bruce's wife, has come to pick him up. We are sad to see Bruce go. We shared so many laughs in the days in Newfoundland. It truly was the dry run for the rest of the trip and Bruce waited on us like queens. We knew not to question the driver and we needed not, as he carefully escorted us through the rain, sleet and snow without a problem. He patiently waited for us at every turn and met us on the trail whenever he could. Our aching muscles will definitely miss him.

Kirk's brother Kevin and his girlfriend, Charlene, are there to greet us. Charlene is a comfortable, traditional person who immediately makes us feel welcome. She invites us inside the big white house and offers cold beer. We parade in, choose our sleeping spots and get acquainted with the Morrisons while Betty prepares a chicken stew and Nora tunes up the fiddle. Something about Jim Morrison reminds me of my father. Whether it is his hyper boxer dog, his unpredictable behaviour or his ability to tell a good story, I recognize their likeness immediately. He is a kindhearted man and his compassion builds as he shares his stories about his life driving the trains for Canadian Pacific.

Jim Morrison - "There used to be a train station about a mile east of here. You got on the train in the morning and you went to school in Iona and you would meet all these characters on the train—all good people, too. Your father bought you a ticket and they'd punch it. Some days, you really didn't want to go to school. There would be the old nuns and they'd be cross and you wouldn't have your homework done on Monday. We'd go right by the school and go to Port Hawkesbury and meet the other fellows. In the afternoon, you'd get off the train with the rest of the kids and your mother would say 'Did you have a hard day today?'

We were in Sydney and I was goin' down with a load of coal, over thirty thousand ton on, and I had the headlight on and there was something on the track. I didn't know what it was but I put on the best brakes that I had and here it was two people making out and they were right between the rails. So, I threw on the emergency and I got out and I said 'What's going on here? I could have killed you.' The guy on the track said, 'Well, she was going and I was going and you were the only guy that could stop us!' That's terrible isn't it? But that's a matter of fact. I threw on the emergency. I was so close to killing them…they were busy.

I was driving in New Waterford, and the brakeman was sitting over there and it must have been grading day because a little girl was twiddling her grading card. I blew the whistle and I blew the whistle and she just stood in the middle of the track. I told myself I had to do something. The brakeman wasn't paying attention because he was on my side and couldn't see. I chucked the train into emergency, jumped down, on the cow catcher and just picked her up and flung her into the ditch. she started bawling and crying and I said, 'Sweetheart, you're lucky you are alive.'"

We enjoy a late supper and some good yarns before tucking into our beds in this great house. Maria, Heike and Nora share the room at the top of the stairs, Betty and I, the room next to Jim's, and Nicholas tucks into his sleeping bag on the big couch in the upstairs hallway. This house reminds me of my mother's family home in Wittenburg, Nova Scotia. The rooms are cozy with patterned oilcloths on the slanted floors. As we drift off to sleep, I think of how familiar I feel in this place among the people we have only met a few hours ago.

May 19

Grand Narrows to Ottawa Brook
Distance: 17.5 km
Wildlife: eagles, hawk

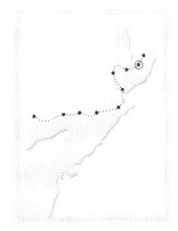

I sit on the large doorstep overlooking the morning sun on the water below and gulp the fresh air coming off the channel. Surely that will help push back the nausea I am feeling from last night's generous supply of rum and pineapple. I struggle getting some breakfast into my shaky body and strap on my pack. A warm wind sweeps up from the narrows as we set out this morning. Unfortunately, our trek today is along the road, which, despite the excellent views, just isn't relaxing. We divert into a small field to have our lunch and stretch out in the sun. It is great to be back in Nova Scotia, every day bringing us closer to the warm weather and less and less clothing to tote along. The grass has grown tall and lush in this protected spot, a perfect nesting place for the ants.

The afternoon hike brings us to high ridges overlooking the water. It is truly a magnificent spot. It is too bad that we have to be so conscious of cars that we cannot relax and enjoy this vista. We continue on toward Ottawa Brook. We promised Kirk we would give him a call and are happy to come to a little side diner called "Cathy's Place II." I wonder what "Cathy's Place I" looked like. There is a pay phone on the outside wall and a sign reading "Open year round." The walkway is overgrown, the doors bolted and the windows are bare and curtainless. The phone is obviously out of order. There is something very haunting about this place. A hawk circles overhead as we contemplate whether to continue on or wait for Kirk. Luckily, Kirk, our gracious host, takes pity on us after 17.5 kilometres of walking, and picks us up in his car. Back at the house, cold beer and lobsters are waiting. What a treat! John arrives with my cousin Billy Redden, our new driver, and Lars Ottoson, our friend from Sweden. Lars has visited us before in Nova Scotia and has met us for hiking in Switzerland. This time he will hike with us across Nova Scotia and Prince Edward Island. We are happy to have his company and his talents of Swedish massage! Maria's friend Iain Caldwell also joins us in Boisdale and will stay with us until Guysborough. This is the first night for the tents to be pulled out and set up, a good dry run for what is to come in the months ahead. Maria and Iain struggle for hours in the dark, trying to fit the vestibule and fly into place. Since it is a replacement fly from LL Bean, it isn't quite like the old one and their patience grows thin trying to make it fit. Nora, Lars and Heike join them later, crawling through a web of strings to get into the tent. This chore of putting up the tent will later be perfected into a ten-minute task.

May 20

Mabou to Port Hood
Distance: 29 km
Wildlife: eagles

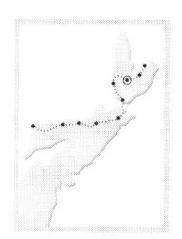

A crew of 12 greets us at the Mabou fire station. They are here to walk with us. My 85-year-old mother, Eleanor (Dolly) Belmore, my sisters Bonnie Price, Dianne Englund and Glenda Burrows, my niece Lisa Price and her husband, Mike Stokesbury, Mike's mother, Liz Stokesbury, our good friends Margie Parker, Peter and Janet MacKenzie, and the MacKenzie children, Erin and Lauren. We exchange welcoming hugs and pose for pictures in front of the local fire station. My mother, who underwent a lengthy bypass surgery on her leg this spring, is dressed

Betty and Heike scramble through alders on the trail to Port Hood.

for hiking and ready to go. If only I possess her spirit when I am her age! Billy is walking with us for the first five kilometres, then he and Mom will meet us for lunch farther along. It is a grand beginning down the old rail bed that threads along the Northumberland coast. The sun is warm and we chatter like a flock of birds just arriving back for spring.

(from Dolly's diary)
It is warm and sunny at noon on Saturday as we drive to Mabou fire station, where our hike will began. The fire chief happens to be at the station and graciously offers to bring out a fire truck and position it as a backdrop. He then snaps picture after picture from the cameras we have piled at his feet. We start out along the old railway, 22 hikers plus Ceilidh the dog. The scenery along the route is beautiful, with lakes and rivers, budding trees and shrubs. Since it is my first day to hike, I want to be careful not to overdo it. I walk five kilometres with my nephew, Bill Redden. It is his first day as the new bus driver. We drive to Hermina's Greenhouse, where we meet the others for lunch. The owner has just put up her sign for the season when we all arrive. She invites us into the greenhouse so that we can be sheltered from the wind. We spread ourselves between the plants and hanging baskets and share some bread, cheese, fruit and chocolate. It is very pleasant. Some of us buy seedlings as souvenirs.

The hike from Hermina's to Port Hood takes a sudden change. The rolling green fields turn to a dense growth of alder bushes. The

Hiking the Dream

previously well-graded trail changes to an overgrown path that disappears into the thickets. We cross over many trestled bridges and scramble through the wooded areas. The ocean is never very far away, offering us spectacular views from time to time.

(from Dolly's diary)
We arrive in Port Hood at 5:30, gather at the Lighthouse Cottages and make plans for the evening. We change our clothes, and pile into the cars to head to Creignish. Kathy had arranged a hall there to be opened so that we can meet with the local people to hear their stories and songs—the first of many venues to respond to a request to meet with townspeople. We are all anticipating an exciting evening. When we get to Creignish, we are greeted by a crimson sunset and a locked hall. Despite previous arrangements, this meeting is not to be, but our spirits will not be dampened. Twenty-five musicians (all family and friends), including Wilfred and Vera Boudreau and Laurettte from Victoria Mines, open up the guitar and fiddle cases and we have our own ceilidh!

Back at the Mackenzie's summer home in Port Hood, the instruments are pulled from their cases once more as steak and potatoes are thrown onto the grill for a late-night meal. Peter and Janet McKenzie will be our hosts for two nights as we trek down the abandoned rail line to Creignish. Taking his new position as support driver very seriously at this point, Billy goes to bed early in the basement below, the music serenading him long into the night.

Back at Peter and Janet MacKenzie's summer home in Port Hood, we roll out the guitars and sing long into the night.

Nova Scotia

May 21

Port Hood to Judique
Distance: 20.8 km
Wildlife: Canada geese, coyote signs, grass snake

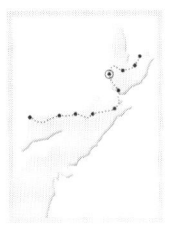

(from Bonnie's diary)
Today the sun is shining but we begin the hike wearing gloves and jackets, as the strong breeze gives the air a chill. Our starting point is a small ice cream stand just outside of Port Hood. Fifteen of us stretch out to begin our hike to Judique. This proves to be more challenging than yesterday's hike because so much of the trail is overgrown with alders that twist and turn together over our heads and around our feet. These patches of alders end suddenly and we find a grassy open path with strawberry blossoms underfoot. At one point we emerge from the alders on a dirt road and are advised to detour to avoid the next section of alders. We soon give up the idea of detouring and head back across a field where we spot a trestle bridge over the river. From there, we decide to put up with the overgrown parts so we don't miss the pleasant surprises of the open stretches, like the glimpses of fields and farm, the low growing clumps of heather, blue violets springing up in the shaded woods, and even the crumbling remains of an old railway station. Billy meets us at the Tin Fiddler, where all 15 of us pile into the van.

We decide to meet at the Mackenzie's tonight for a communal meal, which Margie and Janet have prepared. This is an emotional time for me. Here, surrounded by my family, I realize that we will be parting for the next three months as we continue on the trail. John will return home. Betty, who has been with us

Kathy and John Didkowsky on the trail to Judique.

Hiking the Dream

since the start, will be leaving us. I am touched that so many of my family have come so far to be with us, sad that they are now leaving, and apprehensive about what lies ahead. I have never been good with partings and tonight is no exception. As we sing the old familiar tunes, I fight back tears. When Mum decides to sing, I take a quick glance at Janet, who has tears sliding down her face. I give up! Tears fill to the brim of my eyes, spill over and trace paths down my windburnt cheeks.

After the crowd has gone, I pull myself onto the bed beside Janet and Peter. With Margie on the mattress on the floor, I read them a bedtime story, which is actually a recipe from a cookbook. It lightens my mood, and as I crawl into my own bed, I try to re-walk that section of rail bed to Codroy Pond in my head. It's amazing how vivid it is to me. With each step, I become drowsier, finally sinking into a deep sleep.

May 22

Long Point to Creignish
Distance: 13 km
Wildlife: seagulls, dandelions

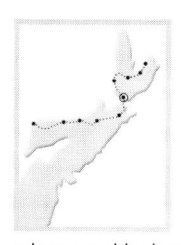

(from Iain's diary)
After two days of walking well over the described 20 kilometres, we have diminished from 16 bright-eyed and bushy-tailed travelers to eight stolid and somewhat shook-up scufflers. A wonderful breakfast of toast, omelets, ham and much-needed coffee has been provided by our hosts, Janet and Peter, before our drive to Long Point. The trail begins beside a horse paddock, and so a short stop is necessary before heading off. We take our first picture beside a field of bright green grass (a welcome sight after so many alders) spotted with dandelions. The trail is well maintained and devoid of the large rocks that are common on other trails. It is a beautiful sunny day—one of the warmest yet—which also brings up people's moods. Betty, who has been walking with the troupe since the beginning, has left, and the void is noticeable. The trail is bordered by the ocean for almost the entire 13 kilometres. For someone who

Nova Scotia

The boys! Nicholas, Iain Caldwell and Lars Ottoson on the trail to Creignish.

loves the ocean as much as I, this is a welcome addition to the hiking experience. Rosehips and evergreens give way to fields of grass overlooking the Atlantic. Although it is warm, it is never uncomfortably so, and a slight wind completes the atmosphere. It's easy to see how people fall in love with the sea in this area. I imagine that its beauty mesmerized train passengers on this track, as well. It is along such a stretch that we spot a long-abandoned house. There are no obvious roads leading to it and it has clearly been here for a long time. Its windows are broken and a portion of it is making its way down the steep slope that it perches atop. But, it still has its rustic charm. It is like a window into the past. Perhaps a family of fisher folk lived here when fishing was still a chief source of income for small families in this area. Perhaps a woman looked out from a window facing the sea, waiting for a husband or a son to return. Nora, Maria and Kathy fall in love with this place.

The path winds farther inland for a portion before making its way back to coastal scenes. The hike ends much earlier than expected. We even have enough energy to play wicker ball. After setting down to a late lunch of bread, cheese and various leftover snacks, we are off to find a camping area across the causeway in the little town of Guysborough. We settle at the Belmont Campground and as Maria and I go off to find groceries for tonight's meal, the rest of the crew sets up the tents. A supper of hamburgers, carrots, and pasta salad are enjoyed graciously by all.

The mist settles around us on the first night of tenting for the whole crew. I sit in the lawn chair that I have brought along, which has been dubbed the 'queen's seat.' Iain has gone to great lengths to find the ingredients to make me a 'Mahito,' a Cuban drink with fresh mint. I have recently returned from a vacation in Cuba and despite the cold air that is now drifting off the Atlantic, the drink brings back memories of the warm beach. Tonight, we split into the "girls" tent

Hiking the Dream

and the "boys" tent. The exact positioning of our sleeping bags on this cold night in May will remain the same until our last night in the tents in late August.

May 23

Guysborough
Distance: 27 km
Wildlife: 3 blue herons

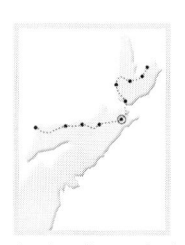

I cannot believe I have slept so long. Nine o'clock and we are just crawling from our cozy sleeping bags…some of us, that is.

(from Lars' diary)
This night we are sleeping in tents for the second time this trip. The first night, I realized that a very nice, light, thin sleeping bag is good when you are trying to fit all of your things in a backpack, but it is not quite as nice when you have to sleep in a cold tent. This time instead I borrowed another sleeping bag, and I was looking forward to a good night's sleep. This turned out to be a false hope, due to some problems getting the sleeping bag out of its cover. I had to use my own once again with the same results as last time—not much sleep at all.

The smell of coffee brewing over the open fire is welcoming and I draw close to its warmth. Billy has already had his toast and is exploring the grounds, which includes an excellent golf course. He bemoans the fact that he has not brought his clubs along.

Ira and Betty Ann Corkum guide us to the Guysborough trail.

Nova Scotia

Wet fog pierces my body. Slowly, bodies begin emerging from the tents. I stir up a batch of pancakes as the tents are stripped of their contents and rolled into their sacks. Ira and Betty Ann Corkum meet us and lead us to the trail head. Betty Ann gives us some homemade cookies and walks with us for a while. Ira is an enthusiastic trail builder with the Guysborough trails group and has been instrumental in its development over the past few years. The trail is well maintained with rest stops, picnic tables and benches. The path leads through a green forest with brooks running down off the hill and into the Salmon River. The trail is along a former rail bed that was prepared for the trains that were supposed to come to Guysborough. Ira shares with us the troubled history of the railway:

> "The Guysborough Railway was first thought about in 1897. It was to run from Pictou County to Guysborough, and haul coal, gold and timber from the harbour in Guysborough and from Cross Roads, Country Harbour. It became a bit of a political football because by 1930 no construction had yet taken place. Between 1930 and 1932, several contracts were awarded to companies to begin construction of the railway. During the construction of the abutments across the Salmon River in Guysborough at West Brook Cove, there was a very demanding foreman in charge. You can appreciate that trying to get the concrete to build a 60-foot abutment on either side of a fast flowing river would be nerve-wracking and tiresome work. Apparently, the foreman was just too demanding, and somewhere along the course of construction he disappeared. The story is that he is entombed in one of those abutments today.
>
> A bridge never was put over the Salmon River. Construction was stopped and funding was cancelled—never to be started again. That was in 1932. The Guysborough Railway was about 87 per cent complete at that time. With our efforts now through the trails association, we are hoping to bring the first train to Guysborough—a caboose that will serve as the trail information center. The only activity on that rail bed until now has been that of snowmobilers and loggers."

We walk past those famous abutments. It is chilling to think that there might be a body entombed in one of these concrete giants. We hurry on. A snowmobiler's cabin provides shelter from the cold mist as we bring out our familiar bread and cheese for lunch. Being in Guysborough and listening to Ira's stories reminds us of the song by Stan Rogers about the legendary Guysborough train:

Guysborough Train by Stan Rogers
c.1973 p.1999 - used by permission of Fogarty's Cove Music/Ariel Rogers

Now there's no train to Guysborough
Or so the man said
So it might be a good place to be
I sit in this station
And I count up my change
And I wait for the Guysborough train

Now I've sat in your kitchens
And talked about walls
And I've sung of your withering pain,
Shattered your temples
And I've brought on your fall
Now I wait for the Guysborough train
Chorus
And I ride for all time
On the Guysborough line
And I grow by the north county rain
And the North Shore's begun
The man I've become
In rags, on the Guysborough train
No train to Guysborough
Now ain't that a shame
Though I know there will be one in time
And the house that's alone
It soon will be gone
Razed for the Guysborough line
Chorus
People are simple
Like the rain clouds sweet
Both grown by that North County rain
The interval is clear
Will it soon disappear?
Under the Guysborough train

Nova Scotia

Back on the trail we catch glimpses of Chedabucto Bay and the gray Atlantic.

Ira has kindly arranged our stay at the Masonic Lodge for the night. For this, we are truly grateful as the rain and fog move in, chilling the spring air. The Guysborough County Youth Fiddlers soon arrive to serenade us as we bustle to make soup. Betty, Glenda, Dianne and Mum arrive. We are so happy to see them all again. We sing and Nora plays the fiddle with Eddie, the Youth Fiddlers' leader. He is a friendly man with an obvious love of the fiddle. We dance and sing. Food arrives for us. Mary Williams, who we have just met, hustles home and returns with a fresh batch of hot biscuits, cheese, and jam. The people of Guysborough town pour their warmth on us. We are so fortunate to have met such hospitable people. Again, we say goodbye to family as they head into the dark, rainy night for the long drive home along the Atlantic coast.

May 24

Tidnish
Distance: 8 km
Wildlife: cherry blossoms, strawberry blossoms, mosquitoes, songbirds

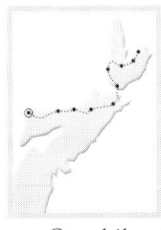

Billy has made coffee on the little stove in the kitchen below the Masonic Lodge. I pour myself a cup and sit on a little broken chair to collect my thoughts. I have an appointment to call CBC Radio's "Information Morning" and I must make arrangements for the interview with East Link Cable when we reach the ship railway.

Our hike today will begin in Tidnish, where the ship railway would have been at the turn of the century. The idea was to build a railway that would transport ships across the 17-mile isthmus of Chignecto that divides the Northumberland Strait and the Bay of Fundy. Ships laden with goods that had been sailed down the St. Lawrence would be placed in a holding basin, then raised by hydraulic lifts onto a cradle. They would then be settled upright onto two 40-foot-wide railcars coupled together. Two parallel tracks, with two locomotives, would haul the "side by side" railcars holding the three-thousand-ton vessel. What a sight this would have been! The ship would be transported to the holding berth on the other side of the isthmus, saving them the five-hundred-mile-long journey around Nova Scotia to the Bay of Fundy. It was an ingenious idea born by Henry George Ketchum, who two-thirds of the way through construction had to halt the project because of lack of funding. Ketchum died in 1896, a disappointed man.

Now, as we file through the narrow pathway that would have been the rail line, we wonder what it might have been like to see large ships being transported through this constricted passage. The trail is dotted with strawberry blossoms, and cherry blossoms form a canopy overhead. The pale, fresh green of early spring surrounds us. I think how this is my husband's favorite colour in the forest, then push back the longing for his presence. The trail winds up and down, over old roots. There is no graded rail bed, since it has long been overgrown. We climb a stairway carpeted with soft green moss and pass through tunnels arched with hanging blossoms sparkling with water droplets left from last night's rain. It is lush and soft underfoot and the earthy smells penetrate our senses. It is a wonderful hike.

(from Heike's diary)
We pass through one stretch of forest where the trees are practically draped in old man's beard. Nicholas and I like this eerie backdrop…it reminds us of something from The Lord of the Rings. We turn around to walk back once we reach the swing bridge, one of the highlights of the day. We think it would be fun to jump off in summer. Of course, it isn't warm enough for those kinds of shenanigans today. Jumping off the bridge is prohibited, anyway.

Our home for the night is fittingly in the cozy caboose belonging to our friends, Trevor and Pam Townsend in Fox Harbour. Trevor's father was a trainman and as Trevor shows me a treasured lantern belonging to his father, he relates stories about his father's life on the railway.

Pam & Trevor Townsend - "I have a lantern that belonged to my dad, William Lloyd Townsend, when he first joined the railway on December 13, 1926. My mom kept it and gave it to me a couple of years ago so I could have it here at the caboose. He was a conductor on the railway between Louisbourg and Sydney. They would get coal in Glace Bay and take it out to Louisbourg where it was shipped to the United States. He lost a thumb when he got it caught in a coupling between the cars on the train. I don't know what to tell you except that he absolutely loved the railroad. He had a heart condition and had to leave it when I was about eight. It was a big blow to his life. Both his father and my mother's father were railway men. They both worked on the same railway—one as a conductor and one as an engineer. They were best friends. The caboose is named the William Laurier, William for my dad and Laurier for Pam's dad."

Pam and Trevor cook up a barbeque with salads and buns. We sit in the caboose relating our trail stories. To the annoyance of the others, Pam and I get out pictures of our recent trip to Cuba, sharing stories that engross us for hours. Tonight, tucked into the top bunk of the William Laurier, where once the trainmen slept, I dream about taking a caboose all the way around the world. I better not mention this to my family until later!

May 25

Wallace to Tatamagouche
Distance: 23.5 km
Wildlife: song birds, stick bug, frogs, forget-me-nots

I awaken to the smell of fresh muffins and coffee, feeling refreshed and ready to tackle another day on the trail. Nora, Maria, Nicholas, Lars, and Billy have been sleeping in "the small boat-shaped cabin, listening to the soothing pattering of rain on the

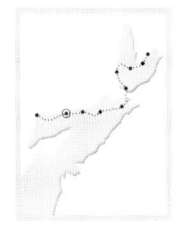

We approach Tatamagouche station, now a cozy inn.

roof" (Nora's diary), owned by John and Marylee Townsend. We only wish they, too, had been here with us last night. Heike is nestled in the bunk opposite mine. Pam and Trevor pack 'real' sandwiches, fresh fruit and drinks for our hike to Tatamagouche. We are delighted that they will join us for this leg of our journey because they offer us 'new blood and new stories,' as Nora puts it. It is amazing that we never run out of things to talk about on the trail and that people just seem to match up with whoever is walking their pace and start up a good conversation that lasts for hours.

The smell of the soft earth reminds us that spring is really here. With the new warmth comes black flies. We exclaim over the freshness of the day, the new green of the bushes and the cherry blossoms that line our path. We stop for lunch at a well-decked bridge over a murky river, which runs peacefully into tall green grasses on its banks. We stop occasionally to tend to the 'hot spots' on our feet. Passing farms nestled between rolling green pastures, we strip our layers as the sun burns through the fog. The trail into Tatamagouche borders the sparkling water of the Northumberland Strait along green fields peppered with dandelions. Forget-me-nots complete the array on this carpet of colours. We approach the old creamery, whose original structure was built in 1925. As we approach the Tatamagouche station, as trains would have in the past, we can see the train cars lined up, and sheets billowing high in the breeze on the line running from the station. An old baggage buggy sits on the platform with vintage trunks. Here, you can truly imagine the excitement of the approaching train.

(from Nora's diary)

We choose to have supper at the Villager Restaurant, which turns out to be a blessing. The food is excellent, our conversations interesting and the friendly service is just what we need. On our walk back home, we notice a sign saying "Coffee House," so we follow the arrow, which points us to the creamery. The lights are off, but candles flicker in the windows. Not knowing what to expect, we enter the building and are greeted at the top of the stairs with coffee. Inside, a man is playing a guitar and a girl is singing. They sound great. They explain that they have been running this coffee house every second Thursday for the past three years. No one is there except for us, which is a shame. The music is top-notch, the people energetic and friendly and the atmosphere, comfortable…comfortable enough for us to brave getting up to sing a few tunes in front of these strangers. This stop is just what we needed to round out a wonderful day. We leave at about 11:00 and walk down the railway line, finally crawling into our caboose beds to fall asleep.

May 26

Tatamagouche to River John
Distance: 23.5 km
Wildlife: deer, apple blossoms, many mosquitoes

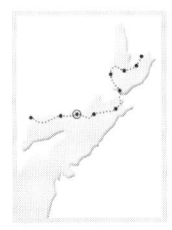

Catching up on email and phone calls is not to happen this morning. Perry from East Link Cable is here to do a documentary on our hike for a program called "Plugged In." He arrives as we are enjoying a delicious breakfast of orange juice, French toast, eggs, bacon, fruit and coffee, which James LeFresne, owner of the Tatamagouche Train Station Inn, has prepared. James entertains me with stories about the Tatamagouche station and his life as a young boy growing up next to the trains.

"Back in the late forties, the train that went by was a one-car passenger train. It was diesel electric and it just went up and down the tracks. You could put your hand out and the train would stop and pick you up anywhere along the track. One gentleman from the area owned some woodlots down the tracks, not near any station, about ten miles from here. As the *Jitney* was coming into Tatamagouche from Wallace, the man put his hand out to wave it down and get a ride into the village. Somewhere along the line something happened and the *Jitney* actually hit him and killed him. The men on the train got out and put his body into the baggage department. They brought him into the station here in Tatamagouche, into the men's waiting room, where there was a doctor waiting to go to River John. He pronounced the gentleman dead on arrival. The doctor then got on the *Jitney* and the *Jitney* left, leaving the body with the stationmaster to deal with. The stationmaster saw that the dead man was a personal friend of the local doctor, so when he called the undertaker, he also called the local doctor to inform him that the train had hit his friend and killed him. Lo and behold, the doctor arrived and found signs of life in his friend's body. He cancelled the hearse and called the ambulance to come down. The ambulance took the gentleman to the hospital in Truro and he remained in a coma for a month. He finally did come out of the coma, went back to normal life and became Senator Hawkins, representing this area in Ottawa. Apparently, when word first came in that Mr. Hawkins had been killed, the stationmaster informed his wife, who called their son in Truro and told him to come right home immediately because his father had been killed. Their son was in school because there was no secondary school here. He began packing to come home when the phone rang again; it was his mother telling him to stay in Truro, that his father was alive and had been taken to Truro. There were several ups and downs that day for the family.

We were always aware of the trains because the first whistles would blow about a mile outside the village. We knew the schedule of the train so I can remember my mother hanging out clothes on Monday—wash day. Usually the clothes went out on the line around ten o'clock because no train was scheduled at that time. But if that whistle blew a mile away, everyone ran to get the clothes off the line before the train went by and blackened them with smoke. It brings back lots of memories.

This station was built back in 1887. It is one of the oldest in Canada. The railway went through between 1900 and 1920. The most prominent dates in the history of the station are 1894, when Governor General Lord Aberdeen was here on a well-documented visit to the area, and 1991, when Governor General Hnatyshun was here at the train station and spent the evening with us. Upstairs was always living quarters for the stationmaster. This train station is of British design and is typical of stations built with living quarters upstairs and commercial quarters downstairs, which would consist of the ladies' waiting room, the men's waiting room, the telegraph room and the baggage room. Six stationmasters lived here over the years with their families. There have been weddings here, and births—the last in 1937.

Stationmasters were always very proud of their stations so they usually had gardens around them. Between trains, the stationmaster would tend his garden. One stationmaster in the 1950s, Mr. Colburn, maintained a community skating rink just outside the station. The rink was actually on the pond that filled the water tower that operated the steam engines. That community rink dated back to the 1930s and had electric lights for night skating. The train coming to Tatamagouche actually killed the shipbuilding industry here. When the trains came, they put a bridge across the French River, where one of the main shipbuilding areas was. The days of the ships were ending, and the railway was coming into its own as the main means of transportation. Back in 1959 they built the Trans Canada Highway and in 1960, just one year later, they closed the passenger service. So, the Trans Canada Highway marks the decline of the railway. It took them almost 30 years to close the railway. We do hold onto a piece of our history where other communities, such as Truro, have lost their old train station, and a big part of their identity with it.

There used to be over three hundred train stations in Nova Scotia. Today there are only 42. We are leading into another era, an era of people who are more interested in the environment and a slower pace of life."

I am glad that James had the foresight to hang on to this beautiful old station. It is such an excellent overnight spot for people using the trail.

Perry, from East Link Cable, films us as we go about our regular 'prehike' tasks...packing our bins in the trailer, stuffing sheep's wool between our toes to prevent blisters, covering already formed blisters with Band Aids and stretching our socks to make sure there are no wrinkles as we finally pull on our boots and tie them tightly to support our ankles. Iain

We are intrigued by this apparent wanderer on the trail to River John.

Caldwell has joined us again and we laugh and joke as Perry runs ahead of us filming our every move. Finally, he departs and we are left on our own. The rain sprinkles down on us and we find shelter in a wooded spot by an old rotting fence. Mosquitoes soon find us, so we hurry on down the trail. Suddenly, we halt in our tracks. Before us is a glorious doe, standing proudly, staring at us as we approach. Her head is high and it is obvious that she can see us, but she doesn't run. For more than 15 minutes, we exchange a curious gaze before she wanders slowly into the woods.

Behind us, a man has also been watching this creature. He is clad in layers of clothing, the outer layer a policeman's coat. He wears policeman pants and in his parcel carrier is a pair of heavier pants and a bag of personal belongings. He wears new shoes, yet his clothes are old and tattered. He appears to be a wanderer. He walks along beside me, pushing his bike as it bounces in and out of the ruts. I try to figure out who he is. It is hot, and sweat from his forehead drips from the end of his nose. He speaks of the law and wonders if we are protected, if we carry mace. He speaks to us about a friend who 'took a bullet to her hip.' We talk for almost two hours as he scuttles along beside me. As we come to the end of the line, we part. I still can't figure him out. I feel I have had an encounter with a hobo from the past.

In just a few moments, we step back in time and enter the Sutherland Steam Mill. Completed in 1894, it was used to construct carriages, sleds and sleighs. Doors and windows were also manufactured in the upstairs of the mill. Powered solely by steam, it could turn out footage much faster than the conventional water-powered mills of the time. Today, it operates as a museum, with demonstrations on the fancy cornice work for house trimming and spools for verandahs.

Billy meets us in River John where we climb into the van, piling our muddy boots into the back of the trailer. After a quick, refreshing stop for some local Scotsburn ice cream, we are on our way to Durham. Margie Parker is waiting for us in her roomy, renovated stone house. We feel at ease in the warmth of her home and soon sit with our feet up, recounting the highlights of our journey since we parted in Port Hood. After plate loads of potato scallop and ham, Margie, Janet and I whoop it up in the kitchen testing Margie's chocolate liquor as the rest retire upstairs away from our noise. Lars, much to his chagrin, shows up in the kitchen and is roped into a little "Swedish massage" demonstration under the guidance of Margie before we all roll off to bed.

May 27

Meadowville to Pictou
Distance: 17.5 km
Wildlife: squirrel, eagle

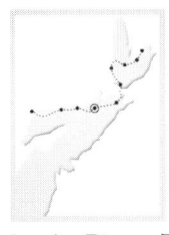

It is a peaceful day and the walk into Pictou is on a well-graded path, passing long stretches of fields before approaching the harbour. Margie, Janet, Lauren and Erin have joined us for the walk and Peter has decided to run it instead. We stop for lunch behind a neat farmyard. This perfectly groomed trail is a result of years of dedicated work by the Pictou Trails Association, my liaison with the Trans Canada Trails Council. I feel proud for them and their early work on this trail. Pictou Harbour boasts the warmest waters north of Florida with temperatures reaching 20°C. For the Atlantic this far north, it is good reason to boast!

(from Maria's diary)
We came to a spot where the Oddfellows House stands on the hill to our left. The house is made of stone in old Georgian style, surrounded by freshly mown grass (the kind that makes you want to take your shoes off and run your toes through). To our right is the harbour. Tall dry grasses wave gently in the slight breeze, adding the finishing touches to the scene, which seemed to be from a romance novel set in the southern states in the 1800s.

It is said that a ghost still lives in the laundry room of this house, which was once a home for needy seniors. Patients are sometimes seen doing their laundry before fading into the walls. The path into town turns to a paved walkway where we can now view a replica of the Hector, the boat that brought the first Scottish settlers to the area. We end our hike on this historic Jitney trail at the Pictou train

The trail into Pictou is on a paved path with a scenic view of Pictou Harbour and a replica of the *Hector*.

station. The original station had burnt down and the new one built in 1996 is its double.

Back at Margie's stone house with 'boots kicked off, feet out to dry,' we are alerted by an approaching noise. What is that coming up the driveway? A 1952, robin's-egg-blue Chevy rolls into the yard. Helen, Janet's mother, jumps out sporting her chauffeuring attire and offers a sightseeing tour of the area. Soon, the car is packed with adventurous hikers, out for a tour of the countryside in the luxury of this vintage machine. Helen plays the perfect role, as she cruises to the scenic look-offs, impressing her passengers not only with panoramic vistas but also the posh ambiance of their transportation. I opt to stay behind to mix up a pot of spaghetti sauce. Clay, Helen's friend, draws a chair up to the table where I am working, pulls out the mouth organ and entertains me as I cook. To my great surprise, John arrives. This is our last night in Nova Scotia before our final return at the end of August and his last chance to visit with us. As is usually the case when we all get together, the guitars and fiddle come out, and tonight, the mouth organ and banjo add to a night of songs. Billy, who has bunked down on the floor in the next room, comments about the pleasure of being serenaded to sleep. After hours of great music, we retire to our assigned rooms for the night. It is so nice to be here in the company of good friends.

Prince Edward Island

May 28 – June 7

On the trail to Hunter River, (left to right): Kristel Englund, Nora, Diane Englund, Christopher MacDonald, Maria, Lars Ottoson, Iain Caldwell, Nicholas, Heike, and (in front) Sonja and Kathy.

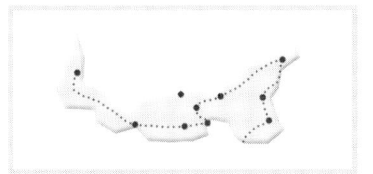

May 28

Wood Islands to Murray River
Distance: 11.5 km
Wildlife: skunk, Canada geese, blueberry fields

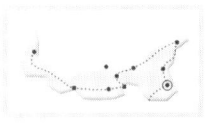

It is Sunday, the day we will begin hiking in our third province. Outside, it is cold and misty. I prolong my rising. John will go home today and we will leave our home province of Nova Scotia. We are so comfortable here in Durham, where people share our sense of humour and way of life.

Margie has made a big pan of scrambled eggs and a pile of toast. The instruments are pulled from their cases for one last tune before we leave. Our parting, as usual, is a scene. The Hike 2000 van is stuck on Margie's front lawn, which is soft from all the rain and it spins a rut as we all push from behind. With this elegant departure, we are off to the ferry, which will take us to Prince Edward Island.

(from Nicholas' diary)
At the ferry, we get out of the van and play hackey-sack with a wicker ball that Iain brought from the Philippines. We call the game wicker ball. This is where Iain leaves us and Topher (Christopher MacDonald) arrives. Topher comes with more

stuff than any one of us has for four months. The stuff will have to go in the back seat with me. After Iain leaves and we board the ferry, Lars, Topher and I decide to explore. We quickly find out that it is cold and windy out on the deck. We go inside and kill time in whatever way we can, which is mainly bugging Nora by pretending to press keys and the escape button while she is working on the web page.

On the ferry, I listen to a tape of train songs that Iain has made for me as I watch seagulls hovering above the ferry. They appear motionless, their sharp black eyes trained on the deck watching for a dropped morsel of food. We are approaching Prince Edward Island, Canada's smallest province. It is an island of rolling potato fields, dark red soil and people as kind and honest as anywhere on earth. It is amazing to think of how varied a people we are in Canada, our environments shaping our characters.

Dot Campbell, a long time friend of my sister Dianne, and her friend Carolyn Stewart meet us at the ferry in Wood Islands. They direct us to the trail, which is the old railway line running into Murray River. It is past 4 P.M., cold, and a mist is falling on our hunched shoulders. It is an effort to begin this late in the day, but we must. It is Topher's first day and he has brought along treats and a new enthusiasm that soon spills over to the rest of us. He is Nora's friend from university and we are glad he has joined us. He has training with the armed services and shares with us stories of his adventures as we plod along the trail.

To our dismay, the rail bed soon turns to a ploughed track. Thick, red mud cakes our boots. It is like walking through a freshly plowed potato field. As Heike said, "it's like walking on platform soles." We trudge along in deep mud for more than 12 kilometres. We pass blueberry barrens and hear Canada geese overhead. Topher sights our first skunk on the trail which brings a minor frenzy as the footing won't allow a fast escape, should we need one. Luckily, the innocent animal is only making its way home and just happened to cross our path.

Billy is waiting for us as we reach Murray River. Much to our weary delight, he has unloaded our bins into the local church hall, which Dot and Carolyn have kindly arranged for us. Inside, the hall is painted a bright violet and is very well kept. We are careful not to bring any of the red clay that clings to our boots and pant legs inside. Our sleeping pads are rolled onto the floor. As I prepare a supper of macaroni and cheese, salad and fresh asparagus, a rousing game of wicker ball takes place. There is always energy for this game, even after a long day on the trail. Garnet Buell, a former railway man, arrives as we are finishing supper. He has come to share some stories about his life on the railway. He is a small, sparkly-eyed man with a kind face and a devilish smile.

Garnet Buell - "I started back in about 1955 on the Murray River line as a section man and we did all sorts of things, like taking the motorcar up the tracks and doing any repairs, shoveling snow, doing the ballast, and replacing ties and spikes. We used to have to shovel out the train to get it hooked up in the morning to get going from Murray Harbour through to Charlottetown. I worked under Mr. Harry Powers at that time. Harry and I are the only two left in this area that worked for the railroad. All the rest are gone. My job was to sit on the front corner of the motorcar to watch for cracked rails. If we didn't have time to replace the rail, we would have to put in a wooden 'puppy,' which would keep the track tight so that an engineer at that mileage post could run over it slowly with the train in the morning. Then, when the train would go by, we would go up and fix the rail. I would work up here on the line at 22 below zero (Fahrenheit, not Celsius). I didn't mind it then. Mr. Powers used to have me there because I could spot the cracks better than anybody. Some didn't like that, because if it was about 4:50 and I saw a cracked rail and put up my hand, we would have to stop and go back to plug it. It wouldn't land us there until after 5 o'clock.

I was transferred from here over to Moncton. The first trip out was a large workman's car and I had two guys with me. It was a large weed mower that used to cut the grass on both sides of the tracks. I worked down through Nova Scotia in Bridgewater, around St. Peters, Inverness, and right down to Sydney and Yarmouth way. I used to work in Musquodoboit down in Nova Scotia. You would work so far along the tracks and then find a place to stay for the night. I got to know a lot of wonderful people down there. I just loved it. We had a lot of fun.

The next year I went with the maintenance gang, and came back into the shops in Moncton with the engineering department. They put me on the heavy machines for a short time, and then asked me to go into the office as a material expeditor—finding parts for all the equipment. Then I went from there to shop assistant foreman. I put in just about 32 years. My pin number was 601682.

Hiking the Dream

As soon as the word came out that the railway here was over, they took the track up and the trains were shipped off. It was just sad. I loved the train...I lived it and worked it and loved it. I still do; I collect a lot of model trains. It grows on you. The old steam train would come up past here and I would run out behind our house, set my clock, and know when to get ready to get to school. We walked two miles to get to our country school. On a cold, frosty morning we would watch the steam on the old train coming up and hear the whistle blow. It was a part of our history here, and a part of our lives. We got to love it and as young people we would jump on the back and jump off again into the swamp. I can still hear the clacketing of it. The passenger trains were taken off in the mid sixties. I was home the last day a freight train went down this line, around '70 or '71."

Before leaving, Garnet pulls the guitar up on his knee and begins to sing some songs for us. He has written his own version of "Old Shep" about his dog, which died when he was a boy. Anyone who knows me, knows the lack of resistance I'll have to this song. Tears begin to form before he even starts to sing. I have given this "weak tear duct" gift to my children as well, so we all listen and blink away our tears as Garnet, his voice churning out the melody, sings of his boyhood friend, his dog.

Regretfully, it is time for Garnet to go home. We hoist him into the air for a quick picture. Before leaving, he invites us to visit his home in the morning to see all of his train artifacts.

We line our sleeping bags in a row on the hardwood floor in front of the hall platform. Billy chooses the little "off room" for his space. Lars immediately puts his headphones on and drifts off to sleep, on his back, with mouth open. Unaware and exhausted, he is soon serenading us with his rare, yet distinct, and somewhat guttural, snoring.

May 29

Montague to Georgetown
Distance: 18 km
Wildlife: blue heron, beetles, ducks, squirrels

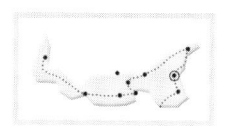

Crash! Billy's radio lands on the floor with a thump. We are suddenly jolted from our peaceful sleep. After coffee and delicious pancakes, we

Prince Edward Island

The trail from Montague is perfectly groomed with railway ties forming the railing.

stop to see Garnet Buell, as promised. He is waiting and entertains us with his array of train paraphernalia…train whistles, train clocks, toy trains and train schedules. Picking up his Martin guitar, he strums another tune for us. We sit on the floor of his tiny living room, among the many train keepsakes, and listen. It is hard to leave. There is so much to see here in Garnet's house, and we would love to stay longer and listen to him sing, but we must go. Garnet laments the fact that he can't come with us.

Our hike today begins at the Montague train station. The path is finished with fine gravel, the best surface yet. It is a perfectly groomed trail, with the old railway ties forming the railing. We admire blue heron on the shoreline of the water and bunnies that dart on and off the trail, as we bounce along with new energy. The blue heron is a large wading bird identified by its long legs, neck and bill. These birds fly south in the winter, sometimes as far as South America, returning in the early spring. We continue, dipping in and out of unexpected forests and back through stretches of perfectly plowed fields with their big white farmhouses proudly facing the sea. We occasionally emerge into open stretches, with the fields now a vibrant green. Mayflowers line our path and we smother our faces in their fragrance.

(from Topher's diary)
We walk a good five kilometres before stopping for lunch. Rolls and cheese, oranges, trail mix and Caramilk bars. After lunch we see an array of animals: bunnies in the woods behind the mayflowers, a squirrel munching in a batch of fallen trees, and even a blue robin's egg. Unfortunately, the egg, being tossed from the nest, will never hatch. Kathy, Nora and Maria sing, "The Sparrow," replacing 'sparrow' with 'robin' to pay their respects. We set the small egg in the tall grass and carry on. Being the woodsman that I am, I spend most of my time trying to learn the names of the local trees and plants in the area. My goal is to learn them all before I'm finished. All in all, the trip lasts about 18 kilometres and ends around

5:30 P.M. We leave Georgetown and drive to the Four Season Cottages in Cardigan River. We meet a guy named Paul who shows us to our 'mansion,' called the Tides Inn, which includes two bedrooms, a living room, the kitchen and a bathroom. It is the spot of our dreams. Kathy, Billy and Heike head into town to buy groceries while everyone else unloads and sets up. Supper is both great and original. Heike invents a dish, which as of yet has no name—a collection of vegetables, smothered in peanut butter with fluffy rice and salad. It is delicious. Nicholas and I spend the evening outside playing a variety of games and chasing 'Freedom,' Paul's crazy dog.

May 30

Souris to Elmira
Distance: 27.8 km
Wildlife: squirrel, rabbits, butterflies, blue heron, red winged blackbird, canaries

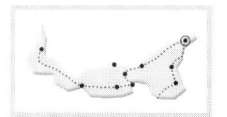

(from Lars' diary)
Breakfast, as usual, is very good—bacon, eggs and toast. After breakfast, some of us work on our Frisbee throwing skills. We also try to upload our journals and pictures to the web page, but without success (at least no success with the uploading; we are getting better with the Frisbee). When the cell phone decides to be as uncooperative as the phone line, we decide to visit a school, on our way to the trail. We want to use their computers and Internet connections for a short time. We go to Cardigan Consolidated School and ask some of the teachers if it is okay. They are very helpful and let us use their computer lab as long as we want. When the teachers find out that there are two foreigners among us, they ask us to say a few words about our countries and answer the classes' questions. Of course, we agree to do it; it was the least we can do in return for their help. So, while some work on the home page, the rest of us answer questions about Sweden and Germany and Hike 2000. I also say a few words in Swedish.

Despite the problems with the homepage, we can't spend the whole day at school, so we head out to the trail and start our hike from Souris. The trail is hard-packed gravel, easy to walk on, and you can keep a good pace...maybe too good, because after three quarters of the distance, my feet and legs are screaming for me to stop. Although the weather is hot, I can't use this sunny day to work on my tan because Kathy had the brilliant idea that today's a 'skirt' day. Therefore, all of

Faithful to our declaring it "skirt day," Topher and Lars stroll along, as natural as can be, in their flowing skirts.

---

us (except Nicholas) are hiking in skirts. I hope I don't turn this into a habit, and no, I did not have a skirt with me. I borrowed one from Maria.

As usual, the views from this trail are beautiful, through fields and hardwood forests, but by the end I am too tired to enjoy them as much as I should. Today the bread and cheese lunch is enhanced with some of Topher's precious trail mix (dry fruit, nuts, and sunflower seeds) and without that I am sure that I would not have been able to drag myself from one end of the trail to the waiting van. While we are hiking, Billy arranges a place for us to stay in the recreation centre near Elmira. My evening passes in a gray shimmer of tiredness, but I can remember a good supper with wieners and beans and a cup of really good coffee. My last memory is Billy walking out from his bedroom (which happens to be the boiler room) an hour after he went to sleep, because it begins the night shift with a great roar.

May 31

Selkirk to Morrell
Distance: 26.8 km
Wildlife: raccoon, snake, seagulls and trillium

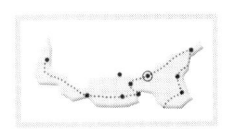

In the cooking area of the kitchen, I am boiling some eggs for breakfast and Billy, as usual, is brewing a fine pot of coffee. The rest are rolling the sleeping bags that have been placed under and around the tables of the hall. This chore of packing up is becoming impressively faster as days go on. Nicholas treats Lars to one of his fried egg specialties, as it is his twenty-fifth birthday. We clean up, leave the recreation centre, and Harry MacDonald leads us to Helen Murphy's trim, white house. She is a wonderful, 90-year-old lady who has agreed to meet with me and tell me about her life and about Percy, her husband, who was a railway man. Helen is still getting ready when I arrive. She appears in the doorway leading to the warm, cozy kitchen. She is small and perfectly groomed. Her appearance reminds me of 101-year-old Mary MacDougal in West Gore, our home village in Nova Scotia. Helen is wearing blue pants with a white blouse that has the vest sewn on. Her hair is puffed up perfectly and she is wearing lipstick. It is heartwarming to see this woman who had put such care into preparing for my visit. I, on the other hand, am wearing shorts and sneakers.

Helen's house is warm and welcoming. On her table is a newspaper with an article about the 1931 Elmira train crash. Helen is in the picture. She was the young teacher at the one-room school in Elmira at the time. Her 'husband-to-be,' Percy, who worked on the line at the time, is also in the picture. The picture was taken seventy years ago and Helen remembers every detail.

Helen Murphy - "I was a teacher at that time and we were going to school with some of the children that lived at this end. The engineer was driving the train too fast and he went by the end of the track and right over the road, ending up on the other side. The wreck happened in the evening, but they couldn't touch it until morning. On the way to school the next morning we had to step on one side of the train—which was right on the road—and right down the other to get past it. The kids were disappointed because they were sure they were going to get a day off school. When we came back at noontime they had cleared it away. Nobody was hurt. It was a big event. It was the only wreck we had.

We had a noon-time train at that time as well— a freight train. The men that were working on the train stayed in Elmira because it is the end of the line in the east of the island. The train station was built around 1921. One young girl died on the train. She was about 18. They wouldn't carry a dead person in the same car with the people; they would always carry the coffin in a baggage car. Sometimes the men would have a drink on the train, and of course if they were ever caught they were put right off."

Before I leave, we look through Helen's pictures showing a barn struck with lightening and the train wreck. She shows me the plaque

Prince Edward Island

> The Elmira station, built in 1921, was the end of the line in east Prince Edward Island.

of appreciation that was given to her for her work at the library. She worked for the library, doing their books, until she was 86. It is a delightful visit and I promise to return when my book is complete.

We arrive at the Elmira station, which is being restored. It has many railway pictures and artifacts on display. 'Scruffy' (Brian Griffin) is here working on the building's restoration and leans back to tell me a few of his tales.

> Brian Griffin - "I'm going to tell you a story about the train that came through here years ago when a bad storm was up. There was a new driver on the train and he didn't see the station light until he was past it. It takes a long time to stop a train, so the train ended up way over in the field. There have been a couple of wrecks down the tracks here a few years back. There's even a phantom train. People claim up around here that they hear a whistle blow and they see a light on the tracks. Then it just disappears.
>
> When we were younger, they used to have liquor cars. We used to get to unload them, but broken liquor couldn't be shipped, so we would always manage to break three or four cases. I used to hook the train—hop the trains and go for a ride—when I fished at the breakwater in Souris. The farthest I got away on a train without getting caught was St. Peters. CN might also be interested to know that it was us that derailed those two cars down at Souris full of grain years ago…a bad prank. We were just kids, only 12 years old. We shifted the tracks and they lost the grain. But someone else's loss is someone else's gain—local boys got to put the grain back in.
>
> It is sad that the train is gone. The road is in such bad shape from the heavy trucks—it would have been cheaper to keep the train. It's pretty hard to pull a train up alongside a potato warehouse today. There was a lot of mixed farming in Prince Edward Island and everybody went by train and shipped their potatoes by train. The last train that I remember was maybe in '83."

We enjoy looking through the old station before driving to Selkirk, our trailhead for the day. Billy drops us off and we make plans to meet in Morrell. This trail is particularly scenic, as it twists along the shoreline, birds diving and circling as they watch for prey. The contrast of the green fields now spotted with dandelions, the deep red earth, the white sand dunes tufted with grass and the clear blue of the waters is a photographer's paradise. Despite the peaceful surroundings, the weather is very hot and our feet burn in our boots. Coincidentally, we meet a biker who worked with Charlie Harvey, Nora's school friend from Kennetcook, Nova Scotia. Small world!

It is almost 7:00 P.M. when we reach Morrell and we still do not know where we will spend the night. Unfortunately, campgrounds do not open on the island until June 1. Like a true hobo, I begin my begging quest. First, I try the hostel. It is now past 9:00 P.M. on May 31. "Nope," the lady at the hostel responds, "The place doesn't open until June 1."

"But that's only three hours away," I plead. Apparently 'a rule's a rule.' I offer to clean, to do anything…but no go. I try the legion. I call the priest. No luck. Finally, I give up. Once more, we have to pull money from our precious and diminishing funds to book a cabin at Cranberry Cottages, in nearby Bristol. We are starving and decide to eat before retiring to our cabin. We drag our dog-tired and scruffy bodies into the local diner. Lars, who has turned 25 today, can hardly walk. Despite our exhaustion, we muster the energy to give Lars a rousing "Happy Birthday" and treat ourselves to seafood and ice cream before collapsing for the night.

Back at Cranberry Cottages, we choose our spots for the night. We pile onto the pull-out sofa bed in front of the first TV we have seen in more than a month. Our eyes remain fixed on the mouths of the characters that appear on the screen before us. We aren't really listening to what they are saying. It is just this tuning in to the 'real' world that has us captivated.

It is this night that I worry again of the condition of my feet. I feel like I have been walking on hot coals. They are completely red and burn from the soles up. I am sitting with bags of ice strapped to their bottoms, trying to cool the fire that seems to be raging under my skin. I fear that if this burning persists, I won't be able to continue tomorrow. It is a frightening thought.

(from Heike's diary)
I think some personal stock-taking is in order: After about a month and almost five hundred kilometres on the trail: My insect bite blister ratio is 42:1; I am slightly leaner (if not meaner); My 'Scottish' sailing tan (face and hands) is turning to a Canadian 'hiking' tan (significant tan line above feet); I'm not getting as much writing done as I hoped I would; My Newfoundland 'survival medal' is still hanging on, weathering sweat and not too many showers thanks to an excellent sheet bend knot. I feel I've settled into this nomadic way of life now and will be experiencing problems going back to a stationary lifestyle. It's already feeling weird to lie in a bed. I'm also better at coping with 'having to be with people' all the time than I was afraid I would be. I just take time out when I need to, but enjoy the company, the talk and the music when I seek it.

June 1

Bethel to Glenroy (through Mount Stewart)
Distance: 19.2 km
Wildlife: cranes, blue herons

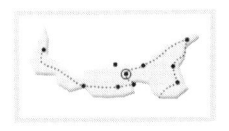

My first thought this morning as I wake up is my feet. The burning seems to have subsided, thank God. I lie on the sofa bed for a few minutes marveling at the miraculous recovery of the body after just a few hours of rest.

(from Nora's diary)
I wake up beside Mum on the pull-out couch, sweltering in my sleeping bag. It is an amazing day outside. I turn over and looked around; Lars on the floor at our feet (his first choice of bed for being the birthday boy), Topher with his head pressed against the fridge, and Billy making himself a ham and cheese sandwich. I get up first, well after Billy, of course, so that I can be the first in the shower, but I become so occupied with our crib games that I end up being the last one in the shower. Cranberry Cottages has been great. The owner is more than friendly and the amenities are outstanding.

We stop at Freda's for sliced bread and packaged cheese (for a change). The day is sunny and most of the walk is through blueberry fields. Until lunch, Mum

Hiking the Dream

Nora and Maria on the trail from Bethel in the midst of colourful barrens and a clear blue sky.

entertains us with stories from her university years. None of us get a word in and none of us want to. We stop for lunch beside rolling, green pastures dotted with dandelions. We are enthralled with a small, friendly foal with its mother in the field beside us.

After lunch we keep walking, but at a much slower and heavier pace. At Mount Stewart, Mum stops at the Trailside Café. Topher and I amuse ourselves by watching a small dog playing in a muddy puddle of water. He looks like a black Benji, with yellow tips on his fur. As we walk away, he follows. Topher and I take him back three times, but with no luck. We decide to keep walking, hoping that he will turn around. Since our diversions have put us behind everyone else, we aren't sure how the rest are doing, but we have a good talk and it is comforting to have this little, smiling dog running beside us. He listens to everything we say. Up ahead, we hear the screech of a whistle. We've reached the 500-kilometre mark, a cause for celebration, since we are a quarter of the way finished our trek. After pictures with Bentley (our new dog), we continue on until we come to Glenroy, a sunny, hilly, farming community. Mom and I carry Bentley up to a farmhouse and ask to use the phone (Bentley's number is on his collar). It turns out that the young wife at the house knows the owners of our little dog and will keep him until they get home from work. The lady is young, friendly and talkative. It would be nice to stay and hear her stories about her animals and her family.

We drive to Anne's Whispering Pines campground in Grand Tracadie, and immediately love it. We are the first visitors for the season and are told we are very special. She gives us special rates, as well as pins and pens. Even better, we have the whole campground to ourselves to play Frisbee, soccer, or just rest in the sun.

For supper, Maria and I make fettuccini noodles, mushroom fried rice, salad and chicken. Later, we sit around the campfire with Nicholas telling us stories of Klondike days in Scouts while Topher toasts S'mores. Doesn't it feel good to get into your sleeping bag when it is cool outside and feel yourself warm up?

June 2

Bedford to Charlottetown
Distance 26.4 km
Wildlife: cranes

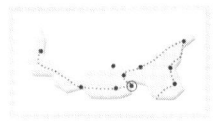

The brilliant sunshine filters through the blue nylon of our tent. I lie on my back tracing the lines of the water droplets, which have formed from condensation, trickle across the ceiling above me. My sleeping bag is so cozy. I hate to leave it, but I must. I have an appointment to call "Information Morning" with CBC radio. Trying not to disturb the others, I unzip the tent door, and crawl into the warmth of the morning sun. Billy has had his shower and is making his daily morning toast over the fire.

As I talk to CBC, the birds chirp around me. They remark how they can hear them in the studio in Halifax. Back at the fire, I put on bacon and French toast. A rousing game of Frisbee has to be interrupted to serve breakfast and dismantle the tents. We certainly have a way of spreading out. By now, we have taken up four camping spots with our tents, bins, fire, van and trailer and of course, we have adopted a playing field. Our hostess at Anne's Whispering Pines is extremely friendly and is unconcerned with our squatters' mess. She treats us like royalty.

Today's route will begin in Bedford and pass through Royalty Junction until we reach Charlottetown. To my surprise, this trail takes us mostly through woodland even though we are so close to a major city. For most of the way, it consists of rough gravel, making our walking slow and tedious. Twisting an ankle at this point would be disastrous. I have allowed only a few rest days and unfortunately, Prince Edward Island has none of them. The trail sporadically appears from the woodland, skirts along a stretch of farmland, squeezes between the barns and farmhouses across endless red potato fields, then winds back into the forest. It is on such a divergence through a farmyard that we meet a farmer who offers us a job grading potatoes. His storage barn is full from last year's crop, which he is now preparing to sell. The long

Hiking the Dream

straight rows of earth will soon be rolled over with new seedlings for next year's bounty.

Farther along, we meet a former railway man who comes down over his lawn just to watch us pass. He is curious about who we are. A jolly man, he leans back with laughter at our every remark. His ball hat sits high on his head, his long arms dangling on his tall frame. He tells us how he walked this line every day, making sure the switches were working. Sometimes this walk would be in deep snow, which he would have had to clear from the switches. This is one man who knows the exact distance of the trail.

His wife, a plump, homey-looking woman wiping a piece of fruit in her apron, invites us in to rest our feet. As much as this is a wonderful offer, we honestly fear we may never get back up if we sit down.

The grade of the rail bed improves as we reach Royalty Junction. We had no idea the trail would be this long. Everyone we ask seems to have varying opinions about how far the trail is from one point to another. We pass the veterinary clinic and wait for a chance to scurry across the busy highway leading into town. It seems strange to me that no crosswalk exists to connect the trailway at this busy intersection.

We finally reach the apartment of Sonja Englund, my niece. Situated on a quiet street, her flat is on the upper floor of a charming, older house. An iron gate leads to a doorway, which opens to the stairway, climbing to a clean, sunny room. Sonja watches us from the patio roof as we sort our bins next to the garbage containers on the street. She is waiting for us with cold beer. My sister Dianne Englund and her other daughter, Kristel, soon arrive. Iain Caldwell has biked from the Wood Islands ferry and arrives, bone tired. He has purchased a new mountain bike, and this first day in the saddle brings more than a little agony. We are happy to have him join us again.

The screen door off Sonja's cozy kitchen leads to a deck with comfortable chairs and big flowerpots. We slide into the padded chairs to relax, watching the sun send a crimson glow over Charlottetown, our second capital city, and the home of Confederation. The sun has disappeared by the time we gather in the spacious living room to a delicious supper of gnocchi with a cream sauce, spinach salad with lemon tarragon dressing and brownies for dessert. Sonya is at the top of her Culinary Arts class at the Culinary Institute of Canada here in Charlottetown. Who better to test your talents on than a group of hungry hikers! It has been such a long day. Our bedrolls are laid out in Sonja's spare room, side by side. We have grown beyond being particular about where we lie down or who we are next to. By now, we are one big family.

June 3

Winsloe to Hunter River
Distance: 23.5 km
Wildlife: blue jays, apple blossoms

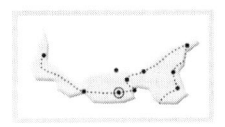

"Why is that phone ringing so early? Who's ringing the doorbell? Heike, the phone is for you. It is your family calling from Germany. Someone open the door for Billy." Billy has stayed the night with a former navy friend, Bernie McGuigen, who resembles Kenny Rogers. He was the best man at Billy's wedding and they have spent the night reminiscing about old times. Billy is now ready to go for another day. Heike takes the phone for a chat with her mom and sister. It is reassuring for them to know she is fine as she fills them in on the adventures of the week.

Now that we are all awake, we might as well get up. Cold rain beats against the windows of Sonja's snug apartment. It is such an effort to leave these warm blankets and think of donning hiking clothes. Brrrr. Dianne, Sonja and Kristel have been waiting on us since we arrived yesterday and this morning is no exception. We are served scrambled eggs, bacon, toast and coffee. It will be a treat today to have family hiking with us, despite the miserable weather. We pull ourselves into the van and Billy drives us to Winsloe, our starting point for the day. The map measurements indicate it will be approximately 15 kilometres to Hunter River, long enough in this cold weather.

Petite Sonja, pulls on Billy's size tall, large rain pants. As she steps from the van, the wind catches the hood of her raincoat, blowing it straight up like the sails on a ship. With her glasses totally fogged over, Sonja is ready for her one day available to hike with us. "Whoever called this fun" she remarks, as the wind steals the words from her mouth. Kristel and Dianne brace themselves against the rain and wind, posing for pictures on this monumental occasion.

We start out, heads bent to the slashing rain. I try to hold a conversation with Kristel about her move to Nova Scotia from Fredericton, to begin her new practice in psychology. It is useless. The wind won't allow conversation without yelling and having to repeat things over several times. We give up and save this talk for later.

(from Kristel, Dianne and Sonja's diary)
It is windy and we can't see much but the rocks directly in front of our feet for the first five kilometres. Thank God that doesn't last. When we stop for lunch, it is actually sunny and clear. We have a lovely view of green fields and red PEI soil. Maria manages to sit directly on a rosebush, which makes lunch a little more uncomfortable for her, but the rest of us enjoy it immensely. We are actually geared up for a short day, and have convinced ourselves that even if the rain persists, we can make it. Kathy estimated the day's hike at only 15 kilometres, which sounded good to us—the out of shape contingent. During the afternoon walk we pass fields with curious horses (one with a new foal) and a few cows. We stop to watch a farmer spread fertilizer on his newly plowed red field. There are lots of cherry trees in blossom and many blue jays—the native bird of P.E.I.—follow us along.

At the 17-kilometre mark, we ask a man at a huge potato barn how far it is to Hunter River. "About eight miles," he says. I could have slapped him! His buddy says, "Well, maybe a long four miles." Leaving them to argue it out, we hope the second buddy is right. It is interesting how everyone still gives you distances in terms of miles. The rain has ended and the sun now shines on the tiny droplets left on the new green of the trees. It is planting season and the contrast of the red earth and this pale green is delightful. The mood picks up and we walk along catching up on each other's lives, hopes and plans. If the long walk has done nothing else, it has given us time to spend together with Sonja, Dianne and Kristel, which we may not have had otherwise. As we end our hike, we can see the van parked by a big grain barn next to the river. We have walked 23.5 kilometres and the van is a welcome sight. We pull our bodies up on the bank and lie back in the final warmth of the setting sun. We have not planned to hike this far and we are all tired.

We stop at the cold beer store for some refreshments, then drive to Sonja's for Greek salad and lasagna followed by rhubarb crisp. As Nicholas says, "hiking all day sure does make the food taste good." And he is right. The food has been excellent. Living here with "chef Sonja" has added a new spark to our menus, something we could become very spoiled by. After supper, Nora, Topher, Lars, Heike and Iain decide to check out the nightlife in Charlottetown. The rest of us pull our feet up on the cozy chesterfield for a warm drink and a good chat before bed. We will leave Sonja's place tomorrow. It is so nice to be with family.

June 4

Cavendish
Distance: 6.4 km
Wildlife: piping plovers, raccoons, squirrels

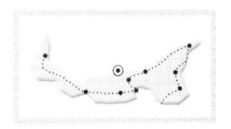

Warm sunshine radiates across the shiny hardwood floors and onto the walls adorned with native artwork, which Sonja has brought home with her from Africa. Tall wooden giraffes stand by the fireplace and colourful throws and cushions are scattered on the big chairs. It is a welcoming room and I linger for a moment, knowing that for the next while, I will, instead, be waking to the interior of our humble tent. I stretch the sleep from my body and begin the pile of dishes that we left last night. We were just too tired to face them. Dianne is making a big pot of oatmeal, as the rest of the crew begins to stir and line up for the bathroom. She has been waiting on us constantly since we arrived, without complaint.

It is a glorious day and we bask in the sun on Sonja's balcony, feasting on moist coffee cake, porridge, rhubarb crisp and coffee. Topher leaves us today, returning to Nova Scotia with Dianne and Kristel. It will be lonely without him, who added his little twist on our already formed 'pack' humour. To live in such close proximity for so long, we begin to develop our own language. There is no longer a need to complete sentences—someone else can do that for you. Matter of fact, we don't really need to talk in full sentences at all, as we all know exactly what the other person means. We pick up little clichés from whomever we meet, developing them into our own jargon, all of us laughing again and again at the quips that have become part of our everyday speech. Those who join us must truly think that we have gone a little mad sometimes. They certainly wouldn't know that some of our jargon might have been picked up in Howley, Newfoundland or Glace Bay, Cape Breton or from any other little community we have passed. To add to this newly formed communication, Billy has added a whole vocabulary of his own. He has found a little saying to match just about every situation that we have encountered and all those who join us find the same little quips coming from their own mouths. It's a study in itself. Our goodbyes to Dianne, Kristel, Sonja and Topher are lingered. We hope they can all join us again, but know this may not happen.

Cavendish Beach is situated on the north shore of the island. Here, the wind has sculpted great white sand dunes that wear a tuft of long marram grass on top. The wind tosses the water and the morning sun dances on the waves. We choose a camping spot out of the wind on a flat grassy corner, protected by the softwood trees. We are close to the beach and the toilets. We are slowly becoming the camping experts, and unlike 'vacationers,' since we are hiking all day and our priorities are different. We look for a place for a good night's sleep, close to washing areas and toilets, late afternoon shade and early morning sun for a quick drying of our tent. It is easy now, as campgrounds have just opened for the season and only the hardy are sleeping out these days.

With tents quickly set up, we enjoy Swiss cheese and buns with a beer. I strap my pedometer to my wrist just wondering how many clicks one beer would give me. To my dismay, to clock distance, a sudden movement of the pedometer is needed and such movements while drinking a beer only result in churning it into foam. So much for that theory. I stroll to the beach for a change of hiking pace. Nora, Lars and Billy challenge Maria, Iain and Nicholas to a game of beach volleyball. It is a rousing game. Billy teases that his old skill is still there from when his team won provincials in 1956. Nicholas, knuckles bleeding, pours himself on the ground time and time again, trying to receive his serves. Maria, her hips bruised from diving on the ground to make saves, is determined to win this match. I'm not sure of the final score but, as I climb down over the sand dunes, their laughter pierces the air and follows me long beyond the sight of them.

My last stroll on a beach was in Cuba in April. I think of the warmth of that sun, the freedom of bare feet and the beautiful people we met there. Here, with wool socks and hiking boots, shorts and a fleece, I face the strong wind coming off the Gulf of St. Lawrence. I click off 6.4 kilometres before resting between two large dunes. I have reached the nesting grounds of the rare and endangered piping plovers. They come to this area in late April to nest in the flat sandy area, where gravel and broken shells provide camouflage. Predators and bad weather threaten this dwindling population and it is encouraging to know they have been given this safe haven to nest. I search the sands for pretty shells and rocks and think about the days I spent in PEI when I was in high school. I had come to Rice Point with the Grove family. Tom and Beverley were playing with the Anne of Green Gables musical at the Confederation Center and I was hired to care for their four children. Dougie was the oldest, a tall, brown-haired boy, responsible for his age. Carol and Nancy were the middle children, always at my side, building teepees and sand castles. We spent endless hours on the beach those two summers. I don't think I ever looked in a mirror and it really didn't matter. We were having fun, each day rolling into the next. And at the end of the day, we would take turns cranking out the homemade ice cream from McLean's farm down the road. Cynthia, the baby, was bright eyed, with vibrant auburn hair. Tom called her 'super baby' and a super baby she was. Johnnie, the youngest son, was born later.

Now, looking out over this stretch of sand and tossing waves, I think of how quickly the time has gone. My own children, 21, 19 and 13 years old, playing on the cliff above me, could just as easily be those Grove children, more than thirty years ago. I think of how the setting is the same, the same red soil and the endless blue sky. Back at the campground, the volleyball game has ended. Heike has returned from the beach where she bravely attempted to sunbathe in her bathing suit. Tucked in the shelter of the dunes, she has been journal writing, writing to friends and drawing in her big drawing pad. She is so faithful with her letter writing. Sometimes I wish my head would stand still long enough for me to do something so peaceful.

(from Maria's diary)
I change into my bathing suit and with towel in hand, head for the beach. Others look for shells and stones, but being so brave, or a bit brain dead from too much sun, I want to go swimming with Iain. I prove to be a poor sea person, as I only run in to hip level then chicken out, rushing, screaming, back to the beach. After drying off, I take a hot shower. It is so nice to be pelted with hot water, cleaning off the salt. I change into my warmest clothes, and quickly fall asleep on the blue mat in the tent. Not long after, I am up again to make a supper of leftover lasagna and salad. Lars and Iain wash the dishes. We make coffee and I stroll to the beach with Iain. We take off our shoes and walk through the sand. Small kernels push up through our toes as we try not to make any footprints at all near the water. I sprint behind Iain, trying to match my stride to his. Then we sit, watching the sun set over the water.

Iain with Maria and Nicholas on his back for the piggyback races at Cavendish Beach.

Lars and Nicholas soon join Nora, Heike and us. We have piggyback rides, all trying to run as fast as possible. I think for sure Iain will hurt himself as he runs down the beach, his footsteps so short, going a mile a minute, carrying Nora or Heike, or me, or even Nicholas and me together. Then I give a lesson on how to make a hand whistle, everyone eventually making a sound or at least an impressive squeak.

A huge crimson ball of a moon sits on the water, sending a glow over the pale blue water. It is a glorious sunset and the beach beckons us back again. I steal myself away from this scene to attempt a phone call to John. On the cliff overlooking the beach and the rolling waves advancing and receding on the pink sand, Billy has made a fire in one of the shelters. There is a big wood stove and we pull the picnic table close to its warmth. It is like sitting on the wood box by the stove at Aunt Erma and Uncle Earle's, when we were growing up in Caribou Gold Mines. They were Billy's parents and he, too, remembers many a cold morning that the wood box was the select seat in the house. We would spend hours sitting next to the fire listening to Uncle Earle's stories while Aunt Erma treated us with hot Postum and fresh biscuits. Now, as we sit next to this fire, it is Billy's turn for story telling.

Born prematurely, in that same little house on December 30 in the mid thirties, Billy was placed in a shoebox on the oven door to keep warm. Our grandmother came by horse and buggy to help Aunt Erma with this little baby. She sat by him for days, feeding him milk with an eyedropper, every hour, to keep him alive. My mother, who was teaching at the one-room school in the community, would come in after work to relieve Aunt Erma and let her get some rest. It was said to be the coldest winter in years.

I can picture Billy, a small feisty boy, loving the outdoors and spending his days in the woods fishing or hunting. He tells me about how all the boys carried guns and about the Davidson boy that fought with him. He tells of Halloween pranks and how a neighbour shot at him as he hid in his woodpile. He shows me the black mark on his shoulder where the pellets are still embedded. I listen with amusement as he tells me of his 'wild west' behaviors when he was growing up in this small mining village in Nova Scotia. He is so calm and patient now; I can hardly imagine this 'Matt Dillon' of a Billy.

At our campsite, the raccoons are taking advantage of our absence. They are invading the food bin. As we approach, one raccoon runs into the bushes, dragging Iain's fanny pack, spewing trail mix in its wake.

(from Maria's diary)
Ralph (the name we have given one of the raccoons) tries to steal a plastic bag from the cooler. When he finally succeeds, Anika (the other raccoon) tries to steal the bag from him, which starts a brief, but loud, fight. They go in their own directions and we, the audience, make our way to bed.

June 5

Alma to Tignish
Distance: 17 km
Wildlife: chipmunk

The brazen raccoons spend the night clawing at our coolers. One is successful in reaching the coffee and spreading it over the campsite.

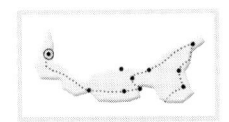

Hiking the Dream

(from Nicholas' diary)
I wake to the sound of a raccoon snarl. Then, I go back to sleep. I've been having extremely bad luck: I spilled half my water bottle in the tent, lost one of the headphones from my discman (later found it) and lost a volleyball (later found that, too). The water spilt in my shoes and my pant leg was wet because I fell down on the shore of the beach. When I get up, Mom tells me to find my toothbrush and clean my teeth—my stress meter is rising. When going to the shower, I drop my deodorant in the poison ivy right beside the trail. When I get to the shower, after having to pick up my deodorant with my shirtsleeve, I make another discovery—the shower door won't lock. Nearly fifteen minutes have gone by when I finally got the lock to do its job. I turn the shower knob and the water is boiling hot. After the shower, I come back to a dry piece of bread and chocolate milk in a bowl, since all the cups are dirty. The chocolate won't dissolve, so it is more like chocolate broth.

When we are on the road, I listen to my discman as Mom tells us the plans. When we get to the trail, it was a long avenue of trees stacked on the sides—I can see forever. I groan and concentrate on right foot, left foot. Never look up—it discourages you. When we get to our first stop, the rest of the group has Spam and a bun. I have a bun. It is different than bread and cheese this time. It is bread and meat and chocolate cookies. The grass is prickly so I'm always scratching my legs and the place is a hot spot for flies. We meet a guy there named Paul who owns Paul's Bike Shop. We talk for a few minutes then we leave. Near the end of the hike, I'm telling Lars why we sometimes wonder why Billy is not around where we actually want him to be, but when we see him at the end of the hike, it's like opening your eyes for the first time. Wow! It's a whole new happy world.

We play volleyball in the park for a brief moment. It is boys against girls, Iain and I against Nora and Maria. We are both doing pretty well and we are just getting to the hot spot of our game when Mom calls us over. Dang, how she does that! We eat at a place called Shirley's and I have my usual cheeseburger and fries. After that, we go to Grampy's ice cream parlor for dessert. Iain just buys another soda 'cause he's lactose intolerant, the

"The trail [to Tignish] was a long avenue with trees stacked up on the sides…I could see forever" (Nicholas).

poor guy. Thirty-two flavors of ice cream. That's a whole lotta sick, as Iain would say. I have strawberry cheesecake ice cream.

After that we go over to Blair Gaudet's house, the guy who invited us to tent in his yard. He has a daughter who has friends over and we have a soccer game, boys against girls. One of the girls has brought her little brother, who was eight. He likes to make up his own rules (hint of the time we had). After awhile, we go inside to listen to music and watch the hockey game. My skin is almost blue because I was out longer than anybody else. They have a puppy that is the size of a kitten. His fur is white and incredibly soft. The bathroom is also pretty good. After awhile I go outside, get into the tent and finally fall asleep, shivering.

The rest of us sit in the comfortable kitchen of Blair and Marcella Gaudet. Blair has made a tape of the "Tignish Tragedy," a song about the train wreck of 1932.

The Tignish Train Wreck
This story is told of a freight wreck,
The worst P.E.I. did ever see!
When freight train number two-eleven
Was struck by express fifty-three.

It was one Saturday night in mid-winter,
A night that was stormy and dreary;
A freight train enroute to Tignish
Rumbled on tho' danger was near.

At last she got stuck in the cutting,
Well into a thirteen-foot bank
A mile and a half from the terminal,
Some two hundred yards from the tank.

Then shovellers were called to relieve her,
And bravely they strove in their fight
To relieve the stranded freight train,
At twelve-thirty they stopped for the night.

Inside the small coach they crowded,
Outside the storm did not abate,

They spoke of the regular express train
Already a few hours late.

The express with two engines and snow plough
Came thundering on thru the storm,
They stopped at the tank for some water
Then started, but none thought of harm.

And then with a crash that was deafening,
She split the freight cars right in twain;
And amid all the debris and wreckage
Men's bodies were found neath the train.

The sorrowful scene that followed
Those at the wreck still do say,
That they will never forget it,
'Twill remain till their dying day.

A relief train was rushed to the rescue,
With doctors and nurses and all
That could be done for the injured was done,
With all haste at the call.

There were Richards, Gavin and Murphy,
Three men as brave as could be,
How quickly their journey was ended
O'er life's long, dark stormy sea.

Frank Murray, the conductor, was injured,
Harold Harper, the brakeman, was too;
But brave Jimmy Hessian, the driver,
He died, the sole one of the crew.

Some of his friends were there with him,
And those words he did mutter in pain,
"I'm going away to a new home
Where I'll never touch a throttle again.

Many homes are now filled with sorrow,
That were once happy and bright

For the train wreck brought death and disaster
That cold stormy Saturday night.

This story is told of a train wreck,
A sight that was gruesome to see;
Four dead and dozen injured,
But it seems it had to be.

(Written by Keith Pratt, 1932)

As Blair gets out his guitar to sing, I am struck by his great voice, and better still, his moving lyrics. His songs reflect his life as a fisherman's son, Tignish, his grandfather and about the island way of life. Marcella accompanies him on the flute and sings along, her true voice complementing his. They sing songs of life and love. I think how beautiful they are together. Their little girl, Felicia, cuddles and brushes her new American Eskimo dog on the floor in front of us. She says prayers with it before tucking it into bed. This home has a warm feeling and we feel genuinely welcome here. We get out the fiddle and guitars and play and sing beyond midnight. Billy enjoys the hockey game on TV in the living room, a rare luxury these days.

As we contemplate going to bed, Blair surprises us with a bucket of fresh clams he has dug today. He tells about this occupation of clamming and the perils it can bring. We are intrigued by the detail of this work and the expense of such an operation. He explains to us that the clams are so fresh, they have not yet spit out their sand. We feast on them, swirling them in bowls of hot, yellow butter and lift them, dripping, to our mouths. They are delicious. I think of how lucky we are to be here in the home of a real fisherman, eating clams on the day they were dug, well after midnight.

Blair and Marcella Gaudet offer us a camping spot, share great songs and feed us fresh clams in Tignish.

Hiking the Dream

Finally, we crawl into our tents for the night. I am reminded how blessed we are to have met these warm, loving people. We are camping in their backyard, and have enjoyed their company all night, sharing stories and songs. Just six hours ago, we hadn't even met them. We are so honored to have shared their lives, if only for a day.

June 6

Wellington to Summerside
Distance: 22 km
Wildlife: beaver, squirrels fox, trillium

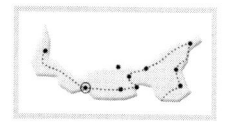

The sound of school children waiting for the bus to pick them up penetrates my sleep. I tear myself from my warm sleeping bag. The children who came by to play soccer last night are now brightly washed and wearing well-pressed clothes. The school bus screeches to a stop—an old, familiar sound. I watch the children file onto the bus and think of how far removed I am from this 'school' scene. Normally, as a physical education teacher, I too, would be off to school at this time. Now, it is far from my thoughts. I have a different mission and a very tight schedule. We have to walk 20 kilometres a day in order to reach our goal of 2,000 kilometres and we really can't get too far behind now— we don't want to have to make them up in the hot summer months.

So, it is time to wake up the crew. Inside the house, Blair is taping music for us. Arnie, Blair's father, arrives. I wish I had more time to talk with him. He is a true fisherman. "Salt water flows through my veins," he tells me. "If you take me away from the sea, you'll kill me." He has to go, but invites us back to 'stay a month.' How I would love to do just that!

(from Iain's diary)
A trip to Shirley's for breakfast precedes our hike. Billy has eaten much earlier, at 6:00 A.M., while waiting for us to get up. He makes me very hungry for a breakfast of bacon and eggs with his description, but unfortunately, Shirley's stopped mak-

ing breakfast shortly before we arrive. Oh, well, I guess since they start making breakfast at 4:00 A.M., they shouldn't be expected to keep serving it so close to lunchtime. So, after an early lunch, we collect whatever snacks we want for the day and set off.

Marcella and Blair tell me about John MacLean, a Prince Edward Island songwriter who lives in West Devon. It is my quest to find this man and see if he will share with me the song he has written about the Prince Edward Island railway. It is a sunny day and the trucks, rolling up this stretch of dirt road, send clouds of red dust into the air. We find John at home on his short dinner break from planting potatoes. A large, strong man, he welcomes me into his home. He has a huge acreage and I promise not to take too much of his time. After a bit of persuasion, he brings out his guitar, perches on the arm of the living room chair and strums the tune. His big hands are agile on the strings and his homey voice sings the words that tell the story of the trains long gone from the province:

> Now this is the story of the railway
> In the western part of P.E.I.
> As the stories are told by the old folk
> Of the times, good and bad, in days gone by
> They cut through the forests
> And they bridged o'er the streams
> They worked long and hard
> To fulfill the people's dreams
> Rugged work and rugged men
> Who have been there and back again
> As they laid down the steel on P.E.I.

John MacLean on a break from planting potatoes.

Lillian, John's wife, looks on with admiration. A picture of John in a field of potato blossoms hangs proudly on the living room wall. It is the same picture that adorns the front of the cassette that he gives me, recorded here on the island. John offers me his second recording, which I happily accept. I am aware of this important planting time and appreciate the time he has taken to sing and chat with me. John is 57 and tells me he can remember everything since he was four years old. He remembers the train taking the cream cans down to Summerside,

Hiking the Dream

and crops and vegetables being transported to the market on the train. He remembers, "The evening train came in at 7:30. People would congregate at the station and tell stories. There was nothing else to do in those days...no television or radio." Lillian also has her hobbies. She takes me upstairs to show me the costumed dolls that she has collected. I immediately feel at home in this neat little white farmhouse. They seem happy I have dropped by and invite me to share lunch. It would be great, but we have to meet our 200 km mark for Prince Edward Island by the end of the day.

Wellington is our starting point for the day. This is our last hiking day in PEI. How quickly time is going. It is warm and sunny and the ground underfoot is excellent. Another blister is forming on my toe. When will these feet toughen up? The trail pierces a forest of spruce, white birch and red pine, its floor now rich with undergrowth. Making a quick detour into the bushes, I spy three trilliums joined at the base. It is too bad that the others don't want to return to this spot for a viewing. Heike also spots a trillium off the trail. This is a protected plant growing in the forest in late spring. The trail is bordered with apple trees, hanging with bright pink blossoms. We stop for a quick snack, but the flies are too thick to linger.

(from Iain's diary)
On the way, we happen along a portion of trail bound by a swamp. Lars spots a beaver swimming in the pond. It is too bad that Topher isn't here to see it, as he was hoping to see one the whole time. Lars also teaches us how to make musical instruments from the stems of the dandelions. We stop for a while to see who can find and play the best 'instrument.' The end of the hike brings us back to the coast where we are happy to see the familiar sight of the van. When we arrive, Billy informs us that both the newspaper and the radio station want to talk to us for stories they are doing. Kathy calls them both back and they soon arrive. The photographer from the newspaper takes several pictures of the whole group, moving us into different poses for their story. Soon, someone from the radio arrives to tape an interview with Kathy. Our final destination for the night is Emily Schurman's cottage in Lower Bedeque. She is a dear friend of Kathy, who is very excited about seeing her again.

We arrive at Emily's family summer home, situated on a jut of land reaching out into the warm waters of Bedeque Bay. Emily and I have been good friends since university. I had just been married when I returned to Dalhousie University in the master's program in health education. Emily was a physical education student at that time. We bonded from the time we met, loving music, sports and generally having a good time. Sharing the same, insane sense of humour, we would spend hours laughing at the most trivial situations. Emily would travel home from university with John and I to our newly acquired farm in West Gore, helping with the pigs, cows and horses. As Billy would say, 'just like we all knew what we were doing.'

Emily is waving wildly from the deck before we even stop the van. We are exited to be together again. I jump from the van and throw my arms around this wonderful friend of mine. There is no 'catching up' to do; it is like we have never been apart. Emily is wearing her comfortable overalls, her blond hair falling loosely around her smiling face. She leads us into the big open room where a wood fire is blazing. The large windows look over the water, which is now churning up some whitecaps. Emily has been preparing our supper after a full day of teaching at the high school in Summerside. A pot of fresh mussels is followed with salad and barbequed sausages, with a treat of ice cream. Emily and I talk and laugh, telling stories of some of our capers as students in university. I beg her now to skip school and stay with us all night. But she devotedly returns home to Summerside, to her husband, Paul and two sons, Charlie and Ben.

Soon, we all go to bed for the night. Nora, who falls asleep on the living room couch, comes to bed in a bit of a daze. Shortly after we get to sleep, she awakens, exclaiming that there is an animal hanging on the wall. A bear, no less! I frantically turn on the light, expecting to see a bat. I am thinking I would rather it be a bear than a bat. It is the curtain. We peel with laughter at our own ridiculousness.

June 7

Leaving PEI, Entering New Brunswick

I have been sleeping with Nora in Emily's cottage. The wind has rocked us all night like in a tiny boat. When I closed my eyes and listened, I could imagine a wild, winter storm. Outside, the waves are crashing and the rain lashes against the windows. We are grateful to be inside, no one wanting to make the first move. We sit in each other's beds, writing, talking and delaying the start to the day. I have an on-line interview with the local paper, then slowly begin packing up. Today, we will leave Prince Edward Island and enter province number four, New Brunswick.

(from Heike's diary)
"Hey, hey, what a day…" After a rocky night, I finally peel myself out of bed at an indecently late hour. After a first glance out the window, I decide I can (should) stay in bed. There is next to nothing left to eat since we did such a thorough job the night before, so we have some leftover salad and ice cream for breakfast while Kathy and Nora are busy getting things up to date on the computer. I have a wee stroll down to the beach, but I never make it all the way down since the tide is in. It is a blustery day, all right. Packing the bins and loading the trailer is not much fun at all."

" We get started eventually and head for the Confederation Bridge. The van needs gas before entering New Brunswick, where they've just raised the price. We stop at a gas station near the bridge. It would be nice to cross the link in nicer weather, especially because in the van we are able to see over the concrete barriers that obstruct your view when you're in a car. Soon after our arrival in New Brunswick, we are in for the first real highlight of the day. Almost mad with hunger, we invade the "Favorite Cup" café in Port Elgin. We stay for quite awhile, ordering course after course. Fortunately, they are doing breakfast around the clock. Perhaps due to the dreary weather, Port Elgin feels a bit like a ghost town after the gold rush.

Then we are off to Sackville, where Kathy manages to secure accommodation at Bennett Hall, a residence at Mount Allison University. It is great to arrive there and meet Kathy's friends, John and Donna McNeil, who are facilitating this luxury for us. John is a don at Mount Allison. Since no one is entirely with it for the entire day, decision-making isn't one of our strong suits. We keep procrastinating our hike until finally we decide to call it a day hike-wise and work on our journals instead. John and Donna drop in after their dinner in honour of John's retirement from teaching and John regales us with excerpts from his speech. In return, they are regaled with readings from our journals, especially Nicholas'. Later that night, Iain, Maria, Nora, Lars and I head for the bars to find that only one is still open. Well, I guess we get going a bit late considering there's no student life happening in Sackville just now. We have some drinks and lots of peanuts at Baldy's before we turn in for the night.

June 8 - June 17

New Brunswick

Shirley-Dale, Julie, Tom, Kathy, George and Elaine Crawford (and their grandchildren) on the trail to Keswick.

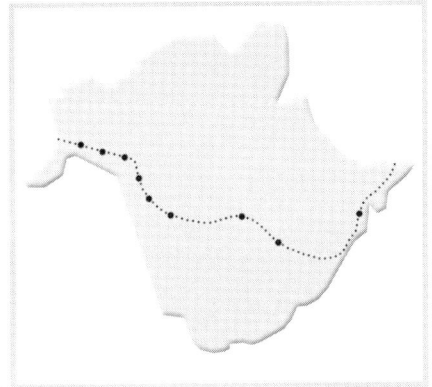

June 8

Place: Waterfowl Park, Sackville
Distance: 23 km
Wildlife: osprey

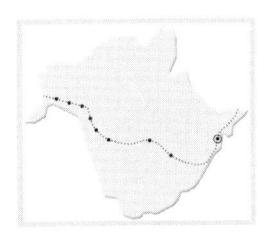

Donna (Langille) MacNeil is my friend from high school in Musquodoboit. We played on just about every school team with each other and shared a million laughs over the years. She is married to John MacNeil, a high school teacher and football coach at Mount Allison University in Sackville, New Brunswick. They are now dons at Bermuda House, one of the university dorms. We can hardly wait to get to breakfast in their cozy flat. When we arrive, a buffet breakfast of fruit salad, bagels, scrambled eggs, and tomatoes is arranged on colourful bowls and platters. Donna passes us tall glasses of freshly squeezed orange juice as we walk in. We take turns checking e-mail on Donna's computer and chat about our latest adventures.

(from Nora's diary)
Donna gives me a delicate, stained-glass purple violet so that I will remember New Brunswick's provincial flower. We go down to the bus station to see Lasse

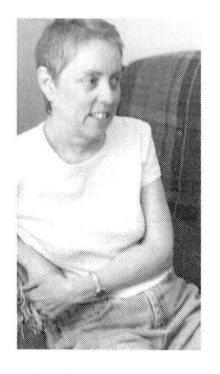

Donna McNeil, a friend from high school, serves us a breakfast fit for kings in Sackville. Below, an eerie house beckons to us from the trail.

(Lars) off and we are all sad at the prospect of him leaving to go back to Sweden. Three weeks just flew by with him. After goodbye tears from us, he leaves on the bus for Halifax, and we drearily head out onto the Waterfowl Park boardwalk. Small birds dart around the reeds and purple loosestrife flowers. The day is gloriously sunny. We get onto our trail from the boardwalk, walking through farmland most of the way. Puffy clouds hover over us. Partway along the trail, amid bushy green trees, towers a huge yellow house, so eerie and ominous that it grabs our attention. Mom and I convince the others to follow a small, overgrown path to the front of the house with us. I can only describe the feeling I get staring at the old unkempt windows as spooked, yet questioning. What happened in this house? Why was I feeling this way? As we inch closer, Mom whispers how it has a foreboding 'Butter Box Baby' feeling surrounding it. Mom ventures to the greenhouse next door and learns that the house is an old school.

We return to the trail, haunted by this mysterious building. Lilacs are out in full bloom and the air smells sweet.

The old rail bed is sandy and our feet sink and spin backwards with each step. The wind is strong on our backs and the long grasses on the marsh wave in time to the wind. We lie back for lunch. There is a solemn mood about us. We are missing the little, sarcastic comments from Lars. Poor Lars, he has forgotten the snacks that he had intended for the bus. We toast him as we share them around. Nicholas builds himself a little model out of dry sticks, as the rest of us lie flat, staring at the mounds of clouds passing overhead. We have to rattle ourselves to standing and retrace our steps back to the Sackville High School where Billy is waiting. He was able to visit an old friend from the navy last night and regales us with stories from that time in his life. Billy was a fitness instructor in the navy and has promised to whip us all into shape with his calisthenics training. It is the pushups with arms stretched straight overhead that we can't seem to muster. Billy, however, finds it extremely amusing watching us try.

A friendly janitor lets us use the school washroom, then we are off in the van to Nancy and Andrew MacInnis' in Lower Jemseg. Nancy and her identical twin, Nora, had been my flat mates in university. Nancy and Andrew share a newly restored home in Lower Jemseg.

(from Nora's diary)
As soon as we pile out of the van, we put our hiking boots back on for a trek around the Lower Jemseg marshes. Nancy's dogs, Matt and Mabou, joined us as we searched for bird nests among the wetland shrubs. Night falls quickly as we push our way through waist-high grasses. It the middle of the field a bird of prey drops its nightly meal of fish. We leave it and continue out onto the dykes overlooking the shimmering water. We walk cautiously, constantly on the look-out for animal burrows, nests, and skeletons underfoot. Large clouds of flies hum around our heads. At one point I look back at Nancy and can barely see her through the hovering haze of insects. Amazingly though, they aren't biting. At the end of our added five-kilometre tromp, we are startled by the screech of an osprey who has made her nest on a pole situated directly on our path back to the road. We keep walking, hoping that we won't get her too upset. Wrong! She begins swooping around our heads, screaming until we are well away from her nest and down the road. By the time we return to their house, Andrew is back from work at Duck's Unlimited. We get a tour of their large, old- fashioned yet classy home. It is absolutely perfect. Every room could be photographed for *Country Living* magazine. The bed where I sleep is cool and relaxing, and I feel better than I have all day once I lie down.

June 9

Place: Oromocto to Fredericton
Distance Traveled: 22.5 km
Wildlife: muskrat, squirrel, lupines, candytuft, flowering crab

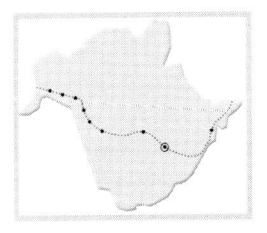

I am lying in a big, brass-posted bed at Andrew and Nancy's. I stare out the window and watch the new green leaves dance on the tree outside, casting the same shadow on the bedroom wall. I wonder if a small child has ever lived here and has lingered in this bedroom, looking out this same window, delaying the beginning of a new day. Below me in the kitchen, coffee is on and toasted bagels await us. The day is fresh after last night's thunderstorm and we are all grateful to have been protected for the night. Nancy takes me into her pottery studio before we leave and gives me five little necklaces, our bonding symbol for New Brunswick. I call Julie, my niece, and learn that Shirley-Dale, my sister, will be arriving at the Fredericton airport at 11:00 A.M. She is flying home from Bhutan where she has been working with teachers and students in the Himalayas. Tommy, Shirley-Dale's son, and his 'Hot Toddy' band members, Thom Swift and Joel Leblanc, will host their CD release party at the Sheraton in Fredericton tonight. What an exciting day it is going to be!

We scramble to pack our bins between outbursts of rain from the black sky. Finally, we are ready, and drive off to catch the four-car Gagetown Ferry. Billy makes good use of our short spell on the ferry to give himself a quick shave with his razor before reaching the other side of the St. John River. We race to the airport as the sun brightens the sky. We want to greet Shirley-Dale on her arrival home after her 36-hour plane ride, but it does not look like we will make it to the airport soon enough. As we hurry into the arrival area, we spot a ruckus in the middle of the parking lot. A woman wearing a colourful woven headpiece, with her back to us, attracts our attention. It is Shirley-Dale. She is wearing a special headpiece given to her before her departure from Bhutan. We spew from the van with a boisterous welcome. The van doors are wide open and Shirley-Dale's luggage lies in a pile as traffic skirts us in curious amusement. Karen Penny, Tom, and Julie are here and we laugh and toss stories around about our stay with Karen's parents, Lorna and Russell, in Port Aux Basques, Newfoundland.

We part in opposite directions; the hikers leave for the trailhead in Oromocto and the others go back to Durham Bridge, Shirley-Dale's home, to prepare for our arrival later in the day. At the Oromocto Park, I dial the school board office in Truro. I have a brainwave that I want to work half time next year, so I will have time to write a book. Standing on the trail, with moose flies bombing my head, I propose my idea to the school board officials on my cell phone. They will get back to me. If they could only see me, talking in my most formal tones, trying to sound

Our approach to the longest pedestrian bridge made from a train trestle in the world, linking Fredericton and Marysville.

professional as I madly swat the horde of monstrous flies that are attacking my hair.

The rail bed is firm and smooth, almost like cement, which is hard on our legs. The trail passes behind the airport where the roar of planes intermittently breaks our steady silence. We reach a flat, green opening surrounded by trees. We munch into our tuna sandwiches and pears. Soon a car arrives and circles up the driveway behind us. We are stretched on his front lawn. We eat up quickly and move on. As we near Fredericton, the path winds along the St. John River. Lupines, candytuft, forget-me-nots, and lilacs border our path. The aroma is a nostalgic reminder of home. Prime property rolls down to the river and climbs above the trail. Perfectly manicured lawns, big, flower-decked balconies, and gardens surround the exclusive homes overlooking the water.

We have reached Fredericton, our third capital city. We cross the bridge spanning the St. John River, which links Fredericton to Marysville. The view from the bridge is amazing. Speedboats make paths in the water below us. On our left is the panorama of Fredericton, with its towering church steeples and university sprawled on the hill. A long pedestrian walk winds along the green banks of lawn on the river's edge and lovers, hand in hand, are strolling in the late afternoon sun. The low sun sends a pink glow over the river and the city. It is truly a magnificent sight. We walk slowly over the bridge. There is a bouquet of flowers tied on the bridge and a small plaque paying tribute to a young boy who lost his life when he fell from the span. It is a sober moment and we all stand in silence, offering our own prayers.

From our vantage point on the bridge, we spot our van in a neat picnic park on the Marysville side of the river. We are relieved when we finally reach our destination, which looked so far away when we were on the bridge. We pile into the van and drive to Shirley-Dale's house in Durham

Bridge. Her house is situated on top of a hill overlooking the Nashwaak River. John Sodderman, who previously built guitars, built this unique structure of saltbox design. The acoustics inside are perfect. Wildflowers pour over the bank and twist around the stone walk leading to the kitchen door. Julie is waiting for us on the big hanging swing seat on the open porch. We file into the spacious kitchen and drop our bags in a heap. Chili, corn chowder, Greek salad and freshly baked bread await us.

We flip in and out of clothes, trying to decide what to wear to Hot Toddy's CD release party. It has been a long time since we wore 'real' clothes. How light we feel in sandals and skirts. Tom Easley, Thom Swift, and Joel Leblanc are pumped, and the energy from the crowd enjoying the music is contagious. We enter the auditorium, where people from all walks of life are reveling in the entertaining mix of jazz, blues, and traditional music. Tom Easley's fingers roll up and down the strings of his bass as the thousands of fans give him a standing ovation. He even throws in a little vocal solo to further excite the crowd of fans who have come out to share the success. Joel LeBlanc pours his heart into the harmonica and Thom Swift moves us with his melancholy song, 'Long Distance Ride.' I think of how this will be us in time on the journey home after our trek, and I wonder how we will be feeling.

The night is excellent for Hot Toddy and we are delighted for them. Nicholas, who has been suffering from stomach pains all night, is sleeping in the van. Billy, always attentive to our needs, sits patiently with him, in case he needs someone. We crawl back into the van after a great night of celebration. Tomorrow will be a true rest day and a time to wash our clothes and tend to our feet.

June 10

Place: Durham Bridge
Rest Day

Waking up on a rest day to an alarm should not be allowed. This hair of mine has to be cut and Julie has made me an early morning appointment at the mall. Nora and Heike decide to join us. After a coffee and bagel on the run, we arrive at the hair salon. My hairdresser is grumpy, and not very enthusiastic about cutting my frizzy, sun-burnt hair. Heike, in the next stall, has an equally grouchy hair stylist. I chat away, hoping to lighten the mood, and by the time she is finished applying a generous supply of much needed moisturizer to my hair, she has become more sociable. Meanwhile, Nora and Julie are spending their morning waiting for us in the washroom stall, due to Larry Little's 'extra-spicy' chili from the night before. Our intentions to float down the Nashwaak River today on inner tubes are not to be realized. I had promised 14-year-old Stewart McNeil that we would give him some business renting his tubes, but it is just too cold. Everyone is perfectly happy just to sit in front of Shirley-Dale's big, open fireplace, listen to music and chat, wearing warm socks and no boots. We vegetate as Tom treats us to cheese and samosas from the market.

Fred McNeil, a neighbor and longtime friend, invites Billy to a game of golf at the River Bend Golf Course. It is a highlight for Billy, who hasn't had a crack at the game since he came with us. He has brought along a fishing rod, hoping to have the chance to drop in a line for a trout some day, but no golf clubs. Tom decides that it is a good night to cook up some hamburgers and pork chops on an open fire outside in the yard. We pull on some fleece and cuddle around the blaze. Down on the interval by the river, Saturday afternoon tractor races are in full swing. The belching and roaring of these machines fill the air. We can hardly hear each other talking. We yell above the racket. Whoever heard of racing a tractor? We finally give up on this unmerciful atmosphere and go inside.

June 11

Place: Fredericton to Keswick
Distance: 19 km
Wildlife: wood anemone, lupines, wild roses, daisies, butter and eggs, strawberries, bald eagle, broad-winged hawk

The kitchen of Shirley-Dale's big timber-frame home on the hill is bustling with

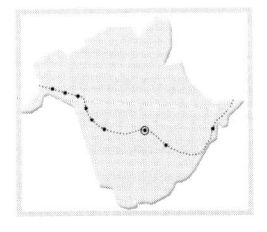

Julie, Tom and Shirley-Dale Easley join us on the trail to Keswick.

activity. We have newcomers joining us today on the trail. Shirley-Dale, Julie and Tom will walk to Burtt's Corner with us. We review their trail needs: sunscreen, water bottle, lunch snacks, extra socks and rain gear. It is interesting to watch them get ready, making sure they have everything in the right spot in their packs and smoothing the socks on their feet. It is a practice that we now take for granted, like brushing our teeth.

(from Julie and Shirley-Dale's diary)
Today was our first day on the trail with the group and how fitting it was to start in front of our old house on Gill Street. We lived there when the train still went by, shaking the dishes in our cupboard twice a day.

Tom, who lived here on the tracks in his late teens, describes his experiences, with a mischievous, exaggerated, western cowpoke tone to his voice:

"I had the pleasure of living right beside the tracks, on Gill Street in Fredericton, New Brunswick. About the time I was 19, I moved into town from the country...a big move for a country boy. My mama, she bought a house on Gill Street right on the tracks and that was back when the train was still running. There was the morning train and the evening train. One of my first experiences in that house was after a good night of whoopin' (I had a few too many); the next day I was feelin' a little ill and the train started comin' and the cupboards started shakin' and the glasses were rattlin' and I looked out my window and I saw four trains comin'. And that train went right through my head and the conductor gave me two aspirins. And that was the evening train, just when I was getting up. I heard from my mama that she used to make sure she was wearing something pretty when the conductor went by. They blew a whistle because there was no actual railway crossing. I lived by the train tracks about four hundred days, or eight hundred trains."

Julie, Tom's sister, takes a more serious approach to my questions about her life when she lived here next to the tracks on Gill Street:

"I actually lived on the railway line while going through junior high school. My friend Jill Palmer and I used to put pennies on the tracks and wait for the train to come to flatten them, then go looking in the bushes for them. We made earrings and bracelets out of the flattened pennies, or gave them to our friends, or sold them. It was quite an experience living along there. We thought it was kind of exciting at first. It wasn't until the first night that my mother and I went to bed that we realized the train came in the middle of the night. I actually thought it was an earthquake because, having lived in the country, I had never even heard cars go by in the night, let alone a train. It shone its light right into the bedroom. I remember bringing friends over and being so scared that the train was going to come— I didn't want to scare them half to death in the middle of the night. You can't really prepare anyone for such a fright.

We thought it was kind of romantic, that we could wave to the engineers and the guys on the train. They would wave every time they went by. We would think how nice they were, and that they were heading across Canada, until we found out that they went five hundred metres up from our house and stopped in the 'hump yard.' We stopped waving in case they came back. Every single time I went out with any of my friends, my mother would say, 'Don't get hit by a train.' It would be in the list with 'Don't talk to strangers,' and 'Don't get in a trunk.'"

(from Shirley-Dale and Julie's diary)
We walk through the north side of Fredericton, crossing the streets at intervals, until we walk out of town. It is neat to watch different people pair up and talk throughout the walk; Tom holding Kathy's hand, Maria and I in the lead for a while, and Nicholas and Julie in the back. Soon the group switches around with Maria and Iain leading the way and Nora and Heike chatting in back.

The walk along the river is fresh and the smell of roses and lupines envelops us. At the outskirts of town, a man appears before us with a camera. His wife and two grandchildren accompany him. The man is George A. Crawford, a former railroad employee. He is the railway enthusiast of all time. An old railway signal light blinks in his yard as he invites us in to view his treasured collection. He passes by the 'peedy' (speeder) he has in his yard and takes us inside. He proudly shows us his train mailbox, train clock, train watch, and even a train cookie jar. In his basement, which has been built to the exact dimensions of a caboose (or a van, as he calls it), the walls are adorned with railway pictures. He has toy trains, signaling as they pass each other, running through every nook of the roundhouse that he has built. He quickly dials a neighbor so that they will return the call to him. A train whistle blows. It is his train telephone, no less. A pot-bellied stove sits in the corner of his 'caboose,' as it would have in the old days. He gives me a video of the last train that came up the Nashwaak. It is a gracious gift, one I will treasure in my own, growing collection of train paraphernalia. If we stayed a month, I am sure we would still not have time to see all of his train treasures. He follows us out to the track, explaining that he moved to this spot, next to the track, on purpose. He loves trains. We leave, amazed by his enthusiasm and collection of information. I think how he should meet Garnet Buell in Murray River. They have so much in common.

Back on the trail, the rain comes even harder and we lean against its force on our last leg to Burtt's Corner. A white farmhouse sits nestled in the rolling hills overlooking the river. We learn that this house is owned by Doug Waugh, who has seen us approaching in our wet state, and with his nieces, Kelly and Sherry, take pity and come out to the trail with tea and cookies. It is exactly what we need. We continue along the edge of the St. John River toward Keswick, picking wild daisies and sampling new strawberries, our first this season.

We rush along the trail. We are anxious because Iain has to catch a bus back to Truro, Nova Scotia, by six o'clock. As we come into Keswick, we ask some people out planting their garden how far it is to Burtt's Corner. They reply, nonchalantly, "about 17 kilometres." We had already walked 19, and didn't have time to walk another step. I hitch a ride from a kind lady at the gas pumps, convincing her to turn around and take me to Burtt's Corner to find Billy. I can't believe how far it is by road. It is another miscalculation by my trail informants.

At the Burtt's Corner Station, I find a locked van and no Billy. He has gone for a walk up the line. A man working at the station heads up the track to find him. We hustle back to Keswick to pick up the others. Iain, who has been with us since Charlottetown, has to go home. He can't take his bike on the bus and we promise to courier it to him as he climbs aboard. We will all miss him. Without complaint, he has prepared suppers, poured drinks, and helped with packing and setting up camp. Billy, Nicholas and Iain have rivaled each other in cards and crib and Nicholas has been trying constantly to beat his record 'hacks' with the soccer ball. As each person leaves us, I am reminded that we will soon be on our own when we leave Fredericton and head to Quebec.

We drop by Thom Swift's house. He is giving me a tape of an actual recording of the conversation between a dispatcher and the engineer of a runaway train, which took place on March 9, 1987. This private tape has become a household item in the community, a legend among the railroaders of the area. It is chilling to hear the helplessness of the engineer and the effort of the dispatcher to keep him calm as the ore train leaving Bathurst Mines—Train 9548—loses its brakes and starts to pick up speed. Luckily, the engineer survived.

We return to Durham Bridge, then Shirley-Dale, Billy and I drive up the Tay for some refreshments. It is so civilized to be able to buy wine in a grocery store on a Sunday afternoon. Back at Shirley-Dale's, I cook up a big pot of spaghetti while Tom and Julie entertain on the piano. Karen Penney brings out her tap shoes and she and Hannah, her three-year-old daughter, give us a little rendition. Julie pulls on her tap shoes and joins in. Nora warms up the fiddle and Maria brings out the guitar. Heike, Nora and Maria sing their latest arrangements, and then Julie and Tom play the piano. Karen and Julie have practiced a few numbers, their voices blending perfectly. It is another late night before we climb into bed.

June 12

Place: Grafton to Hartland
Distance: 21 km
Wildlife: beaver, loons, ducks and ducklings, monarch butterflies, and strawberries

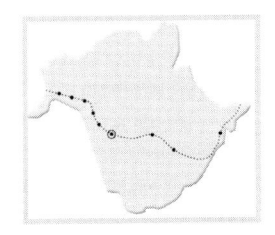

The warm sun filters through the window of Julie's attic room and sends a wand of light across the bodies lined up on mattresses on the floor. It is early morning. Today, we will move on…this time from the security of family. There is no turning back now. Slowly we begin wandering down to the kitchen where Tom is making breakfast. Rounds of coffee are poured and I sit, feet up on the big rocking chair, like a caterpillar afraid to leave the cocoon. Slowly, very slowly, we pack, lingering at every chance. Julie and Karen sing us some great songs, and we join in on "Midnight Train to Georgia"…just not wanting to make the break.

It is late afternoon when we finally pull out of Durham. We drive to Fredericton to find Walter Long, a railway man of 45 years. He is a kind, gentle man. He speaks of his life on the railway with a smile of remembrance on his face. He had been a 'car man,' fixing broken railway cars and hauling derailed cars back onto the track. He recalls horrendous train wrecks in the area and speaks about how things were in the days of the steam engine:

Walter Long - "My father was the conductor on the steam engine and it was what they called the 'way freight'; it ran between here and Newcastle. They left here early in the morning in May and right at the end of the bridge there was a washout in the night that they didn't know about. A bunch of logs had got away and dug into the bank and it was soft and tipped the track. When they came along, the engine dropped off the track and two or three cars followed it, cars of lumber and pulp. So, the engineer was killed and the brakeman had his foot caught between the engine and the tender. When the train went down, the coal door in the floor opened up and the brakeman's foot got caught in it. The engine just slid down into the cold water. They got two or three doctors out there, but none of them could make up their mind to do anything. By that time, the water was coming up on the brakeman, so the fireman held his head up out of the water. They couldn't decide whether to cut his leg off so they just left him. After about three hours, he died from shock. They cut the leg off with an axe and took him home. The doctor figured if they'd a done that first, he wouldn't have survived anyway.

Another wreck happened in 1936. The engineer was Murray Hoyatt. The passenger train was coming from Newcastle towards Devon on the fourth of June. They hit a soft spot in the track that lots of times they'd put culverts in. The engine jumped off the track and it ran along a ways, then it went down in the ditch and upset. One of the steam pipes broke in the cab and the engineer was caught by the throttle and it sort of jammed him in. The steam scalded him and he died shortly after. The fireman that he had with him lived for quite a few years after him. He was thrown out but he climbed back up in the cab to try and help and shut the steam off. He got burned quite badly too but he survived.

My job was 'car man.' We repaired and maintained all the equipment, except engines. I started full time in 1944 at the age of 16. My grandfather had worked on the trains for 44 years before me. Sometimes there would be a wreck and you'd have quite a bad mess and we only had a little crane here. It was a lot of hard work but everybody would work together.

The first summer that I worked on the 'extra gang' in 1944, there were still quite a few hobos traveling. At that time, they would be going by on the train. They would be in a 'hopper car,' that's a low-sided car, or they'd be in an empty box car. They'd have the door propped open. We had a little hobo that used to come in here for the first eight years that I worked here. Nobody knew where he came from and it didn't matter. He just said his name was Joe. He was probably about 50.

When I left, I was the last one down here in the equipment department. When I walked out and locked it up that was the end. It was a sad day. There were 25 little stations between here and Newcastle at one time—a little station every three or four miles for a hundred miles. At Durham, it was just a little shed. At Penniac, another little shed. Taymouth had quite a big station, as did Marysville and Devon. A lot of people would be just traveling back and forth. They would come into town maybe or just go down to visit a neighbour. When the express would come in, they would always unload and see who was coming in, who was getting off and who was going out. Then they would cross the track and right there was the post office. They would go into the post office and wait for the bag of mail to get unsorted to see if there were letters from home. It was sort of a ritual with people. Lots of times when you get thinking back about the different things that happened, there was a lot of exciting times and a lot of sad times."

Walter shares a poem on the tragedy that took two lives on the outskirts of Marysville, written by the late Helen Rickard.

"May 10th 1920"
The 10th of May was a sad, sad day,
When the startling news spread round,
Of the terrible railroad accident,

And the engineer was drowned.
George Greer and I in George's car,
Went quickly to the scene,
We could not plainly see the wreck,
On account of the awful steam.
The poor man's leg was pined in tight.
And held the poor man fast,
After three long hours he breathed his last.
His aged father bent with years,
Stood on the opposite shore,
And watched his dear boy perish ~
For once and evermore.

The angel of death cast its shadow,
And carried away his soul,
And carried it off to Heaven,
To its everlasting goal.
(Written by Helen Rickard)

Nora and Maria are going door to door with the Russian quilt we have brought along to raffle off. John, who has been working in Russia, has brought the quilt home with him. It is made by hand with a rich

---

The St. John River mirrors the mackerel sky above on the way from Grafton to Hartland.

blue pattern. The people in this area are particularly generous. We will eat well tomorrow.

Billy drives us on to Grafton, just beyond Woodstock. Here, there is a junction between lines going to Hartland and Millville. We query over which line to take. I finally ask a woman who lives right at the junction. She calls to her son, just to be sure. He is an avid four-wheeler so she is certain he must know. He assures us of the way and we set out. It is 5:20 P.M., our latest start yet. I have brought along a flashlight, just in case the trail is longer than expected. I ask at the local garage, 'How far is it to Hartland?' One man pokes his head from under the hood of a rusted-out truck and says, 'I only know how far it is on a four-wheeler.' 'Wouldn't it be the same distance when you are hiking?' I ask, without trying to sound rude. Never mind, we are hiking it no matter what the distance. Nicholas decides to stay with Billy and keep him company. Their mission is to find a tenting ground in Hartland.

The trail from Grafton is perfect underfoot and the softly packed mud road is easy on our legs. It winds along the St. John River, which resembles a mirror reflecting the new green on its banks and the changing sky. We stop to watch two loons diving and gliding on the river. I think of their romance, mating for life in this perfect spot. Nora and Maria are walking ahead, arms linked, sharing one set of headphones and listening to the tape Iain has made me of train songs. They stop occasionally to pick up pretty stones. This has become one of our little entertainments on the trail. At night we spend time seeing who has found the most unique stones then store them in our bins, which become heavier each day. As Nora and Maria belt out the song, 'The Last Train to Clarksville,' a beaver resting on the bank bolts into the water, slapping its tail, frightened by their approach. They jump to the other side of the trail in equal surprise, headphones flying apart.

As the sun sinks deeper in the sky, the light on the river and gullies of green take on an iridescent glow. We stop, take pictures, and admire the warm hue this light has caused. After 19 kilometres, we walk into Hartland, a small town with its row of brick-fronted buildings facing the river. Spanning this river is the longest covered bridge in the world, which opened in 1901. We stop at the little garage to ask about the campground so we can find Billy and Nicholas. A customer who has been getting gas pulls away with the nozzle still attached to his car, ripping the hose from the tank and dragging it down the road behind him. A small boy watching the scene from his bike turns to us and states flatly, 'That can't be good.' This little quote becomes part of our 'pack language' in the days to follow.

We cross the historic covered bridge and walk into a picnic park right next to the river. It has a perfectly mown lawn, picnic tables, a small parking lot, and a neat row of toilets at the end. It has three large signs indicating no overnight parking, no tents, and no fires. It also has a sign stating that the park is still closed for the season. Sitting directly in front of the signs is our erected tent and Billy with supper on the go. Nicholas is happily playing hack with the soccer ball. "What are they doing here," we ask? 'Well, it's a long story…' Billy begins. As we were hiking, Billy and Nicholas began their search for a camping ground. The campground indicated on the map had long since closed. It is suggested that the local motel has a lawn where we could camp, but it isn't open, so there would be no toilets. The golf course is suggested, but that also isn't open. Billy becomes discouraged and frustrated and says emphatically, 'Get me the mayor!' Mayor Betty-Lou Craig listens to his story. As Billy puts it, 'By the time I was finished with my story, she was crying and so was I.' She kindly secured this picnic spot next to the famous covered bridge just for us. We are honored. She later returns with pins for us to remember our stay in Hartland. This was not the end of Billy's dilemma, though. There were no stores open at this time in Hartland and he has to cook supper. Another man, feeling sorry for Billy's predicament, opens his store and sells him hamburgers and hotdogs. By the time we arrive on the scene, a big pot of chop-suey is bubbling on the camp stove. With daylight still in the sky, Nora, Maria and I head up the hill to round out our distance before supper. The late sun sends a deep alpen glow onto the covered bridge. We walk to the big truck bridge farther up the river. Vibrations rattle through our bodies as we cling to the side rails. There is no walking lane here and the closeness of these trucks is too unnerving, as is that momentary insanity that strikes you when you think you might jump off something this high. We retrace our steps.

Supper is ready when we return to our perfect camping spot. We sit down to not one but two and three plate loads of Billy's legendary chop-suey. We are starving! It is 11:00 P.M. when we finish cleaning up

| May 2 - June 17 | **Eastern Canada** |

Newfoundland - (Above)
The climb to the summit of the Discovery Trail, Woody Point in deep snow was well worth it. The view of Bonne Bay was breathtaking. From left to right: Kathy, Glenda, Nicholas, Nora, Maria, Heike and Betty.

(Below) Maria breaks trail through the snow in Woody Point.

(Inset) Maria huddled against the cold on the trail to Come By Chance.

Hiking the Dream

Newfoundland - We hike the Moose Garden Trail to Western Brook, Gros Morne.

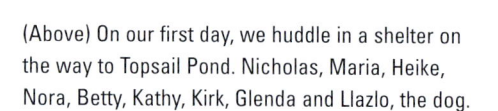

(Above) On our first day, we huddle in a shelter on the way to Topsail Pond. Nicholas, Maria, Heike, Nora, Betty, Kathy, Kirk, Glenda and Llazlo, the dog.

(Left) The trail to Codroy Pond is closed. We scale the poles across the river and continue on well beyond sunset.

Hiking the Dream

Nova Scotia - Twenty-two hikers break for lunch on the trail from Port Hood to Judique.

(Above) Lars Ottoson and Nicholas climb the moss-covered steps on the old ship railway, Tidnish.

That eerie abutment on the Salmon River, Guysborough.

Hiking the Dream

Nova Scotia - Hermina's Greenhouse provides shelter for our lunch on the trail from Mabou to Port Hood.

At sunset in Creignish, Nora and John tune up for our own ceilidh.

(Left) Family and friends join us in Mabou for the hike down the Cape Breton coast.

Hiking the Dream

Prince Edward Island - Red earth, turned over for potatoes, stretches to the skyline.

(Left) Lars, ever smiling, body aching, pulls on his boots for the long trail ahead.

(Inset) The daily "bin parade." Charlottetown.

Hiking the Dream

Prince Edward Island - (Above)
Nora and Lars on the trail from
Selkirk to Morrell.

Sunset, Cavendish Beach.

(Inset) Emily (Wainwright)
Schurman, Lower Bedeque.

Hiking the Dream

New Brunswick - Kathy, Heike, Nora, Maria, Nicholas, Iain. Oromocto Trailhead.

(Below) Nora and Maria stroll ahead on the trail from Grafton to Hartland, singing their hearts out.

(Right) Kathy and Heike swap stories at the evening campfire in Mulherin.

Hiking the Dream

New Brunswick - With the St. John River always in view and waterfowl and soft green along its banks, the trail to Hartland is perfect.

(Left) A long boardwalk takes us through Waterfowl Park in Sackville.

(Lower left) Nicholas makes use of every opportune moment to read—this time, on the trail to Florenceville, *The Lord of the Rings*.

(Lower right) Sisters Joanne Delong and Meg (Delong) White; the perfect hostesses in Florenceville.

and crawl into our tents. We have shut the gates leading to the picnic park in hopes that no one will notice they are not locked. Soon we hear the squeal of tires approaching. A drunken man stumbles out of his car to have a leak and smash a few beer bottles against the signpost leading to the park. He and the driver of the car obnoxiously laugh at their antics. We hold our breath, hoping they don't spot us. They drive off. The town clock chimes the hours through the night as we drift in and out of sleep.

June 13

Hartland to Florenceville
Distance: 21 km

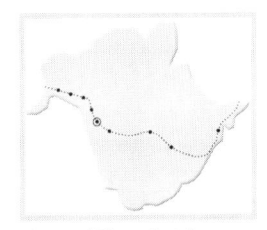

The sun pours down on our little camping place by the river. Billy has the coffee ready and is restless to get going. I pour myself some coffee and take my diary to a sunny spot on the green lawn down by the river. The river is a pale blue, quiet, with a glassy haze, mirroring the great covered bridge above. This bridge, nearly a quarter of a mile long, was officially opened in July 1901. It was a toll bridge until 1906 with fares costing three cents/person, half a cent for a head of sheep and three cents for a head of cattle. Warnings were given for going faster than a horse's trot. Later, a fine of $20 was imposed for driving faster than a walk. Shortly after 1921, electric lighting was installed because no one would venture across at night, even on a bet. During

Hartland Bridge; the longest covered bridge in the world spans the St. John River.

Taking a break on the crumbling platform of the abandoned Florenceville station. Heike, Maria, Nora, Kathy and Nicholas

prohibition days, the eastern approach was an ideal location for road blockades to catch the 'rum runners.' Sitting alone here next to this grand structure I think, "if only this bridge could talk."

Slowly, everyone crawls from the tent and I muster up some pancakes. We pack up our gear and take a quick jaunt up the hill to visit the local souvenir shop. We cross the river to fill our water bottles at the same little gas station where we were entertained yesterday. At the station, the pastor, Paul Kelly, who invited us to see his museum on covered bridges, meets us. He has built several replicas with the help of his son. He has put the project together to help put his family through university. He is such an interesting man and a fountain of knowledge on covered bridge history.

The hike today is along the St. John River, an easy walking path bordered with large cedars. It is unbearably hot, though, and my feet burn in my boots. Nora is feeling dizzy from the heat. We stop for lunch in the middle of the trail in a trickle of shade from one of the cedars. The trail seems to stretch on forever after lunch and our pace slows. As we approach Florenceville, the trail opens across some newly planted fields. A man is filling a water truck from a little pond next to the trail. I beg him to spray us. I anticipate that he will raise his hose and let the cool water sprinkle over our salty bodies. Instead, he directs the hose with full force directly into our faces. It is a shock and we gulp the water that has been blasted straight into our mouths, as we scramble out of its force. The man leans back in delight at his little prank as we wring the water from our shirts. Heike, who is hiking on ahead, is oblivious to our little encounter.

We reach the old Florenceville station, standing abandoned and boarded shut. Sisters Joanne Delong and Meg (Delong) White arrive just as we drag our tired bodies into the station. It is perfect timing. I met Joanne at Shirley-Dale's in Durham Bridge in the fall and she immediately offered to help us out when we arrived in Florenceville. Joanne and Meg lead us over the bridge and up to the high ridge overlooking the river to their home. The house is situated on a slope surrounded by fruit trees and cedars with cool green lawns carpeting the grounds. We fall from the van and lie back on the cool grass. Squirrels scamper on the branches of the trees overhead. It is so peaceful here, I could fall asleep.

I enjoy a refreshing shower before supper. I imagine the salt that's rolling off my body would probably be enough to keep our steps free from ice for a whole winter.

Joanne and Meg have prepared a spinach lasagna and salad. We sit around the big picnic table on the deck overlooking the spacious lawn. It is a warm summer night and the mosquitoes are out in droves. After the main course, we are treated to rhubarb crisp and ice cream. Joanne and Meg's mum arrives and immediately begins making railway contacts for me. She contacts Myles Meed who agrees to open the Florenceville station.

Myles is waiting at the station when we arrive. His truck resembles a large tool kit. There is hardly room for him to sit for the tools that are piled in the cab. He reaches in and brings out a big power tool and begins pulling the screws from the station door. Inside it is dark and broken glass and old papers are strewn on the floor. The eerie glow of the flashlight sends shivers through me. I wonder who might have stood in this women's waiting room—perhaps a young woman on her way to see her loved one or on her way home for Christmas. And in the men's waiting room on the other side of the station, what yarns would have flowed, with the spittoon strategically placed in the middle of the floor for all to reach. We descend the rickety steps to the basement where lumps of coal remain strewn on the floor. An old broom leans in the corner, next to the coal chute, as if just propped there for the night. Myles tells us they want to move the station up to the nearby village of Bristol. No small task. As we are about to leave, I spy a poem, written by a switchman, among the rubble on the floor. I wonder about the circumstances of the person who wrote this poem.

Hiking the Dream

My Job
I'm not allowed to run the train,
The whistle I can't blow.
I'm not allowed to say how fast,
The railroad train can go.

I'm not allowed to shoot
off steam,
Nor even clang the bell.
But let the damned train
jump the track,
And see who catches hell!

We leave, promising to meet Myles at his machine shop in Bristol tomorrow. Joanne drives us up past the McCain's plant, a multi million dollar food business. More people work at this plant than live in the entire community. Back at Joanne's we choose our sleeping spots. Nicholas and I retreat to our separate rooms in the basement. Heike chooses the sun porch. Nora and Maria are in the cozy bedroom upstairs and Billy's private room is next to theirs. We will sleep like kings and queens.

Among the rubble on the floor of the Florenceville station we found this poem, date unknown.

June 14

Florenceville to Upper Kent
Distance: 25.5 km
Wildlife: muskrat, squirrel, albino robins, cedar trees

(from Heike's diary)
After a good night's sleep on the porch (seems to be my favorite spot), I awake fairly early due to the

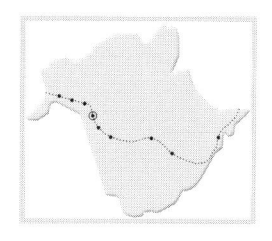

104

New Brunswick

Bristol station, Shogomoc line: Nicholas sits at the counter in the old auxiliary train.

warm and bright morning sun. A fantastic breakfast consisting of rhubarb muffins and really good coffee awaits me and my fellow travelers. We then set out across the old bridge to stock up on provisions. No bread and cheese today, but fancy sandwiches to keep up the troop's morale! We start our hike where we finished yesterday. We are in for another scorcher, which makes me long for the Newfoundland climate once more. My right foot comes up with a new surprise for me by reactivating an old blister. The worst with these little ailments is that you can never tell how bad it's going to get—it's not the actual pain that gets you down. What else was there to do but go into autopilot and just keep on trudging.

We first pass a lot of buildings belonging to the McCain Company. I didn't know that their headquarters were in a little town in New Brunswick. Then, a windfall for Kathy: she finally manages to replenish her "medical" foot wool supplies at the 'Lamb 4 Ewe' sheep farm.

I head out, my two bags of sheep wool tied to my backpack. This will come in handy in the next few months. The sheep's wool is especially good for separating and cushioning the toes, preventing blisters. The lanolin helps to keep the feet from callusing, a little trick I learned from my friend Elizabeth Nagel-Hari in Switzerland. Now in her seventieth year, she has climbed every mountain in the Berner Oberland. Growing up in the mountain village of Kandersteg, she always had a good flock of sheep to supply her needs. Elizabeth and her husband, Heinz, have become our dear friends and this summer will be the first in many years that we will not visit them.

Maria treats us to some ice cream at a little trailside stand. The ice cream in this heat is especially delicious. After a few more clicks on the pedometer, we come to Bristol, where Myles Meed is waiting. He shows us the old Canadian Pacific Railway cars that the Shogomoc Railway Club plans to restore and turn into a museum. The name Shogomoc, is derived from an Indian name given to a stream and lake near Nackawic, New Brunswick. The name was first applied to a railway passenger car of the Intercolonial Railway around 1890. The CP rail line that passes through this area is called the Shogomoc Subdivision. Myles shows us around the 'support cars' for the train wrecks. They would be hauled in to the site of the wreck so that people working on them would have a place to stay. The cars had been sleeping cars, decorated with ornate wooden carved armrests. The final car had been used as the baggage car on the royal train that carried Princess Elizabeth on a trip across Canada in the 1930s. Myles leads me through the cars, explaining their history as we go:

"One of these cars was built around 1930. We got it up here after the railway announced that they would no longer allow any railway cars to be given away because people would jack them up and move them maybe 25 feet sideways off the track and leave them there and not bother to do anything with them. They just got rattier looking all the time. About a year after that, when we were looking for one, one of our club members was retiring in six to eight months and figured that if he gave out a car, by the time they discovered it, he'd be gone. Originally, it was built as a sleeper car. It had 14 upper births and 14 lower. The whole inside was painted with this weird green colour. Even all the mahogany was covered in green paint. We succeeded in scraping and sanding the paint. We hope to eventually do all of it. In the sixties when the shine was pretty well all gone, it wasn't acceptable for passenger use anymore but it was still in good condition. Because it was so heavy, they said we might as well do something with it, so they took all the beds out from here to the end and they put in a lunch counter and they made it an auxiliary. An 'auxiliary' car is one that travels out with the wreck train so that workers at the wreck will have a place to eat and sleep.

I grew up about a quarter of a mile down the road from here. Although it isn't evident, when you are coming up along the track, it's got considerable upgrade. Back in the village, the original station was down the other side of this bridge, probably a couple of hundred yards. It was burned around 1910. Up until that time, the train stopping at the station in some cases couldn't get moving again up the hill. They had to back the train up to get a run for it so they could go on down the road. The people reasoned that if you're going to have to back up here why not build the station here to begin with? So, when they built the new one, around 1911, they built it here. Then the trains could go up the hill. I lived part way up that grade down in the village and it was amazing to watch the steam locomotive going up there with the black smoke flying out of it. We just grew up that way. In 1946, we moved over to the house here and it was still right beside the track. We still had steam trains running here then. In 1947, there was a train wreck, and two men were killed just around the corner on the river. We have some photographs of that wreck. In the fifties when they discontinued that steam service, they put on the diesels then after that they had the dayliner. Then they did away with the passenger service all together. Later on they went to nothing but freight. They were actively de-marketing, trying to discourage use so that they could claim it was a money loser. They created artificial bills against this piece of track, and there was no justification for them other than creative bookkeeping showing they were losing money on it.

One spring, the water running down over the hill had undermined the tracks. It didn't wash out in the sense of leaving the track hanging, but the ground underneath was all just soggy. When the freight train was coming down from up river, the whole side hill, track and everything went down to the river. There were two men killed. We saw it because we were living here at the time. We were just having dinner and we looked out the window and could see the steam coming from down on the river shore. It didn't blow up but it certainly was a bad wreck. One of the cars our group owns was actually part of the wreck train that went to that wreck. When we got the car, we discovered this fact because they had the record book that went with it ….essentially a daily diary for the wreck car.

The Princess was over in Canada on a royal tour and this car was part of that royal train. It might have been used for staff or it may have been a dining area and one part was all for luggage. The queen was a princess at the time but her suitcases would have been in this car. The door that was on the end of the car has since been vandalized."

Back on the trail, four-wheelers whiz by us, kicking up the dust. We enter Bath, where the stately old railway station has been converted into law offices. Continuing on, the heat is unbearable and we are in desperate need of a washroom. Hiking in a civilized area can sometimes be an inconvenience in this regard. The school in Bath is the perfect spot. We enter the cool building and are met by some teachers just packing up for the day. They treat us with packs of juice and relate their own stories about the trains. Judy (Little) McNally is from Harvey Station. She recalls the train when it ran by their cottage:

"The cottage that we have is on the mainline between Saint John and Montreal, which was a CP rail line but is now owned by Irving. There was a station there. My father bought the station house and took the freight shed end of it and moved it to the village of Harvey, to Harvey Lake and made a cottage out of it. And that cottage still exists there on our lake. We watched the train go by our cottage every summer for years. Irving's trains are still running there—two or three freight trains a day. The train used to be the main communication link between Harvey, Saint John and Fredericton."

Judy Guest, from Zealand Station near Millville, just up from Burtt's Corner, remembers when the Jitney was the passenger train:

"We would get on that and go to Woodstock to shop. The tramps were scary. One thing that was real special to us was the big inspectors and their big fancy car with flags on it. It would go on the rail just like a car to inspect the rail lines. They came quite often. I was up to Grandpa's a week or two ago and I saw a car coming down the line just like I'd seen when I was young. It's probably 50 years ago since I saw those cars. They just drove it right along.

Mum was making cookies one day and one of these hobos came up the track and he came in and he wanted to have something to eat and drink. It really scared us that day and it stayed in my mind. Mum never had much counter space, so she was making them on the kitchen table. That man stood over her the whole time at her back and really made her unsettled, especially because my dad was on the railway working. When somebody came walking up the tracks you would get out of the way…Mum would say 'come on in.' Not that they were bad, but it was the impression that they gave, they were dirty and quite corrupt looking. In a big city you might be used to it but we were in the country.

I spent a lot of nights in the railway cars. My dad used to go 'over cross,' we used to call it. Going across to Carlisle. If he was the cook they would let us use that cook car and a sleep car for my aunt and uncle and my family. We would go over for the weekend for a '48,' (to go across the border for 48 hours) so we could bring back things. That used to be a fun time because we got to sleep in the bunks and my dad cooked. We never went anywhere back then because we were poor, you know, in the fifties and sixties.

Dad was really lucky. He was right in Bristol here and he found a twenty-dollar bill right on the track. It was over at the train bridge, too. There are a lot of memories."

(from Heike's diary)
From now on, I've basically been going into autopilot and only wake up to explore a long, metal stairway leading up the bank to my right where I am rewarded with

a view of a dam, a power station and the Trans Canada Trail. Before that I spotted a tiny figure in the distance on the trail which later turned out to be our Billy, who'd come to find out what had become of us. It must be boring to spend a good part of the day waiting for us. He put his time to good use, though, as we find out when we arrive in Upper Kent. It turns out that Billy has almost managed to acquire "local status" by getting down to some serious socializing. He has tracked down Ervin G. Canam, who is waiting to chat with Kathy about the railway.

Ervin is 84 years old. He is finishing his supper when I arrive for a chat. I wait on the swing seat on the porch. Soon, he joins me, sitting very straight and stern with his small dog on his knee. He is most serious about his answers and sometimes impatient with my requests for more stories. His father worked in the railway, as did his grandfather.

Ervin G. Canam - "My father was born at Big Shore down here and he worked all his life on the railroad. He was a big, two-hundred-pound man when he was fully-grown. When he was 13 years old, he started to work on the railroad. He worked on the railroad all his life until he was pensioned off at 65. He had a foreman over him and they would go out in the morning and up here to Upper Kent to what they call the handcar shed. A handcar has one set of handles on the back and one on the front. Two men stand on the back, two on the front and they pump it up and down. They'd go work with that handcar. My father's section was always up to kilter—five miles and one mile down below Upper Kent. They had to patrol that to see that it was safe for the trains.

In the wintertime, the station here in Upper Kent, up by the crossing, was the main thing. We had in the winter here what they called the 'up express train.' It had about five cars with fruit and vegetables in the front end. They'd stop and put bananas and oranges off at each station. We called it the 'up' express and the 'down' express at two o'clock, one went from Fredericton or McAdam up to Edmunston and at three o'clock, the down express came down and brought whatever people wanted to come down.

Down between here and Woodstock, 38 mile, down by Hartland, 20 mile there was a terrible train wreck. The train was comin' up there in the night and a big freshette. It had rained all night and washed the track out and it went down in there and killed the engineer and fireman and brakeman. In them days they had two brakeman on the train, one controlled the rear in the caboose and one had to stay with the engineer and the fireman. The three of them were killed that night.

You'd see the hobos going by underneath the trains. There was big rods that go underneath and the hobos would be in there. Every train you would see them in there laying on them rods. Every once in awhile, the brakeman would be asked to walk on top of those cars from the caboose while the train was going. They all hated it, but they had to do it. Between every car there was this space about four feet and they'd have to jump across that. One fellow was coming up one night from Woodstock and he knew there were hobos on the train and he was watchin' for them, doin' what his boss told him to do—get them off the train. They were afraid the hobos would unhook the coupling when they were going along the road and leave half of the train behind. This fella was coming up and he was looking in between the trains; sure enough, the hobos were standing on the coupling. On top of every car there's a big wheel that turns the brakes off and on. This fellow from Aroostook, he saw the hobo there and he reached down and took a hold of the wheel and gave it a big lurch. The tramp didn't know anyone was up there; he lost his balance and fell down. The next morning they found him all cut to pieces where he went down in between."

Soon, Ervin's daughter and wife come out to go for a walk along the railway line. Maude is wearing a neat white cardigan buttoned to the top. Her mother links her arm in Maude's as they stroll out across the yard. The wind has picked up and swirls of dust play across the driveway. Something very heartwarming strikes me as I watch them disappear down the tracks. It is probably a scene that repeats itself every night at this time. Finally, it is time to say good-bye to Ervin. He poses with his dog for a picture before I leave. I know I want to see this man again. I know I have only touched the tip of the stories that he has tucked away in his memory.

(from Heike's diary)
The rest of us go to the store for treats and refreshments and some banter with the locals. Upper Kent certainly is a friendly place! People are easy to talk to here. We are also given some crackers—a welcome salty snack. While we wait in the van for Kathy to come back, we see a mottled white bird we take for a small pigeon or a robin. We learn from Kathy that it was indeed an albino robin. Then we are off to Muniac campground, our home for the night. We make good use of all the facili-

ties and all the available space. Billy gets to make a fire, we have supper and everybody is happy.

June 15

Upper Kent to Perth Andover
Distance: 20 km
Wildlife: squirrel, carpets of blue flowers

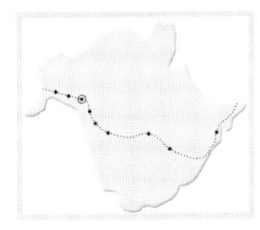

(from Nora's diary)
For the first time on this trip, Billy doesn't wake us up to start the day, and it feels odd. Instead, we are allowed to sleep while Mom interviews Jim Dunlop, a schoolteacher who stops by our campground on his way to school.

As Maria makes breakfast, I sit by the fire with Jim Dunlop. It is very windy and I hug my fleece close to my body as he tells me about the trains. Jim is a real history buff, a mine of knowledge about the trains. He tells me about the famous royal train:

"The royal train went across Canada in 1939 with the visiting king and queen. It was a celebratory kind of process. That would be King George VI and Queen Elizabeth. They had all kinds of people that accompanied them and a separate train was put together. The steam locomotives on the front were Hudson-type locomotives. And with the king and queen coming they put crowns on the front of the locomotives and so you'll hear the name 'Royal Hudsons.' Today, when you go to Vancouver, if you ride the line from North Vancouver to Squamish, you'll ride a 'Royal Hudson, 2860.' It's a 2800 class and they had a series of sleepers and diners and had a couple of cars for the press. It was a full, 12-car train and it would stop wherever the schedule said across the country, mostly the big cities to meet dignitaries. There was a two-day stop in Ottawa. I think the trip was 14 days long, coast to coast.

Then there was the 'spud express' bound for Montreal. Many nights it would have 90 cars on, all potatoes. That was a six-day-a-week train. One day at Perry's

Bishops Cemetary, where thirteen unmarked graves, moved to this spot due to the flooding river, stand side by side.

Potato House in Grand Falls when they were getting ready to go out on the boats with seed potatoes, they loaded 38 carloads in one day. My father was a section foreman and one of his jobs was to make sure the cars' heaters were ready. When they went from steam to diesel, there was a bit of apprehension. One engineer didn't like the way the diesel took the turns so when he filled out the trip papers he filled out three hundred miles on a trip that would normally have been one hundred. When questioned about it, he said well, she was swinging a hundred miles that way then a hundred miles that way over the hundred miles down the track."

(from Nora's diary)
The trail starts close to the side of the highway, yet our view of the road is quickly blocked by full, lush green trees on one side. For much of the way, I walked beside Mom, neither of us talking. Some days, you feel like hiking fast and furious, other days you feel bubbly, sunny and talkative. This is not one of those days. On days like today, you have no impulse to walk quickly. It doesn't matter if you have someone to walk beside you or not, because you spend most of the time in your own head anyway. The feel of the walk engulfs me. I could have been in Wittenburg or Caribou, Nova Scotia, or any other town that was once busy with people but now lies dormant and sleepy. It is like stepping back in time. The old shingled houses are deserted and sag in the middle. Lilacs of purple, violet and white hang over the doorways. Vines crawl around the old barn doors. Small, blue flowers carpet the ground and follow us the rest of the way to Perth Andover. Mom and I stop in curiosity at the old Bishops cemetery. Most of the people there died in the 1800s. Thirteen unmarked graves stand side by side. There is so much unknown history. Later we learn that the graves were moved here because of flooding along the river.

As we approach Perth, we meet an old woman bundled in winter clothing. She holds herself like she is walking in a winter storm. We, on the other hand, are wearing sleeveless shirts and still exclaim about the heat. She tells us how the 'great flood' had flooded her home by the river and they just plowed it under. Her husband died three years later and now she lives alone up across the tracks. She complains of the cold wind on her ears and trods on home. We watch her go, her small body gnarled with age and a hard life, making its way along this lonely stretch of track. The late afternoon sun chokes out any hint of a breeze.

(from Nora's diary)
We arrive in Perth Andover very warm after 16 kilometres in the sun, but happy to see Billy. We drive over the bridge to the old Andover side for groceries, then back again. Maria, Mom and I decide to walk to our campground to make up the 20 kilometres. First, we stop at the Home Hardware to ask if anyone knows where Maria's university friend, Dave, lives. They do!

At our campground, we set up the tent while Mom makes stroganoff over the campfire and Maria makes a salad. It tastes wonderful. Also wonderful is to finally have a shower. Evelyn Broad, an avid trails person and snowmobiler, stops by to welcome us and help up plan our walk for tomorrow. Maria's friend Dave picks Maria up and shows her around the town. It is still early when the mosquitoes finally drive the rest of us into the tent to sleep. A short time later, I hear Maria zipping up the tent while I'm slipping into sleep to the sound of Nicholas reading *The Lord of the Rings* to us.

Nicholas is intent on his reading to us. I try to listen each night, falling asleep before the end of the chapter. He stirs me awake to quiz me on what he has read. I try my best to remember the characters and the plot, but to his disgust, I never seem to get them all straight. I have been home schooling Nicholas this year and have told him that for his English assignment, he is to read to me each night. I tell him I will mark him on my ability to understand what he reads. This explains his disgust with me. How can he possibly teach someone who can't stay awake to listen? Welcome to teaching, Nicholas!

Heike lies in her sleeping bag, intently listening every night. Like Nicholas, she is interested in this story and during their 'down time,' they draw fantasy pictures that would rival those in the books any day. Heike has purchased Nicholas some drawing pencils and they spend hours discussing this fantasy world. It is a great escape and I envy this peaceful yet creative hobby of theirs.

June 16

Perth Andover to Brooks Bridge
Distance: 24.5 km
Wildlife: muskrats, squirrel, red-winged blackbird, ducklings, seagulls

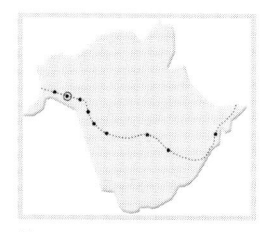

(from Maria's diary)
The day begins early with Billy's friendly beckoning outside the tent, "Is anyone up in there?" he questions. No answer. "Anyone up?" No answer. "Kathy, are you awake?" "Nope," comes a muffled reply to my right. Back to sleep in my case until Mom's call comes from outside. "Girls? Nicholas? Are you up? The newspaper reporter is coming." Groan on our part. I think that I could sleep all day. We crawl out of the tent and toast bread over the fire that Billy has made. The reporter talks to Mom and takes pictures. Evelyn Broad brings maps for Mom, and we pack up our gear. We are driven across the river to Andover to start our hike. Nicholas opts out for the day, and I think that is probably a good decision for him. I pull on my clean braces, already twice worn socks, hat, and eighties Vegas-style sunglasses and am off.

The heat immediately pelts us until drops of sweat roll down the nosepieces of our sunglasses. The packs leave wet imprints on the backs of our tank tops, and even the tapping of my braids seems too much to bear. Not long into the hike, I eat my chocolate bar and have some water. I bring more than usual on this hike and, looking back, thank God. As we arrive in Aroostook, our attention is immediately drawn to the old station. The roof is slanted down to meet the curlicue braces. The windows are boarded shut, but the front door has been beaten in. We quickly made our way inside to inspect the ruins that are left behind. All papers, documents and instruction manuals have been left in the station, but vandals have pulled most papers off the shelves and they are piled in a corner. We rummage through, looking for dates on the stamped tickets for freight cars. 1950 is the oldest date we find. The objective turns into finding significant dates, like birthdays or holidays. It is so sad to see so much detail in such disarray. I would love to help clean it up.

New Brunswick

We were called to keep moving. I try to prolong the leaving as long as possible, as it is much cooler in the old station. Soon, we are back into the heat, plodding along, telling our favorite sceneries of the trip, and discussing our travels to date. When we reach the twisty train bridge, we decide to stop for lunch down by the abutments. We make our way down to the water's edge, strip to our undies, and enter the water. God knows what is floating in it. I'm glad that I don't know or I probably would not go in.

Once out, I write on a small piece of paper from the train station: "The sound of peepers, crickets, frogs and birds surround us as we sit by the water clothed only in our underwear. The sun shining through the trees behind us dots our crisscross of tan lines with light. Heat dries our skin as we share the bread and cheese. No boots hinder the movement of our toes. To our left, birds dart in and out of the abutments, which carry the bridge we will soon have to cross. The river ripples in front of us behind thick blades of grass that barely move in the nearly non-existent breeze. Fallen trees border us on the right, so perfect to sit on. We chose the sandy plateau covered in sparse tufts of grass. Clouds build above us in the deep blue sky, creating a feeling of an impending thunderstorm."

We pick our way back up the trail and set off. New underwear and socks make it feel like we were starting a whole new day. The heat quickly saps water from our pores and our water supply runs out. Feet become too sore, and delirium is looking past my sunglasses to the back of my eyes. I quickly try to ingest a chocolate bar from yesterday, but because it looked like a melted bear turd, laughter twists my sides and I double over in a fit of tears. I have absolutely no control. Mom's feet feel like her toes have melted together into one huge rotten potato and Nora's feel like they are bending over backwards. Mine feel burnt, like I have walked over hot coals, and Heike has nice blisters. To my awe, she continues on without complaint. The heat becomes too great, so we stop and ask a lady if we could fill our water bottles. She kindly tells us she has a hose connected to the house around back if we want water. I guess we are too dirty to go inside. After filling our water bottles, we are off at a brisk walk/hobble/run as swarms of mosquitoes gorge themselves on our flesh. We stop again later. We are so tired. Do we walk on the road? Do we hitch-hike or go to the nearby house to ask how far it is to Brooks Bridge? From this house, it is one mile.

When we meet Billy and Nicholas (who have spent the entire day waiting for us), they are worried and glad to see us. We get some ice cream and drive to the campground. After setting up the tents, Nora, Nicholas and I head for the pool to ease our aching muscles and fly bites. We play and do stunts in the pool, eventually pulling ourselves away for supper. Mom makes great spaghetti and we sit around the campfire that Billy has made. This is where I sit now. Everyone is making their way to bed as the moon reflects its light on the pond by our tent.

June 17

Place: Mulherin to Grand Falls
Distance: 16 km
Wildlife: crazy partridge

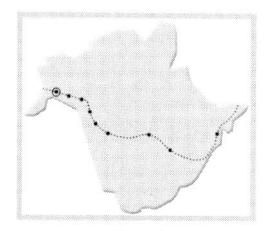

I lie outside my sleeping bag thinking about this being our last day in New Brunswick. It seems so hard to believe that we are actually doing it…walking across Canada, just like we said we would. There seemed to be so many obstacles when I was planning this journey, but now, we just get up and move on every day. As Billy says, "Just like we knew what we were doing." It is almost eight o'clock and the heat is already forcing us out of our tent. I scramble up some eggs as Billy brews some fresh coffee and makes some toast over the fire. Very juicy oranges and orange juice round out our breakfast. Last night's wash is strung on the line we made from the little lighthouse to the big pine tree. The morning sun will hopefully dry these before we have to pack up. One washer and dryer at a campground just isn't enough sometimes. Oh, oh—showers. We scramble to get the 'almost' dry clothes from the line. Phew. We throw them in the back of the trailer until breakfast is over. The sun is shining again. We hustle to get the clothes back on the line to catch the warmth. Oh no. Rain again. It's hopeless. Take them down. There's the sun again…hang them out! That's it, they're staying, rain or shine. We will walk from the campground and surely they will dry before we return.

So, we give up on wrestling with the clothes and put on our hiking boots. As I sit on the grass and pull out my bandaging supplies, I can't help but feel a little sorry for my feet. My right foot has three blisters, four large 'square' calluses, one with a blister on top, one toe is missing a toenail, one toe has lost many layers of skin and is down to a raw, red, tender layer. There is one corn on another toe and a hotspot underneath the pad of the foot. If I were exaggerating, this might seem funny, but putting the boot on let alone walking hurts this foot. The left foot seems to be faring a little better and isn't giving me half as much grief. Oh well, after the first five kilometres, the feet tend to go a little numb anyway, so I'll try to ignore the misery for the first bit.

The road from Mulherin Campground leads straight up to the highway. The hot sun scorches down on us and we lift our arms and comment on how the hot air is preventing us from sweating. In fact, we are accumulating white rings of dried salt not only on our clothing, but around our mouths, on our cheeks and the straps of our packs. It is too hot to stay damp from sweating. We are on a mission. We must accumulate 15.5 kilometres today, if we are to reach our two-hundred-kilometre goal for New Brunswick. We walk briskly along the dusty road that rolls up and over long stretches of farmland. In the hazy distance, we can see a rise of hills that reminds Heike of the terrain near her home in Germany. It is a peaceful open landscape and we talk of how difficult it must be on these remote farms in winter.

A big friendly farm dog lopes out of one of the farm lanes and ambles after us. Appearing fearful, like a wolf, he is just too hot and gives up his idle pursuit. We take a side junction up a long dusty farm road to the right. It leads over a plowed field that is now dry and dusty. The blue sky meets the brown earth with nothing in between. We could have been walking on an arid desert. We stop to replenish our sun cream and veer down the lane, which we hope will return us to a main road leading back to the campground. We are without a map. A half-ton truck is rumbling down the road, kicking up a dust storm behind it. I will hail down the driver and inquire about the distance back to Mulherin's on this road. The thought of back-tracking through the dust bowl on the plowed field was anything but inviting. Suddenly, as I begin to flag down the truck, a partridge flies out of the bushes and chases me, squawking. Screaming with surprise, yet not wanting to lose the only contact we have had all day, I run toward the truck with the partridge in pursuit. The young woman driving the truck slows to a stop and rolls down the window. Her young children appear nervous as I run toward them wild eyed. The partridge has not given up, flopping and squawking at my legs. They must think I am insane! The road, I learn, doesn't go back to Mulherin and we must retreat up that same desert-like stretch of farmland.

It is almost one o'clock when we reach the campground. We are now soaked in sweat as the breeze has died and the sun is even hotter. Quick showers and we climb into the van. It is such a relief to put my bare feet up on the dashboard and stretch the backs of my legs. We had been hiking on hills all morning and it was just too hot to stop and stretch. We drive to Edmundston and hunger hits us. Greek pizza at Pizza Delight is our choice and we devour it in minutes. Tonight we want cabins. We must download our website and get an early start in the morning, our first day in Quebec. Auberge du Jardin in St. Jacques will be our resting place for the night.

Located directly behind the hotel unit are seven neatly painted cabins, each with its own distinctive character. Our cabin is number six, the little red and gray one. Billy and Nicholas are sharing cabin number five. The owner of the cabins has given us a good deal and by the time we leave I bet he wishes we had never arrived. We encounter one problem after another. I am so excited to have an oven, I have purchased the ingredients for a cherry pie. Thus begins the saga. First we need a phone line to download our website to the net. "Hello, this is cabin number six, can you explain how to get an outside line on your phone?…Hello, this is cabin number six, is this the operator? Oh, the main desk again? Sorry. Hello, I'm from cabin number six and our oven won't work, can you help us? Hello, this is cabin number six, are you sending someone over to fix the oven? I've bought all the ingredients for a cherry pie and now I don't have an oven. What should I do? (as if they cared!) Hello, I'm from cabin number six, I'm here to pick up the microwave. No microwave dishes? Hello, this is cabin number six, when I turned on the microwave, the TV went off in cabin number five and our lights went off. Hello, this is cabin number six, we have no phone or lights."…and on and on. We lie back on our beds and laugh at the irony. We have been sleeping in a tent for more than a month with no thought of an oven, electric lights, let alone TV. Now, we have splurged to enjoy the luxury and nothing works. The microwave has given me enough power to make a cherry crisp, which I cover in melted ice cream since the freezer also doesn't work. Grateful not to have a tent to dismantle in the morning, we count our blessings and go to bed.

June 18 - June 28   Quebec

The Trans Canada Trail marker on the New Brunswick/Quebec border.

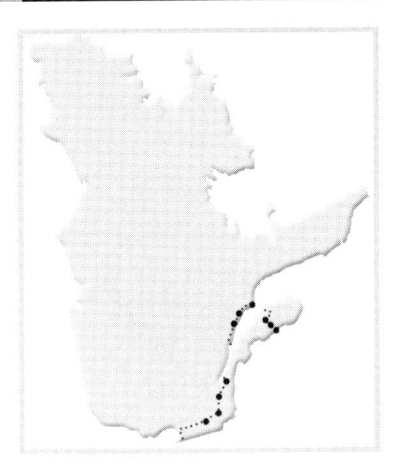

June 18

St. Jacques to Dégelis
Distance: 27 km
Wildlife: chipmunk, rabbits, hummingbird, Indian paintbrush

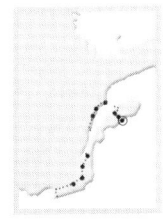

It is early morning in our brightly painted cabin number six in Auberge du Jardin, St. Jacques. Bacon and eggs are cooking on the little stove in the corner by the sink. Today we will cross the Quebec border, our fifth province. We have been trying desperately to get our website up to date but with little luck. Today is no exception.

It is noon when we leave our cabin and cross the street to join the trail, which is an old railway line. It leads to a well-groomed park with ornamental trees and flowers, boardwalks and benches. We pass the transport museum, which has a train in the yard. There are a lot of bikers on the trail today, skirting by us on both sides and from two directions. As hikers, we are definitely outnumbered.

(from Nicholas' diary)
The day promises to be cool without many flies. When we are hiking, we come to an historical site with an airplane in the middle of it, surrounded by a fence and

119

some picnic tables. We decide to eat here. Lo and behold, I forgot my chocolate bar—nothing but a two-day-old apple in my backpack. Mom gives me her chocolate bar.

As we are hiking, we start to notice the slowly increasing temperature and the rapidly increasing flies. We are swatting like crazy and before long my whole neck is dripping with blood. Two mosquitoes decide to perch themselves on my arm to work on a previous fly bite. I introduce them to each other the hard way. The flies are coming in armies. As I type, Mom has a fly stuck in her eye.

By this time we are already over the border and at least we've had a stain of hope. Near the end of the hike, my hip is really starting to bother me. Before long, I am limping at the end of the line. When I look past Mom and Maria, I don't see Nora and Heike, who are up ahead; they must have turned in to where the van is parked. I limp my way over to the van, grasping hold of the passenger's seat and pulling myself up. I stagger my way over the spare tire and collapse on the back seat. We have reached Dégelis. It has been 27 kilometres.

Before long, we are on the road searching for a campsite, despite Billy's information that no campgrounds are open for the moment. It doesn't matter to me—I'll sleep in the van if I have to.

We are exhausted after our long, itchy walk to Dégelis. We are told there is a place to camp called "Le Centre de Plein Air." It is a long drive before we find a little winding, dirt road snaking down a wooded hillside overlooking Lake Temiscouta. There are fancy chalets tucked into the trees on the slope above the lake. I explore the grounds, looking for someone to designate a camping area. A narrow path sprinkled with pine needles leads down to the shore of the lake. Here, I find a large boathouse with kayaks, paddleboats and canoes. There are boats tied up at the dock as well, which makes me think someone must be around. Just up from the lake, a grassy path leads back through the trees to a group of flat clearings with a sign "campground." Perfect. The main building is open with running water and washrooms. We chose a flat spot for our tent, close to a water supply and fire pit.

(from Nicholas' diary)
My hip is in agony and I am useless as we set up camp. It looks like a very good campsite—they have wooden chalets, plenty of tenting spots and boats lining the "Lake du Fly." By suppertime, we are seriously thinking that if we're lucky, maybe the campground staff won't see us here at all. I highly doubt that, due to

our noise. A blind man could find us. Soon I go to the tent and rest my troublesome hip. The flies are fewer in the tent and I am really thankful for that. Billy's supper is really going good and Mom's supper has settled in my stomach. I am ready for the next day.

As the tents are set up, Billy builds the fire and I cook up some Spanish rice and stir fry with salad. Some fine French wine complements our meal as the moon appears in the sky above us. Loons cry mournfully across the tranquil lake. Tonight we are lucky.

June 19

Dégelis to Notre-Dame-du-Lac
Distance: 16 km
Wildlife: chipmunk, cowslips

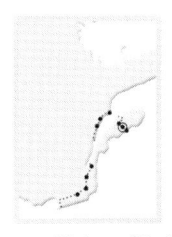

The tent is chilly inside. It isn't even eight o'clock yet and everyone is awake. The time has changed, one hour back. I crawl from the tent. The grass is cool and damp. Billy has a fire going and coffee on. I explore the woods surrounding our tent. This camping spot is pretty remote and I contemplate the possibility of the presence of bears.

Nelson Dubé, one of the staff members at the facility, is working at the main building which houses the washrooms. He is not alarmed to see us as I explain our project and how we happened to be parked on their land. He is friendly, and in conversation tells us he only knows one person from Nova Scotia. He had worked with this person on a project a few years back and we both consider it a long shot if I know him but I say, "You never know." As it turns out, that person is Kevin Stokesbury, the brother to my niece Lisa's husband, Mike. Amazing. Nelson quickly writes him a note, which I will deliver on my return to Nova Scotia. We discuss the best approach to today's trailhead and Nelson offers to deliver us to the beginning of the Trans Canada Trail across the lake in his boat. This is a first for Hike 2000.

We scurry back to the campsite for breakfast, clean up, doctor our feet and make plans to meet Billy at the end of the day. Tom, Nelson's chocolate Lab, joins us for the trip across the lake. He stands on the bow, nose sniffing the morning air. The lake is like glass as our small boat cuts a wedge through its stillness. Nelson diverts a little, showing us a new dam that has been built to control the water level in this large lake. Our boat pulls up to the dock at a marina on the far shore. Nelson brings us ashore to show us the trail beginning, then sets off with Tom in his command position at the bow.

(from Heike's diary)
The day is just another scorcher. The trail runs along the shore of Temiscouta Lake the whole way. Many signposts for little secluded swimming beaches are beckoning. I certainly am sorely tempted. Exploring down a little path to the lake, I find one where I could spend the whole day. But alas, our quest allows for no delay. We find a nice beach with good skipping stones where we have our lunch, though. The trail is laid out especially for cyclists. The underfoot (wheel) conditions are perfect, and at the picnic sites (all with picnic tables and outhouses) there are sturdy bicycle stands to which one can lock a bike while taking a refreshing swim in the lake. This part of today's hike takes us through forests and cuts in the rock, whereas toward Notre dame du Lac, there are more and more cottages and private beaches.

    Soon after lunch, we meet Donald and Ursula, from Quebec, who are spending a week cycling on La Route Verte, the trail between Edmundston and Rivière-du-Loup. As it turns out, Ursula is originally from Dusseldorf in Germany. She tells me that when she arrived in Canada in the late fifties, everyone thought she was crazy because she cycled everywhere. Today there are more people cycling in Quebec than in any other province. Her husband, Donald, tells us a story about a New York businessman who kept a mistress in a big fancy house in Notre dame du Lac. Her name was Marie Blanc, an exotic beauty from Martinique. She was famous for her shopping sprees in Montreal. The gentleman kept his family from coming to his 'cottage' by telling them that it was too dangerous and unsafe in Canada. The house was conveniently situated right next to the railway line and has been converted into an inn named after its former occupant, Marie Blanc.

Billy is waiting when we arrive in Notre Dame du Lac, as planned. Here there are large marinas and the trail is lined with flowers. On the opposite side of the trail, large flower gardens adorn the front entrances to the doorways. People are tying up their expensive water-

Nicholas cools off in the clear waters of Cabano.

craft as we trudge in with our sweaty packs and dusty boots. My pedometer isn't working properly so I walk another kilometre to check its accuracy. The trail is well measured with signposts every kilometre, which has helped us on this day. No luck with my pedometer. I will have to buy a new one. We drive to Cabano and choose a camping spot with an electrical hookup for our computer and a close water supply for cooking.

(from Heike's diary)
It is my turn to cook again. (Looks like I can't hide forever …), and I make sure that they are hungry when supper is finally lifted. The marinated chicken (soy sauce, fresh ginger and garlic, spring onion) isn't so much a problem as the 'soup mix' (dried lentils and beans) I intended to use for the base of the curry side dish. Making/waiting for supper today is a prolonged affair. The rest of the gang makes good use of their wait by going for a swim in the lake.

The cozy pebbled beach is inviting. Nora, Maria and Nicholas wade out in the cool water. The hills in the distance remind me of Stresa in Italy where we vacationed last year. Only there, the water was warmer and there was not the pressure of walking 20 kilometres or more each day. The dark clouds roll in as we head back to the campground for supper. Today, we have reached the end of the Ramsey's wool I have brought along for our feet. Ramsey, our ram at home, has been the source of the wool we use between our toes to prevent blisters. Maria offers to wash the wool we have secured in Florenceville and takes one of the three bags into the washroom. Before she goes in, we talk of her trip home when she reaches Quebec City. Her friend, Mel Lombardo, will graduate from high school. For Mel and Maria, it is a milestone, as Maria has been tutoring her since grade nine. Maria has promised she will be with her on that day. Maria discusses whether she should get her hair cut short when she is home. When Maria was in primary school, Rawdon District, they had a closure due to an outbreak of head lice. Maria was a victim of this problem at which time I had her head practically shaved to get rid of the tiny bugs. At the time, Maria was horrified. I promised her that when the lice were gone, she could grow her hair as long as she wanted. Now, 14 years later, her hair has never been more than trimmed.

I am writing in my journal when Maria returns from washing the wool. She stands in front of me and says, "I'm finished, and here's your wool." Without looking up, I thank her and continue writing. She repeats herself, "Mom, here's your wool." This time I look up into Maria's face. She is standing holding the wool and her own hair. She has cut her hair with fingernail scissors in the washroom where the tiny mirrors prevent a full view. It is chic, as if done at a beauty parlor. I jump up and hug her. Tears stream down my cheeks. "Maria, you are so brave. I am so proud of you." Billy grabs Maria, hugging her tight and telling her how beautiful she looks. We can't believe she had such nerve to cut off her long, thick braids in these conditions.

(from Maria's diary)
During the hot days of hiking, the tapping of my sweaty braids on my shoulders drives me crazy. My head is constantly hot, and my neck aches. My thick wavy hair is too much to handle. As we sit around waiting for supper, I think, "Should I cut my hair, just a little?" I go through the positives and the negatives. Finally, I decide that I will cut a bit off, but I don't want anyone to know. I grab the wool, which we use to stuff between our toes to prevent blisters. It needs to be washed so I will take it to the washroom with me. I stand in front of the mirror, and lose my guts to cut my hair and begin cleaning the wool. Slowly, I cut off the bad parts of the wool and wash the cleaner bundles. And there it is again, the brushing of my braids on my shoulder. I can't stand it, so I take the scissors and cut off one of the little braids I had in the front by my temple. Immediately, I am shocked! What have I done? Sharp bristles of hair stick out above my ear, no longer than an inch. I can't believe my own insanity! I can't just leave my hair like this. So, I undo my large braids and continue to cut my hair. Handful by handful, I lift my hair and cut it off, no longer than about a finger's width from my scalp. At one point, another camping guest enters the washroom, and her jaw drops open as she watches. I'm sure she thinks I am crazy. Once all of my hair is cut, I am terribly scared at what I've created. The part in the middle of my head is still there from where my braids were, and the short hairs on either side stick up, like mohawks. I wash my hair, dry it with the dishtowel I brought to dry the wool, re-part my hair, grab the leftover wool, and go

Quebec

Philippe and Lucie Latulippe: This exceptional couple was kind, warm and incredibly energetic.

back to our campsite. Everyone is extremely supportive and surprised, which makes me a bit nervous, but Billy jumps up and gives me a huge hug and tells me how proud he is and how beautiful he thinks I am. That made it all worthwhile.

Up at the main desk, I am told a man who has walked across Canada is in number three. I am excited to meet this man and immediately try to find him. There is a small trailer on the site next to ours, which I believe to be site three and in the window, behind the curtain, I can see two forms gyrating up and down. I think this man really has a lot of energy after walking all day. Should I knock and interrupt his 'cool down'? How else will I ever meet this man? I knock and wait. A woman with wild orange-coloured hair and tousled clothes appears at the door. She appears disarrayed and obviously annoyed by the interruption. I wish I could quickly rewind the clock and disappear. She tells me the man I want to see is next door. How embarrassing!

Nora, Nicholas and Maria join me as I knock on the door of the trailer across the driveway. A small woman, named Lucie, greets me at the door. She assures me that I am in the right place and calls to her husband Philippe, who has already gone to bed. Lucie sits in the large chair with her housecoat tucked around her small body. Her eyes are bright and her manner warm and comfortable. Philippe Latulippe appears before us, now fully dressed. He sits down beside us and begins to tell us about his life. He is 81 years young and is a medical wonder. Until the age of 49, he was a heavy smoker. His doctor told him he had better do something about it or he would be sorry. He quit smoking and began walking. He has since traversed Canada three times, twice on foot and once by bike. As he spells out his physical milestones in humble complaisance, we sit in awe of this "Einstein of the body." His name has graced the pages of the Guinness Book of Records four times, twice for long distance walking and running and twice for long distance cross-country skiing. In 1999, at age 80, Philippe biked across

Canada with Lucie driving the support vehicle. Lucie says she knows what he needs best and is comfortable looking after his needs along the road. Philippe tells us about his 24-hour skating competitions and the 24-hour skiing events. I think about our four-month trek across Canada, which pales next to this man's accomplishments. Phil and Lucie tell about his 200-kilometre walk into the year 2000. They chose 50 locations in Quebec and Philippe ran or walked 40 kilometres in each location during the months of November and December. I can hardly imagine completing 40 kilometres a day for 50 straight days in dead winter in Quebec. To say this man is a phenomenon is to say the least. In July, Philippe teamed up with his two friends, Jacques Amyot, a 75-year-old swimmer from Ste-Foy, and Buddy Coutreau, a marathon biker, also over 75 years of age for the Double Ironman Triathlon, held in Quebec. When I asked Philippe how they made out, he said, "Fine, there wasn't anyone else in our age class. We came in two to three hours under the average time limit."

In just a week's time, Philippe will compete in an in-line skating competition. He donated his bike, which he used on his trans-Canada tour, as a prize. Philippe never accepts money for his endeavors. He has donated more than two million dollars to humanitarian causes. As we are leaving, he hands me his latest medal for good luck as we make our way across Canada. He signs a book, written by Serge Richards, "L'homme qui est allé au bout des Routes."

We retreat to our tent. Tonight we are definitely blessed to have met this adorable couple and this amazing human being.

"Philippe's note"

Quebec

June 20

Cabano to St-Honoré
Distance: 27 km
Wildlife: an odd unknown rodent

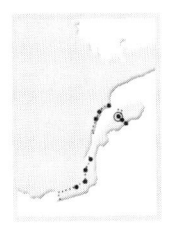

It is 5:00 A.M. and roasting in this tent. I need a shower and to get breakfast started. The weather has become very hot and a late start to the day is unbearable. By 6:30 A.M., we are eating our breakfast of fish cakes, croissants, orange juice and coffee. We will hike directly from here today. As we are cleaning up our dishes, we see Philippe returning from his one-hour, ten-kilometre 'walk.'

(from Nora's diary)
After breakfast, we go to say goodbye to the wonderful couple we met last night, Philippe and Lucie Latulippe. Philippe and Lucie are not only an amazing couple, but enthralling as individuals as well. I thoroughly enjoyed myself in their company—her smiling and telling stories with a twinkle in her eye as he teases her and adds in extra tidbits. It is hard to believe he is 81 and she is 85. He has given Nicholas a shirt he wore when he crossed Canada by bike. That is an honour in itself but it gets better ...

We decide that it is best to start hiking before the day gets too hot. We say goodbye to Lucie and kiss both cheeks, but when we turn to say goodbye to Philippe, he walks off. "Where are you going?" Mom asks. "You don't think I'd let you walk alone, do you?" he comments in passing, as he donnes his sneakers and water pack. How exciting for us! Then it hits us…this man wakes up every morning at 5:00 A.M. to train. Every morning he walks ten kilometres in an hour. This is fast. He is an ultramarathon man. He can run over one hundred kilometres at one time. He can run for more than a day. His first time running across Canada, at 63 years old, he averaged 63 kilometres every day. How are we ever going to keep up?

We are giddy as we prepare for our 'walk' with Philippe. This may be the challenge of our life. Philippe leads us out of the park on a route that takes us to the old train station that is now a country inn. We step inside for a moment to admire the pictures of Philippe on the walls.

He is definitely a celebrity in this town. Philippe tells us it is the first time he has been in to see them.

(from Nora's diary)
We started off at a good pace, probably our average pace. "Hey, we are doing it," I think. The pace gets faster and faster. Philippe doesn't walk so fast that we can't keep up, and doesn't make us feel as if we are holding him up, but we can tell that he is holding himself back and could walk a lot faster. The thing is, that Philippe's stories are so interesting that we don't notice we should be feeling tired at this pace. He is funny, unique, humble and incomparable in most ways. This is definitely one of the highlights of our entire trip.

Billy is waiting at the picnic park in Saint-Louis-du-Ha! Ha!. It is the 8.6-kilometre mark. We stop for a quick nectarine. Nicholas decides to stay behind with Billy at this point as his hip is still sore and this pace is just too painful for it. They will meet us at St-Honoré.

At this point Philippe goes into overdrive. We don't dare stop to fix our boots or even have a drink of water. This 81 year old is tromping out effortlessly. At one point, I walk directly behind him, trying to put my feet where his were, even swinging my arms the same. I mimick his every move. I just want to make my body feel like his does, I am in such total awe of this man. He is wearing his water pack and sips on it occasionally, never changing his pace.

We pause at a little rest stop where we refill our water bottles in the cool stream, below the wooden deck. I can feel Philippe waiting patiently above for us to get on with the hike. I purposely linger behind. Last night's curry dish has caught up to me and I scurry into the nearby bushes for relief. Now, I will never catch them.

Billy and Lucie are waiting for us at St-Honoré, 27 kilometres and five hours later, including our short rest stops. Philippe shows us some stretches, the secret, so we're told. As we part, he tells us it has been his honour to hike with us. We know, as we watch them drive away, that the honour has definitely been ours.

In Rivière-du-Loup, we search out a sports shop where I buy a new $40 pedometer. Pointe Campground is just out of town on a jut of land overlooking the St. Lawrence River. The paved driveway circles up a big hill with neatly mown sites. We choose our spot and begin setting up for the night. Maria and Nora are making fettuccini alfredo and salad for supper. Some fellow campers stop by to see what we're all about. One couple, from Saint John, New Brunswick, has biked up and will begin their journey home tomorrow. They are an interesting couple. He tells me that he is a dancer and that he sometimes entertains at the senior citizens' home in his community. I challenge him to demonstrate some of his moves if Nora plays the fiddle. They are heading down the hill to have supper at the tiny restaurant, so decline my invitation.

After supper, Nora and Maria get out the guitar and sing. Heike joins in and gets out her pad to jot down the words in her book where she is collecting songs. Nicholas has curled up on the lawn chair with his book. It is one of his favourite ways to relax at the end of a day. We take a short stroll to watch the sun set over the St. Lawrence. The campers roll in with their train-sized recreation vehicles and extended trailers. I can't imagine maneuvering those buses on the tiny roads we have traveled. The lights and the televisions flick on and these hardy souls settle into the campground for the night. We watch them from our humble tent, in pity, rather than in jealousy.

(from Nora's diary)
Tired, we crawl into the tent to sleep…how is it that we always set our tent up on a downward slope? Poor Nicholas, who lies perpendicular to us, always ends up with his head squished into the corner of the tent in the morning. What an eventful day!

June 21

St-Simeon
Distance: 12 km

This morning, I must set my new pedometer. Before the rest get out of bed, I strap it on and march out at our usual pace to set the stride. Billy measures out an accurate kilometre and I test the distance. One try and it is right on. Excellent.

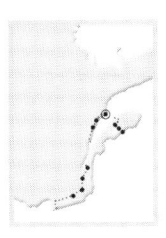

(from Maria's diary)

We are up early to get the van packed and to catch the ferry to St-Simeon, on the other side of the St. Lawrence River. When we get to the ferry terminal, we drive past the entry line of cars, so we stop and asked directions. "Keep going," is what we understand, so we drive a bit farther. Then, it is obvious that we aren't in the right place, because we are parked in front of all the cars that are waiting for the ferry. So, we stop and asked directions again. "Keep going," is the reply. So, with Mom back in the van, we drive to where the boat is going to dock and there is enough space to turn around. One of the workers jumps out in front of us. I'm not sure whether he thinks Billy was on a suicide mission or what. But, since he blocks our way we can go no further. Sorry Billy, better luck next time.

We successfully made our U-turn and drive into the correct lineup of cars. Two seconds later, Nora gets out her fiddle to accompany the tap dancer we met at the campsite the night before. He flies around the parking lot, arms outstretched and smiling. We clap and laugh while people clamber out of their cars to see what is going on. Ladies and gentlemen, Hike 2000 has arrived!!

On the ship, traveling is much less interesting. The 65-minute crossing of the St. Lawrence River involves little talking as we sit in our group of chairs. We are all glad when Mom suggests that we get a bite to eat on the other side. The waitress is friendly and pleased to hear us all order (or attempt to order) our food in French. Then, we are back in the van with full stomachs and indecisive minds on what to do. However, since the information bureau is closed and the trail is not to be found, we opt for a road hike. The weather is perfect for hiking; cool crisp air but with a warm breeze. Mom, Nora and I have a wonderful hike along the highway, as cars, buses, trucks and motorcycles beep and people wave as they pass. We stop for a while to check out the unique pottery in Port de Peril. Then, on down the road we go, chatting and waving as we walk. Billy,

Nora plays a jig on her fiddle as our new tap dancing friend entertains the crowd at the ferry terminal; his wife doubles over with laughter at this spontaneous display of talent.

Quebec

Heike and Nicholas are waiting for us after a very short 11 kilometres. We clamber into the van and are off to La Malbaie. Our campground is "Chute Fraser," and as we drive in under the huge power lines, I feel very weary. But soon, the view of power lines turns to rolling fields of long grass, then to trees before we cross a bridge over a waterfall. Our tent is set up on a grassy plateau on the bank of the river. The sound of the river breaking over its rough bed is a wonderful backdrop noise for our supper of hotdogs, steak and baked potatoes, all cooked to perfection. The rain falls on our shoulders as we sit around the fire. Wine is held in divine plastic cups and the mood is merry. I talk briefly to Iain, a broken conversation. Mom tries to tempt me for marshmallows. We make our way into the tent once the conversation ends, to fall asleep to the sound of pattering raindrops overhead.

June 22

Chute Fraser to La Malbaie
Distance: 16 km
Wildlife: squirrels

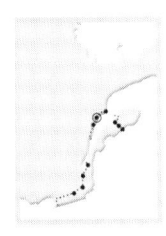

Beautiful sunshine warms our tent this morning. The rain in the night has left everything looking fresh and green. The rush of the river and the sound of the rain on our tent in the night made me feel like I was in a little cocoon. Today, we will stay in this area to hike. With the green rolling hills surrounding us and this perfect camping spot by the river, there is no need to move on. It will be a nice break for Billy to spend the day relaxing. Maybe, with a bit of luck, he will even catch a trout for supper. Also our towels and tent could use a day of drying in the sun after the rain.

I want to hike early today to avoid the midday heat but in searching for something in the van, I get a sudden urge to clean it. I spend an hour, re arranging, sweeping and organizing. Billy promises to scrub the outside later. What a great guy!

Nicholas has decided to stay behind today as his knee is bothering him and the idea of hanging out with Billy by the river is much more inviting than walking into La Malbaie in the heat. Nora, Maria, Heike and I leave the campground and stroll down over the curving hills,

Chute Fraser, La Malbaie: Billy exclaims over the amazing view from this rolling field of clover.

under the swinging power lines. Billy comes with us for part of the way to enjoy the vista from the top of the hill. He stands with his arms outstretched breathing in the fresh air. The view is spectacular looking down over the fields of clover with clumps of puffy clouds floating across the blue sky. Billy says this spot reminds him of the Virgin Islands, minus the sea.

The road borders the Malbaie River, passing neat little homes that front it. White picket fences with lilacs drooping over their peaks separate the tidy yards. People are sitting on their verandahs, looking cool and relaxed as we hike by with our backpacks and hiking boots. They greet us with curiosity as we pass. We are obviously 'from away' and the villagers give us a sympathetic smile as we walk on in the heat.

We walk into La Malbaie, a bustling village with stores, banks, schools and pubs. We are on a quest to find an Internet source. We try the bank and the elementary school with no luck. We try the larger school and walk straight into a school concert. Little children, dressed in their painted tinfoil costumes, are putting on a play. How far removed I feel from this scene. We leave this school and go to the library.

Inside the library, we meet a friendly young janitor named Alain. He patiently listens to our best French explanation to our dilemma. He doesn't have the authority to let us use the equipment here. We continue to plea with him until he lets it slip that he has a computer at his home. Poor Alain! What a mistake! We jump at the idea of using his computer. He is unsure of our motive and makes it quite clear to us that he is not 'that' kind of guy—that would be entertaining strange women in his home. We assure him that we are not a devious group of women and he agrees to pick us up tonight when he finishes work and take us to his place to use his computer. Before leaving the library, he gives us a personally guided tour. He is proud of this library and of the work he has done to keep it in order.

Alain Lavoie stops by to visit before we leave La Malbaie. Our wet clothes from the previous day dry in the background.

We leave Alain at the library and stop at the local pub for a beer. The beer is deliciously refreshing. We sit back and chat with some of the villagers in the bar before taking a look at the blackening sky. We hurry away. Eight kilometres uphill on a half run leaves us breathless as we reach the crest of the hill leading to Chute Fraser. We make a quick detour to the falls of 'Chute Fraser,' which tumble over flat tables of stone before cascading over the rugged cliff and into a deep pool. I can only imagine the freshness of a swim at its base on a hot summer day.

Back at the campsite, we scurry to make hot dogs and beans before the rain. We also don't want to be late for our date with Alain. At the appointed moment, Alain arrives, freshly washed and wearing his new wire-rimmed glasses. Nora and I climb into his sporty car. We are the appointed website fixers for the night. As Alain swerves down the roadway, Nora and I exchange amusing glances, apprehending what might be in store for us tonight. We arrive at Alain's neat apartment where three pairs of newly purchased slippers are lined up at the door, each tucked into its mate. We take off our sneakers and choose our slippers. The table in the kitchen/sitting room is set with fresh fruit, cheese and crackers. We imagine that this must be for us. The apartment is impeccably neat, with everything in its exact place. Alain shows us into his bedroom where the computer is located. Nora begins to work on the website as I sink down on the end of his bed to wait. As Nora works away, Alain proceeds to show me his collection of books depicting the male and female anatomy. Each book is carefully bookmarked at his favourite selections and we open them and discuss the details of everything from childbirth to copulation and menopause. Charts and posters on the sexuality of men and women decorate the walls. Alain is well read in the topics and we discuss our varoius views. He assures me that he has had no practical experience, just theoretical. He amuses us with his unique views of life and sense of humour.

Hiking the Dream

For the entire time we are at Alain's apartment, we must keep absolutely quiet. It wouldn't be good for Alain's neighbours to get the wrong impression. Nora and I are amazed at Alain's extensive knowledge of the physical and mental intricacies of women. We stay until about 12:30 A.M. Alain thanks us for coming and we assure him that we are the ones who are grateful for his generosity. He carefully drives us back to Chute Fraser in the rain and promises to see us before we leave tomorrow. We hurry from his car and crawl into the tent, trying not to wake the others. We whisper about this unusual acquaintance we have made due to our dire circumstances with the computer.

June 23

St. Irene to Les Emboulements
Distance: 21.7 km

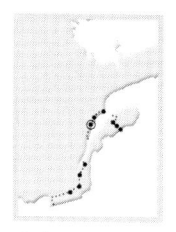

(from Nicholas' diary)
I wake up to extreme temperature in my tent. I could cook a turkey in my sleeping bag. Not to my surprise, everybody else is already up and has evacuated the tent. Mom calls me out to meet a guy called Alain, whom they met last night. We shake hands and say hi. After I have breakfast (French toast), I play with the soccer ball. Alain comes over and starts to play, too. Before he leaves, he gives Nora a gift—a pin and a note (I have no idea what the note says).

After a bit of driving, Billy lets us off at the top of a tall hill. We can see some kilometres in the distance. My knee is in pretty bad shape, so Mom puts a wrap on it. I had never have a wrap on before. It is tight and feels like it is pushing my knee upwards. There is a spring to my right foot, which is quite uncomfortable going down that steep hill. We stop at a boutique to look at woodcarvings. I wait on the doorstep, reading a book. When we start out again, the going is a little easier, but I still feel like I am marching military style due to the wrap. We are walking along the road that leads to a fishing village on the St. Lawrence River, and the sun is getting noticeably hotter. After some time, we come to the base of a very high hill. Ironically, there is no spring in my step anymore. For about an hour, we trudge up that hill, but the view is pretty good. The sun is beating down on the St. Lawrence River far below us. I appreciate the view but I would have appreciated the feel of the water more.

The road from St. Irene twists down into small quaint villages with big open-verandahed houses. Artists' signs hang on the doors and woodcarvings decorate the doorways. At one wood carver's shop, tall, carved giraffes, cats and birds greet us in the entrance. This is the first day for this shop to open for the season and we are the first customers. We are saddened by the fact that we haven't carried any money in our packs. We walk to another village bordered by a beachfront, the rail line separating the houses and the water. A large teepee has been constructed on the beach, perhaps ready for burning at the St-Jean-Baptiste celebrations tonight. Nora, Maria, Nicholas and I walk along the boardwalk talking to the people along the way. Heike heads up the beach alone to the far end.

As we walk on, the hills seem endless. Heike discusses with me the idea of cutting the hike short today so that we can enjoy Quebec City a little earlier. We are only at our ten-kilometre mark when we reach Billy. He is unconcerned about our journey into Quebec City and assures me he will happily wait for us if we want to continue walking. Much to Heike's chagrin, we decide to continue on for at least another five kilometres. Nicholas decides to stay with Billy and rest his leg, Heike stays back, upset with our decision and Nora, Maria and I continue on. Now, the walk becomes more pleasant. We walk through rolling countryside and into small villages. The roadway turns to streets where colourful doorways are only an arm's length away. The cozy French settlement shops reflect the early settlers' skills of woodworking and weaving. Art students sit in the sun, painting the backyard gardens or a neighbour's house, their canvas and paint depicting the scenes before them.

It is nearly six o'clock when we reach the cobblestone streets of downtown Quebec City. Without a single navigational mistake, we reach our hostel and a parking place by the water. By now, people celebrating St-Jean-Baptiste are reveling in the streets. After parking the van, Billy and I climb back up through the crowd to a little sidewalk bar. It is time for a cold beer, or as Billy would say, "Time for an apple."

We sit at the outdoor bar just below the towering Chateau Frontenac. The late sun reflects a golden glow from its roof, making it resemble a castle from a fairy tale.

When we arrive back at the hostel, we take a quick shower and dress for supper. It will be such a treat to saunter through the streets of old Quebec and be served French cuisine in an outdoor restaurant. We amble down the cobblestone streets in the warm evening air. There's no urgency to find the perfect spot and we pop in and out of tiny cafés, testing the ambiance. Finally, we settle on a spot with flower baskets hanging overhead in a cozy artist's corner of the street. Maria sits at one end near Billy and Heike. Nora, Nicholas and I share a menu at the other end of the table. We chat and enjoy the passing crowd, basking in the luxury of our surroundings. After supper, we meander back up through the streets, stopping to watch dancers and magicians in the Frontenac square. Chateau Frontenac appears majestic on the hill above us, an historic landmark for Quebec City.

June 24

Victoriaville to Warwick
Distance: 19 km
Wildlife: 2 muskrats, red winged black birds, many wild flowers—wild roses, Indian paintbrush, daisies

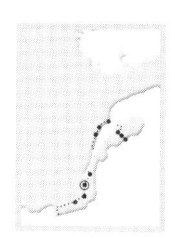

(from Heike's diary)
After a noisy and stuffy night in the youth hostel, stepping out into the bright clear morning air is a very invigorating experience. I accompany Billy down to the harbour, where the van was parked for the night. On the way there, we take in the view over the 'low town' (Bas Ville) and the Fleuve Saint Laurent from the balustrade at the Chateau Frontenac. How different the place looks from last night's festivities, the traces of which are still being cleared away, the occasional body littering benches and green spaces. To brace ourselves for the day, I decide to fetch some coffee and croissants from a nearby patisserie. Billy and I have our *petit déjeuner* in the van while we wait for

the rest of the gang to arrive. We watch life begin to stir on the *Rembrandt*, a Danish cruise ship that arrived last night.

Thus fortified, finding the airport is a piece of cake. We are taking Maria to catch a flight to Nova Scotia. We arrive there with enough time for a second breakfast, which in my case consists of a buttered bagel and cranberry juice. I also manage to write and send two of the three postcards I scavenged from the pub on the tour of the city the night before. Maria is excited about spending the next few days at home and attending her friend's graduation. I hope she gets a window seat, since the cloudless sky will lend itself to some aerial photography (of all the trails she's hiked so far).

On to Victoriaville, the starting point of today's hike. Those of us who aren't busy navigating and driving manage to catch a few winks to make up for the lack of quality sleep. Victoriaville turns out to be a lively town centring around a grand cathedral. The trail, which runs through the town's centre, is paved and laid out like a road for cyclists, with a yellow centre line. It is pleasing for me to see how many people are using it—not just professional-looking "hardcore" cyclists, but also families with children and people in wheelchairs. We turn out to be the only hikers. Outside the town area, the trail is comfortably packed fine gravel, easy to walk as well as cycle on. Haymaking is in full swing, and the smell of hay mingling with numerous wild flowers growing along the trail contributes to the "summery" feel of the day. In some places there is beautiful red-tipped grass growing higher than my head. Hiking through this summer scenario, I recall all the seasons we've experienced on our journey so far. Although we are outside every day, some days, like this one, still hit you with an unexpected intensity. At some point I just go off into my own head and at my own speed (which I break into when inside my own head). I hope that by now everyone knows that this state of mind I get into sometimes when hiking doesn't have anything to do with my surroundings. Just after contemplating asking some people sitting on a balcony for the use of their pool, I find Billy waiting in the van, which is parked appropriately next to the old Warwick railway station. The building now hosts a local youth club.

Nora and Kathy decide to pile in a few more kilometres on the trail, while Billy Nicholas and I explore down streets in search of ice cream. We find a little supermarket where Billy buys a whole tub of butterscotch ripple, which we share between the five of us. Nora, Kathy and I go back to the shop to buy some groceries. Then we take off in search of the campground in Kingsey Falls, which isn't quite as simple as the map would make us believe. When we've passed through the town without any sign for the campground, we stop at a beautiful farmhouse

Hiking the Dream

with two very happy geese living in a pond to inquire about the way. When, at last, we arrive at our last port of call for the day, we find it to be situated near a river with lots of trees for shade. Nicholas and I go to cool off in the pool. We are treated to a very special supper prepared by Nora and Kathy: potato salad, fresh green salad, bread, and bacon.

June 25

Kingsey Falls to Danville
Distance: 16 km
Wildlife: raccoon

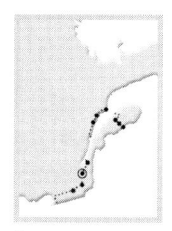

8:15 A.M. "Is anyone up in there?" Billy calls. This has become our alarm clock. Some mornings we all lie awake in the tent waiting for Billy to call us. He calls and we lie still, no one wanting to answer. He calls again and we giggle. He knows exactly that we are waiting for him to call us again. Answering is admitting you are awake and being awake means you now have to get up. How easy it would be some mornings to sleep forever.

I crawl out and make my way to the toilets. No toilet paper. Back to the van for our horded supply and back to the toilets. We are becoming the expert campground analysts and have developed a rating code for many aspects, especially the cleanliness of the facility. This lack of toilet paper will definitely cost them some serious demerit points.

I return to the campfire and pour a fresh cup of strong coffee. I have become so spoiled waking up to a blazing fire and coffee every morning. Billy is having his toast, which he has made over the fire in the double toaster we bought in Perth. We are certainly becoming high-class campers. Heike soon joins us and we begin discussing this venture of mine.

Nora, Maria, Nicholas and I have been traveling together since Nicholas was only three. We have lived in the mountains of Switzerland in a village where few people speak English. We have traveled with 11 large packs by train from Switzerland to Russia. That journey taught us a lot about sharing responsibilities and working together. We have lived in Moscow in a small Russian flat where survival depends on your ability to look beyond your own needs. For Heike, who is coming to us from a totally different way of life, it must, at times, seem overwhelming to join a family on such a demanding adventure. Nora, Maria, Nicholas and I have worked together so long, there is no necessity of drumming out responsibilities. There is an unspoken understanding that we all share and contribute equally, which comes from experiencing many adventures together.

Now, there are many issues that have to be discussed with Heike. The responsibilities that we discussed previous to the hike seem to have faded and more and more there is a growing dissention between us. My time is consumed with daily planning, hiking, looking after our nutritional intake, keeping the finances straight and in general, trying to keep things running smoothly for everyone's sake. It is no small task. I feel uncomfortable now approaching Heike, as I appreciate her reasons for joining us, yet, it is not a tour and I cannot go on with this feeling that I am doing someone an injustice.

Now, as Heike and I sit on the little campstools watching the drops of rain bounce in the dying campfire, we must come to an understanding. It isn't easy. The rain comes even harder and we move to the back of the trailer. We put towels over our heads to protect ourselves from the pelting rain. The importance of this conversation far outweighs the misery of getting wet. I have taken a whole year off work to plan the details of this trip. It is not a journey where we will have time to visit museums, craft fairs, village markets and stop at quaint cafés. As much as all of this is very inviting, time restraints just won't allow it if we are going to hike 20 kilometres a day and reach our goal of 2000 kilometres.

Heike has come to Canada on a teacher exchange. Teaching German at Acadia University in Wolfville, Nova Scotia, she has had little opportunity to travel during the university year. Now, with an extension of her stay permitted, she has chosen to see Canada with us. I realize her frustration of being so close to so many interesting sights, yet not having time to really enjoy them. However, she has chosen to travel with us and I have to follow my timeline. I give her a choice now and it is one she has to make. Will she continue with us as part of a team or will she go off on her own? I want her to stay. She has become a good friend for Nicholas. They draw, tell stories and joke together. Nora, Maria and Heike have worked out a repertoire of songs that they sing together. Sometimes I lie back and laugh at her unique view of our journey. She has in so many ways become 'one of us,' yet we appreciate the individuality that sets her apart. I can't imagine her not being with us.

Emotions rise and fall. It has to happen. We cry, we laugh, we shout, we whisper. We exhaust ourselves with this battle. In the end, we hold each other tight and promise to communicate. We are two, strong-minded women with powerful emotions. We are soaked from the rain, but it is the best I have felt in days.

(from Nora's diary)

The day starts out very frustrating. The rain pours down, then stops, then rises again with no warning. Nicholas, Billy and I sit in the van and play golf (a card game) and wait until the rain lets up enough for us to take down the tent and pack up. As soon as the rain leaves, it becomes so muggy it is almost unbearable. It feels thick to breathe the air. Billy drives us to our starting place on the trail. Heike, Mom and I get out, jump over the ditch, and begin our walk through the 'keifer' pines. The mosquitoes are ravenous. The salt-and-pepper-coloured trail twists through pine groves. It is humid. The warm smell of flowers, sweet smelling ferns and the forest wafts around us. The sky gets heavier and heavier, until it just opens up and pours down on us. There is no sense in even trying to put a raincoat over our wet clothes, the rain comes so fast. Within a very few minutes, we are soaked from head to toe. It feels like we are walking on sponges, and our Band-Aids float in our boots.

At the former Danville train station, which is now a rest stop, we find shelter from the rain with two bikers. There is a picture on the station wall of Marc Sennette, a comedian in Charlie Chaplin's time. He was from this little community and had won an Oscar award.

The rain slows to a drizzle as we continue on our way. We aren't minutes from the rest stop when the skies lash out again, pelting us. It feels like someone is throwing small stones at our faces and legs. It is a welcome sight to see the Hike 2000 van. Billy and Nicholas are sound asleep. Water dripping from head to toe, we strip off all our clothes outside before getting into warm, dry clothing. We look like wizened prunes...like we have been in the bathtub too long. The casino across the parking lot certainly gets a show. The windows in the van steam up as soon as we get in.

Kathy and Nora on the trail to Danville just before the skies opened up.

Billy drives us to Magog, where we eventually find a less pricey hotel in the centre of town. We begin the 'bin parade' in the parking lot behind the hotel, pulling them out to be viewed by the public while we rummage for our underwear and toothbrushes. A man wearing a stretched green shirt over a bulbous stomach sees our instruments and yells over in a strong accent, "Hey! When does the concert begin?" The conversation turns to some bantering about the price of our concert to the price of our last egg. He says he'll pay a nickel, definitely a low wager. He eventually comes over to stand beside us as we rummage, telling us jokes non-stop and laughing, exposing a row of very long teeth on the bottom and none on top. Billy laughs so hard he gets right into the trailer on his hands and knees. The meeting gets more and more absurd, with him telling about his former lives and how he was engaged to a princess in Africa, then back to his jokes. He tells us that he was a Jew in a past life and had been stoned to death, and in another life, he had been drowned in a river. He invites us into his room to show us the pictures on his wall, then wished us well. He repeats, "You have to come to Quebec five minutes to laugh, eh? eh?"

Our hotel room is sufficient. You get what you pay for, I guess. It is situated at the top of a wide staircase. Two beds are an arm's length apart, facing the only other piece of furniture, a television. A big metal fan that is blowing in the hot sultry air supports the open window. A small bathroom and some hangers round out the living space.

We stuff our hiking boots with newspaper, watch the Simpson's, then head out on the town for some supper. We eat outside in the centre of town. We could be anywhere in the world, the night feels so majestic. Our waitress has only been working two days and is very nervous but friendly. I didn't think I could fit anything else in my stomach after supper, but manage a big ice cream cone from the small shop across the road. The crosswalks here are more like run-for-your-life walks. Back at the hotel, we climb into bed. It is hot and sticky, but at least we are dry.

Magog: We choose to hike around the lake today wearing our bathing suits for a quick entry into the cool water.

June 26

Magog to Eastman
Distance: 19 km
Wildlife: red-winged black birds

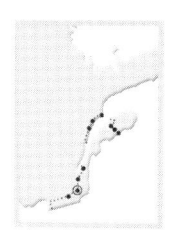

I look around me in the night…a room of restless bodies, twitching and turning, trying to find a cool spot on their pillows, or the faintest hint of cooler air that might be coming from the fan in this stifling room. We are relieved when it is finally a reasonable hour to get up. We take turns in the hall shower then go out into the bright morning to find a breakfast spot. Magog is bustling with people, some hurrying off to their shops, others relaxing in the spacious open-air restaurants. We stop at an inviting, rustically decorated spot called Jessie's. The prices are good and the decor reminds us of a place we might find in Spain or France. We are delighted when the large breakfast platters arrive, laden with unexpected slices of melon and strawberries. We gorge ourselves on this rich meal. After breakfast, Nora and Heike hustle back to work on the web pages while Billy goes searching for new sandals.

I want to find trail maps and am told the information centre is the place to go. This centre is much farther out of town than I expect and the long walk in my sandals is very slow and hot. I return from the centre along the bike path that winds around the lake. This is a much nicer path than the main street that I chose on the way there. I dodge bikers and rollerbladers that sway their way up and down the stretch.

We decide to hike the extended bike path around this lake today and juggle our footwear. It is now extremely hot. I opt for my hiking boots, thinking of my Achilles, Nora and Nicholas choose sneakers, and Heike chooses her sandals, which are cool and light. The way is varied between gravel and pavement, winding through a wooded area and back through town, where bikers, rollerbladers, wheelchairs and strollers share the way. We stop at a little ice-cream stand for a treat, then continue. Billy is waiting at the beach at the far end of this lake, and we anticipate that cool water on our sweaty skin.

The humid heat surrounds us and the combined smells of summer flowers hang in the air. We reach the lake and tear off our footwear. We run over the cool grass to the lake. We have been hiking with our bathing suits on to save time at this moment. I submerge my body in the water. I can feel the salt leave my skin as the water streams by me. It is such a relief from the hot sun. Our feet, free from boots, glow white under the water, the hiking sock ring distinctly contrasting the colours on our legs.

Back on shore, I get out the maps once again to decide on the camping spot. I choose a place in Eastman. The area is thickly wooded with the rise of hills of Mont Fort to our right. We drive to our campground, which resembles an upper-class trailer court. There are no tents around but we view the lake and decide this is the place for us. We park our tent on a well-groomed piece of lawn overlooking the lake. It feels like we are camping in someone's back yard. Faces line the windows of the large, modern, trailer homes as we drag our bins from the trailer. Our paraphernalia is soon scattered on our site. Our lot is a definite contrast to the folded-out, more permanent structures around us. These campers are more like summer homes, with window boxes, flower gardens, paved walkways, and large lawns. The only difference is they have wheels.

It is hot and the lake beckons. Nora, Nicholas and Heike go down to cool off, as Billy and I pull up a lawn chair and open an apple (beer). I sprawl back on the "queens' seat" as Billy pulls another lawn chair from the trailer. It is a great time of day. Everyone is off to do their own thing, free from hiking boots and packs. It is a time to reflect, share stories and generally do as we please. Today, Billy and I chose to just sit and do nothing.

After supper, Nora, Heike and I go for a walk. We walk up a trail in a wooded area and collect some firewood for the night. The blackfires are outrageous and we retreat on the run. We sit around our fire with Billy and discuss the attributes of tenting as opposed to vacationing in campers. Before retiring for the night, Nora and I go down to the two back-to-back toilets, which have been erected especially for the tenters. The doors begin at knee-level while sitting. So, privacy was not a priority in the design to say the least. Having had typical 'campfood' for the last few days, we are in great need of relief. While walking all day, you must plan the right moment. Feeling we are alone (since all other campers have their own private bathrooms), we decide to practice some of our songs on the toilet. The acoustics are perfect. We sing in loud harmony, paying little regard to the other natural acoustics that are escaping our bodies. Suddenly, we hear voices and laughter directly outside our doors, which send us into gales of embarrassed laughter. As we laugh, we lose all control of our extra acoustics. The scene gets worse…long high pitches and low base tones as we laugh uncontrollably. We wait until it is quiet to make our escape. When we peer out our doors, we see the swing swaying in the still air. Our listeners had waited behind the toilet and had heard it all. We race back to our campsite, delirious with our embarrassment.

We crawl into our tent under a starlit sky, only to be awakened by flashes of lightening, crashing thunder, and rain pounding our tent. We all wake up, questioning our safety in relation to this electric storm, which seems to be centred nearby. We are sleeping on the ground, steel rods running through our tent, on a hill, above water, under two trees. After a few moments of discussion, everyone but me seems to drift back to sleep. Too tired to make a move to the safety of our van, I lie awake for what seems like hours, counting the seconds between the flashes of lightening and the clap of thunder until it finally rolls away. As it echoes in the distance, I fall asleep.

June 27

Place: Eastman-Waterloo
Distance: 20.5 km
Wildlife: Purple irises, forget-me-nots, daisies, buttercups, pet pig

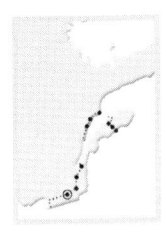

It is absolutely pouring rain. Dishes, with remnants of food still on them, left over from last night's supper, are floating in water. Our candles, stove, food bin and pots are soaking in puddles of water. Intermittently, the rain lets up and we race to put our things into the trailer. There is no halting it. We stuff the wet towels in a garbage bag and load our tent, dripping wet, into the back of our trailer.

(from Nicholas' diary)
It starts to rain a little bit harder and Mom tells me to get the ice-packs out of the campground freezer where we left them last night. I walk up the road to the campground convenience store and get the ice-packs out of the freezer. By this time it is pouring extremely hard and the ice-packs are very cold on my arms. It is raining so hard I can't see the road so I take a random guess at which one to go down. I ran up to the van and by this time my arms are freezing. Mom tells me to get into the van because it'll be drier in there. After we take the tent down in the pouring rain, we drive to the spot where we are going to hike. I reach for my hiking boots—they are dripping wet on the inside and when I look down, there is a puddle on the sole. It looks as if I will have to stay back in the van.

(from Nora's diary)
After the skies finish pelting us with water, Heike, Mom and I start walking to Eastman. The trail is beautiful. We are in the middle of the woods but the wild flowers lining the path are amazing—bright purple vetch, fresh white and yellow daisies, vibrant orange Indian paintbrush, and Queen Anne's lace. We decide to walk more once we meet Nicholas and Billy in Eastman. Mom buys a map of the trails in that area and scours them with Billy for the best route. The trail we choose runs straight on the map. It seemed easy enough. Then something weird happens. Before we get out of the van, Mom says to Billy, 'Good Luck.' She never says that. I suppose that doesn't seem so weird, not knowing the end of the story yet.

The first part of the walk is beautiful. The old farms we walk past could have been down that old road in West Gore where Andrew MacInnis used to have a house. At one point we come upon a lady walking a pig like a pet, while a dog, which looks like a German Shepherd-poodle mix, waits on the lawn. Farther on, we come to an unforeseen "T" in the dirt road. There is no direction about which way the bike trail is, or where to get onto the 241. A lady wheeling a baby carriage hasn't even heard of the 241, and she is a local. We come to some men working on a barn and watch as they maneuver the tractor, with its cables attached to the barn. Suddenly the whole front end of the barn collapses. Mom applaudes them, then goes to ask them if they know where we should be going.

The men at the barn tell me the fastest way to get to the 241 is on the power line. We cross the barbwire fence and are delighted to find pockets of purple irises growing in the wet areas. Among these purple-blue flowers are sprinkled yellow buttercups—such a pleasing contrast. Forget-me-nots and baby's breath grow out of the mossy spots along the water holes. We walk through the tall grassy flowers until we reach Highway 241. We decide to walk toward Highway 10, as planned, expecting to find the trail and Billy, but to our surprise and dismay, there is no van. We walk on past Highway 10 toward Lac Brome. Still, there is no van. We walk back up Highway 241 and trudge past the power line. Where can they be? We stop at a little flower shop to ask about a road or a trail. No positive answers here. We walk to the corner where route 241 ends and enter a little corner store. In my best French, I ask the young boy at the counter if he has seen a van. No luck. Finally, I decide our only hope is to call the police. I dial 911. After being re-routed three times, I am able to talk to someone who takes pity on us in our dilemma. A policeman arrives, fully clad in a bullet-proof vest and instructs me to get into the back seat of his car. We tear off, me telling my story as we fly around the country backroads in search of our beloved van. We check rail lines, Highway 241 and Highway 10. Then, the officer remembers there are three Highway 241s…all crossing Highway 10. How ridiculous. We drive at least 20 more kilometres and there we find Billy, Nicholas, and the van. Billy and Nicholas have erected a makeshift clothesline for our towels and tent. They are sitting back in the shade, patiently waiting for us, as unconcerned as can be. The police car screams in beside them. The officer jokingly yells out the window at Billy, 'You're lost!'

Billy replies, also in jest, 'I don't think so, Tim.' The officer instructs Billy to follow us back to where Nora and Heike are waiting at the shop. We had screamed by them three times in the police car, me in the backseat like a convict or the queen being escorted through town.

(from Heike's diary)
While Kathy is in search of our van with the policeman, Nora and I try to keep ourselves entertained by playing tunes on my little recorder and waving at passing tour busses of senior citizens. The helpful policeman wanted only one of us in his car. Our entertainment program is so effective, in fact, that we notice Kathy zooming by in the police car only once. The trudging around and looking for the van and not knowing where and if we are going to find it has actually been more tiring than the announced 30-kilometre hike. I'm quite content to just hang out on the grass in the late afternoon sun with a drink of pop, trusting others to set things right. It is interesting to watch the people who come to shop for groceries at the little store. Some of them leave the engine running while engaged in their shopping. If Kathy waited a little longer, we simply could have highjacked one of these cars and looked for the van, and get involved with the law in quite some other way.

With Billy behind the wheel and everyone in their familiar seats, we begin our journey into Chateauguay, Montreal. The highway maps are spread on my knee as I instruct Billy on every turn. Winding this oversized, 15-passenger van, which hauls a trailer, through narrow streets, is no small chore.

We will spend tonight in Chateauguay, Montreal, with my husband's mother, Katherine Didkowsky (Babushka) and John's brother, Peter. Babushka and her husband, Vladimir, came to Canada when John and his younger sister, Mary, were young children. John's father, who was from Russia, died in 1974. Babushka is from Czechoslovakia, and after marrying Vladimir, fled to Austria. It was 1945 when they reached the tiny village of Geretsberg, Austria, where John was born. This would be their home until they moved to Canada. Peter, the youngest son, was born in Canada.

We are anxious to see Babushka and Peter. Babushka still carries her European ways and we can hardly wait to sit at her table. She is waiting for us and directs us into the house. Beds of flowers and vegetables border the fence. Her pet squirrel, Misty, chats his curiosity to us from the large tree in the front yard. Peter soon arrives home and

Hiking the Dream

we pile around the kitchen table and eat until we can't move. Tonight we talk long into the evening. It is so nice to see Babushka, but sad that we are staying for such a short time.

June 28

Place: Montreal

(from Nora's diary)
I wake up at 9:30 and looked around me: Heike and Nicholas spread out on mattresses on the floor in the living room, Mom on the couch, and Billy and Babushka already up. Babushka comes and talks to us while we lay in our sleeping bags. Then, she goes into the kitchen to make us my favourite type of pancakes—blinchekies. They are like thin crepes, and you can roll fruit, yogurt, syrup, cottage cheese, sour cream, or anything into them. Yum! We cleaned up after breakfast and basically veg out for the rest of the day. Heike and Nicholas draw some more of their 'Lord of the Rings' characters, Mom does some laundry and goes for a walk, Billy relaxes outside, and Babushka and I talk about everything under the sun and more. It feels really good to be there. In the afternoon sun, Babushka and Mom bring us tea and cookies in Babushka's garden. The work that has gone into the garden is amazing, and it shows in the beautiful flowers. Back inside, Babushka brings out her homemade Christmas decorations...each of them her own design. To my delight, she shows us exactly which way to cut the base and stitch the yarn and beads. I am going to try and figure out how to make them. She gives each of us one; our special gift from Quebec. When Peter comes home from work, the seven of us sit around the table and enjoy supper. Not long after supper, and after Peter has driven Mom to get medication for her cold, we all tumble sleepily into bed. We have great plans to get up by five o'clock tomorrow morning to start on our way to Hull, then into Ontario. Yawn!!

Babushka: Katherine Didkowsky opens her home in Montreal to a vanload of vagabonds. We wash clothes, eat like kings and all leave with a special gift.

148

June 29 - July 9   **Ontario**

Nora, Kathy, Bonnie, Julie, Shirley-Dale, Maria, Nicholas, and Heike on the ghost trail at Magnetawan.

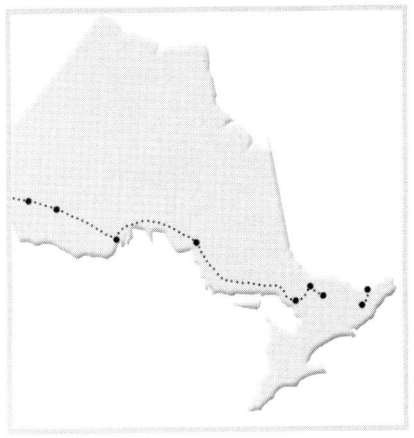

June 29

Hull, Quebec to Ottawa, Ontario
Distance: 14.2 km

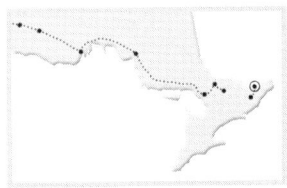

As planned, we are up early to beat the rush hour of Montreal city. Peter has already left for work. We don't take time for breakfast; we'll stop once we're on the highway, away from the traffic. We drive through the Kahnawake and come across the Mersey Bridge. Driving through busy streets, with the 15-passenger van hauling a trailer, is not one of Billy's favourite things to do, to say the least, and this Monday morning the cars are bumper to bumper in every direction. It is the week of the Montreal Jazz Festival, just to add to the numbers arriving into the city. "Love a duck" Billy repeats as we swerve in and out of traffic until we are beyond the city. We stop at a small doughnut shop for a quick breakfast and take it along with us to save time.

Charlotte Allen has been my friend since university. She has offered us a place to stay with her in Ottawa, as we reach our mid-way mark across Canada. We will spend three nights with her as we wait for my sisters Bonnie, Shirley-Dale and Glenda to arrive. Also, Maria

149

Dolores Doucette and Charlotte Allan: Warm friends pamper us for three days at our halfway point in Ottawa.

will return with them. It will be nice to have Maria return and have my sisters walk from Ottawa to Winnipeg with us.

Charlotte (Charlie) drives over to Hull, on the Quebec side of the Ottawa River, to meet us and guide Billy back to her house, which she shares with her friend Dolores. Charlie arrives in her sporty jeep and greets us, her infectious smile unchanged in all these years. She assures Billy she'll lead him through the most non-congested part of the city. I have bought a map of the city and I study it with Charlie to choose our route back to her house once we reach Ottawa.

Billy climbs into the van without me, his trusting navigator. His eyes focus only on Charlie's jeep as they inch their way across the busy Alexandra Bridge linking Ottawa, Ontario and Hull, Quebec. The parliament buildings stand high on the hill on the right as Nora, Heike, Nicholas and I cross the bridge spanning the Ottawa River. We stop for ceremonial pictures on the bridge. We are halfway across Canada, in our country's capital city. I only wish Maria were here to share our feeling of accomplishment. We pass the parliament buildings and walk down to the famous Rideau Canal. Our hike will take us along this waterway, which dissects the city. Small boats are tied up along its banks and ducks glide back and forth in the dark water. In winter, the canal is a highway of skaters with people on their way to work and some just out for some exercise. Now, rollerbladers whiz by us on the walkway running parallel to the canal. We stop to look closely at some tree branches that are extending into the water. There, on one branch, on the edge of the still water, is a turtle. Who ever would have thought that after all the wilderness we have walked through that we would see our first turtle in Ottawa? Christopher MacDonald (Topher), who hiked with us in Prince Edward Island, watched for turtles the entire time. We snap a picture of the turtle so Topher can enjoy it on our website. We can also see large fish lounging under the canopy of algae in the murky waters of the canal.

Ontario

The halfway mark across Canada on the bridge between Hull and Ottawa.

It is a long, hot, walk to Charlie and Dolores' house on Huntersfield Street. The concrete underfoot is heating up the soles of our boots and our feet burn. Hiking in the city, we have to be aware of lights, cars, bikes and people. The stink of the exhaust chokes us and the noise becomes too loud even to enjoy a conversation. It is not like any other walk we have taken. At one street corner a car backfires, setting all of our eardrums ringing. We can actually feel the vibrations right through our bodies.

Charlie and Dolores live in a two-storey home on a quiet street fronting a large park. Billy, Charlie and Dolores have already had a few 'apples' before we arrive. We pile into the front foyer of the house and unload our packs and strip off our hiking boots. We sink into the chairs on the back deck, which is shaded with a trellis of grapevines and overlooks a neat lawn with flower and vegetable beds. It is great to be here, knowing we don't have to pack anything up for three days. It is our first break in a long time. Charlie has the entire menu planned for our stay. Soon supper is laid before us: asparagus with ham, and some cheese rolled in crepes with salad, rice and carrots. We gorge ourselves. After supper, Nora and I work on the web pages, then climb into bed.

I am sleeping in Charlie's room on the top floor. I lie in bed thinking about Charlie and our crazy behaviour as teammates on Dalhousie University's field hockey team. There is little we wouldn't do for a laugh. She was a fast winger and I was the goalie. Now, with inherited lung degeneration, she is barely able to walk across the room without gasping for breath. She is unable to work and spends her time keeping as fit as possible in the fitness room in the den on the lower floor of their house. Charlie's two cats, Rudy and Kristy, keep her company during the day while Dolores is at work. Kristy, curious to our presence, shies away from us, climbing to the high platform of a scratching post and reaching out with outstretched paws as we pass.

Rudy is a bit more sociable, rolling and twisting with his make-believe mouse toys on the floor. I fall asleep to the sound of rain on the windowpane. I am so happy to be inside tonight.

June 30

Place: Ottawa to Bells Corners
Distance: 21.5 km
Wildlife: Canada geese, ducks, one-eyed river snake, 18 gophers

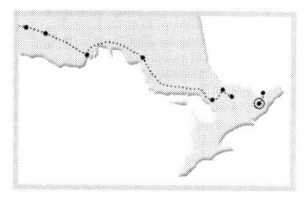

This morning, French toast, sausages, orange juice and coffee await us. Charlie serves us like kings and queens. After breakfast, Nora and I struggle with the web page, then pull on our hiking boots. We are the only two to walk today as Nicholas opts to stay behind and watch TV, read, draw and basically relax. Heike wants to spend the day exploring Ottawa and Billy is content to be staying in one place, just relaxing.

Charlie drives Nora and I to the National Capital Commission, near the parliament buildings, where we will begin our walk. The trail begins just below the canal, then curves along the Ottawa River. Rollerbladers swing around us and we meet bikes and lovers strolling hand in hand. A popular walkway, it winds along the river through parks and small wooded areas. The hiking path leads away from the city centre to Bells Corners.

The day is warm and we stop often for water breaks. At Britannia Bay Park, we stop to check our map and lie back on the cool grass, in the shade of a huge maple tree. It is a peaceful park with sprawling lawns stretching to the water's edge, and giant trees providing restful shade. Canada geese have also found this park and pick away at the grass close to the river. Suddenly our tranquility is interrupted by the shadow of a man standing above us. We glance up and directly over our faces, there is a man dangling his jewels. If only I had my hiking stick handy! We are too surprised to tell him how unimpressed we are before he darts away and climbs into his car.

Back on the trail, we cross a busy highway, then travel into a wooded area. It is hard to believe we are so close to civilization in this remote stretch of backwoods trail. The trail pops out of the woods at the Queensway where the traffic is a steady roar. We are reminded that it is Canada Day weekend, the busiest for this capital city.

At Nepean, we stretch out our maps once more on the edge of a large ball field. A couple of friendly ladies are biking the same trail and stop to chat. We exchange addresses with them, then part ways. We walk on to the highway that crosses above the Queensway. Trucks roar underneath as we cling to the guardrail above. Finally, we reach Bells Corners. We are tired, hot and thirsty. We hobble into a store to replenish our water supplies, then call Charlie who has promised to pick us up and drive us home. We plunk ourselves down on the grass and wait for our faithful hostess to arrive.

We learn, when Charlie arrives, that Maria has called and is in urgent need of a new pair of hiking boots, which have been ordered at Mark's Work Wearhouse. Charlie drives us back to the coolness of her house, where we sink into comfortable chairs with a cold drink. We wait for the call from Maria. Soon, Dolores drives me to pick up the boots where we meet Julie, my niece, and Maria. My sisters, Shirley–Dale, Bonnie and Glenda, are packed and ready to begin their extended hike with us through this large province. We make plans to meet in the morning.

Back at Charlie's, we eat grilled chicken, potato salad, green salad, and buns and, to top it off, a strawberry torte. Can things get any better?

July 1

Place: Ottawa
Distance: 5 km
Wildlife: Groundhogs

Charlie has prepared coffee and muffins for our morning start. It is a rest day, at least from hiking. Canada Day in the capital city can hardly be considered a rest day. We decide to get a taxi downtown, where celebrations are underway. Nora, Maria, Nicholas, Heike and I all leave in one taxi, driven by a tall turbaned man with a huge knife strapped to his side. How relaxing! We stop at the bus stop to pick up my battery charger, which Babushka has forwarded to us, then walk the five kilometres to Parliament Hill. It is funny that a five-kilometre distance is only considered a stroll now, not really a walk. We go straight to the Terry Fox monument where we have promised to meet the others. They have been camping all night at a nearby camping ground in Nepean. Iain Caldwell will also be meeting us here. He has driven to Ottawa with his friends to celebrate the national holiday and, of course, to see Maria.

(from Maria's diary)
People with painted faces, cheerfully waving flags, line the streets. Venders on every street corner are selling sausages, hotdogs, lemonade, and pop. Iain is waiting for us, dressed in very cool red and white sneakers and armed with a map. We make our way past buskers and face painters, through throngs of people and to the grounds where multiple bands play.

Julie, Shirley-Dale, Bonnie and Glenda are among the revelers on the street, getting red maple leaves painted on their faces and shoulders. We join in the celebration. Rob, Shirley-Dale's son, and his girlfriend, Liese Johanson (from Sweden), are driving from New York City to join us for this one day. Kirk Newhook, our friend from Newfoundland, will arrive with them. Marcy, Glenda's daughter, and her boyfriend, Scott Tilford (from Pennsylvania), are driving from Washington and plan to meet us here and travel with us to North Bay. We are excited to see them all and return to the appointed meeting spot at the Terry Fox monument several times to see if they have arrived. With the bodies packed into the streets, will we ever find them?

On one of our searches to the Terry Fox monument, we spot Iain's friends, Chad, Paige, and Blake. They have driven to Ottawa with Iain to celebrate Canada's birthday. As we spread ourselves on the ground in front of the entertainment stages, the sky darkens. Nicholas reminds us several times that it is going to rain but we take no heed, enjoying the music and the good company. Suddenly, lightening splits through the sky and loud rumblings are heard over the noise of the band. The storm is definitely coming. We grab our bags and rush to find shelter.

We are too late. The sky opens and rain pours from the black clouds overhead. The entire crowd begins moving as one, pulling anything they can find over their heads. Bodies push one another without seeing feet. There is a panic to find shelter from this fierce electrical storm. We edge our way back with the crowd over the canal and to the monument. Here, throngs of people are gathered. We spot Glenda and Shirley-Dale, join them, huddled under the trees next to the little outdoor bar. The rain pelts even harder. In desperation, I curl under one of the little bar tables. We have no raincoats and become soaked. The rain lets up for a moment and the sun appears from a break in the clouds. We emerge from the trees, our clothes clinging to our wet bodies. Warm water rushes in the gutters of the street.

(from Maria's diary)
The sun immediately shines through a break in the clouds, and we play in the rivers which run through the streets. Warm water splashes around us as we jump and laugh in our drenched clothes. We hang our outer layers to dry on the parliament-building fence, but it begins to rain again. This time we decide that being wet isn't any fun, as cold wind joins the huge drops. We decide to go home and change before the fireworks.

But, the sky darkens again. The storm is not over. This time we run for the shelter of the information centre. We decide to find a bus and take our cold, shivering bodies back to Charlie's. Broken balloons and paper Canada flags float in the gutters as we hurry down over the canal to the bus stop. A taxi pulls over and we opt for this drive. The lightening flashes and the thunder rolls as water streams down the windows of the taxicab. We watch from inside, our wet hair dripping on clothes that cling to our bodies. Back at Charlie's, we strip and run to the showers. That is it. Canada Day in Ottawa! I pour a glass of wine and sit back on the extended chesterfield with the built-in footrest. Charlie and Dolores join me, as the rest crawl in for a snooze.

(from Maria's diary)
Back at Charlie's, we get changed into our warmest clothes and eat supper in front of mindless game shows. Blake, Chad, Iain, and Paige pick up Nora, Heike and me and drag us off to Parliament Hill. We make it close to where the fireworks are, but they start exploding when we are still by the canal. Heike, Nora, Iain and I run into

Rob Easley and Louice Johansson drive from New York City to celebrate Canada Day with Hike 2000.

the crowd, trying to make it to where the gang is waiting. The fireworks are phenomenal. It is absolutely amazing, and I have never seen anything like it before. I think I used a whole roll of film trying to catch how huge and bright the fireworks are.

We eventually make it to the Terry Fox statue, after squeezing through the biggest crowd I've ever been in the centre of. Our gang, plus Rob, Liese and Kirk Newhook, are waiting for us. We go to get some fries and walk over to the war memorial. Covered in flags and stickers, the tomb of the unknown solider lies in front of us. People come by and kiss the tomb and one elderly man leaves his hat on the grave. It is so sad.

On the way to catch the bus, Rob poses with the statues, catching the interest of strangers on the street. Nora and I don't know how to make connections to get home, so we decide to call a cab. After hasty good-byes, we jump into our already moving cab. At first, he is very snappy with us, afraid we would hassle him for taking the wrong roads, but not being from Ottawa, we don't care. Mel, our driver, turns out to be very friendly, as we ask about his family. Charlie is waiting up for us, but we quickly go to bed, as five o'clock (our wake up) call will be here in less than three hours.

July 2

Place: Magnetawan
Distance Traveled: 23 km
Wildlife: frog, salamanders, deer flies, black flies, mosquitoes, blue heron, shadfly

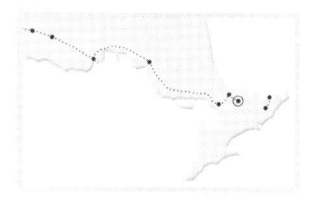

The alarm is ringing on the little stand beside Charlie's bed. I am rattled awake. It is 5:00 A.M. I lie for a moment, collecting my thoughts, and then rally the troops. Today, Bonnie, Shirley-Dale, and Julie will join us in the van. They are

Ontario

camping at the Nepean Ottawa Municipal Campground, where we have promised to meet them at 6:00 A.M.

We pack our bags, and, sleepy-eyed, hug Charlie and Dolores good-bye. We are sad to leave them and hold on for just a few more minutes. Charlie has planned our meals and packed lunches for us for three days. Dolores has also been wonderful, amused by our travels and mindful of our comfort. Five unruly vagabonds have invaded their organized life, the contents of our bins spewed on their garage floor, for three days. They have been such good sports, feeding us, waiting on us and giving us full range of their comfortable home. We have shared space with their two entertaining cats. We hold each other in a tearful goodbye. When will we see them again?

Our van winds through the wet Ottawa streets and pulls onto the highway leading to the campground. We pile from the van to greet the other sleepy-eyed travelers. Kirk Newhook will return to New York with Rob and Liese. My sister Glenda has decided to drive to North Bay with Marcy and Scott.

Shirley-Dale, Bonnie and Julie pack their belongings in the back of the trailer. Shirley-Dale and Julie have brought along an extra tent and foam sleeping pad that we stuff above the rest of the gear in the trailer. Finally, we climb back into the van, each person sliding themselves deep into their seats for a nap. Having to navigate, I never experience the luxury of a power snooze in the van.

We drive to North Bay, then swing down Highway 11, which leads to Magnetewan. Today, we will hike the "ghost trail," on the old Nippising road. This road was originally a cart path that brought early colonizers up from the south. The people would be put off the train and walk up this long road, making small settlements along the way.

We arrive in Magnetewan, a community remotely situated yet bustling with people. I inquire here about the trail and, as is usually the case, most people know nothing about it. There are no maps and details are sketchy. We are told that a van can drive through this old road, which suits us fine. Our start is late. Nicholas is not feeling well and being the first day back on the trail for Shirley-Dale, Bonnie and Julie, it is best to have the support vehicle handy.

We decide to eat lunch in the van, away from the swarms of mosquitoes and black flies waiting outside. Billy parks the van, partially blocking Nelson Lake Road as we pass around the bread, meat and cheese that Charlie has packed for us. We joke about Billy becoming lost and how no police would ever find him here. No sooner are the words out of our mouths than a siren wails behind us and a police car screams around the van. An ambulance follows it with equal urgency. Cars and other vehicles rush by, all appearing to be escaping from something or being called to an emergency. This sets up a myriad of suggestions… a forest fire, an escaped convict, a murder? It is the topic that consumes our lunch period and well into our walk.

Billy will meet us at the 5-, 10-, 15- and 20-kilometre marks, just in case anyone wants to take a break. It is a good plan. By the ten-kilometre mark, Maria's new boots are giving her problems, Nicholas is feeling sick and Julie decides to take a rest. The rest of us walk on. We are on an old winding road with large maples and pines hugging its narrow sides. Under their drooping branches is a floor of new ferns and moss. I imagine how majestic this road must be with a soft falling snow. We occasionally come to swampy areas with white water lilies poking their heads from the still dark water and blue irises huddling in clumps along the spongy shoreline.

(from Bonnie's diary)
Mosquitoes and moose flies arrive forcing us to reapply repellent many times on the route. We meet a man in brand new coveralls standing at his gate. The sign in the background says it is a breeding kennel for Rottweilers. The man tells us that the ghost trail is named such because of the many people who were buried along the way due to an epidemic. The rain begins to fall steadily not far into our hike. We put on rain gear, some of us trying out the weatherproofness of our coats for the first time. Our first glimpse of the Canadian Shield appears as a flat gray spread of rock, partly covered with pale lichen and small yellow flowers.

In the pouring rain, we come upon the first small graveyard. A decaying fence surrounds Devon Methodist Cemetery and the old gravestones are covered in moss. We stand in the graveyard, quiet and motionless, then walk from headstone to headstone, running our fingers over the names…Ellemanda, Dorcas, Charles, Albert, Minnie, and Earl. The oldest is ten, the youngest, one. I stare at this plot of earth that holds these tiny children. I can only imagine the grief of their parents. In another small plot, surrounded by a rusty iron fence, are the graves of three other children, Charlie, Laura and Emily. How

Eleanor (Dolly) Belmore and Juanita Campbell, reunited in North Bay, Ontario.

this tiny community must have been wrung with sorrow at that time, winter 1902, just after Christmas. What toys were left behind to remind the parents of their loss? Had there been a school with the children's empty seats reminding the others of their friends' deaths? How would a parent go on, losing six little children to some strange illness in just five days between January 14 and January 19? Did the children have fevers? What were their symptoms? In the pouring rain, we stand, silently holding our own sorrow for these families. We walk on to another graveyard, this one a Baptist plot. More young children, dying in that same dreadful time period, are lined with their siblings under the tiny stone slabs that mark their site.

It is seven o'clock when we reach the van. We are soaked from the rain. Shirley-Dale removes her boots and winces in pain at her toes, which have turned under in cramps. Experiencing our own endless foot problems, we offer her little sympathy.

The two-hour ride to North Bay is quiet. The darkness and the rain lull us as we ride along. Our destination is Juanita Campbell's, where Dianne, Glenda, my mother, Marcy and Scott are waiting. Juanita is a first cousin to my father. My father, Bernie Belmore, was 17 when he first went to northern Ontario to work in the mines. At that time he lived with his uncle Sam and his family, who he stayed in touch with all his life. Now, Uncle Sam's daughter Juanita is the only one left in the family and she has been waiting for us all day. She is a slender woman with an immaculately coifed hairdo. She greets us with a sharp, witty sarcasm about our lateness, "It mattered that you were late at first, but it doesn't matter now." She welcomes us in and invites us to sit down at the table. It is an invitation she doesn't have to repeat. The food is ready on the table when we walk in. Dianne has made endless trips bringing all the food to the common room in the basement of the senior's complex. A supper of salads, ham, homemade squares and tea is devoured in minutes.

Glenda has located a reasonably priced hotel for this night in North Bay. We chat with Juanita almost to midnight. Mum and

Dianne stay with her and the rest of us make plans to share three rooms at the Voyageur Hotel nearby.

(from Bonnie's diary)
Later, we come to the front entrance to leave Juanita's and see that the glass doors and windows are completely covered in white fluttering shapes: shadflies!! They cling to buildings and lampposts, falling in heaps to the ground. In the headlight's beam, they whirl and spin like falling snow. Tomorrow we will definitely have to find out more about this particular shadfly phenomenon.

Scott, Marcy and Glenda lead the way to the Voyageur Hotel as the van bumps along behind Scott's truck. Our van brakes roar and squeal as we accelerate and brake behind them in search of the hotel. The girls (Nora, Maria, Heike, Julie and Marcy) share one room. Scott pours us a nightcap of gin and tonic. We climb onto the beds in the girls' room and listen to Marcy and Scott tell about life in Washington. They are both teaching there and have entertaining stories about the challenges they face in their schools. Nicholas, Billy and Scott share a room and Glenda, Shirley-Dale, Bonnie and I share the third room.

As I lie back in this hotel room, I worry about the van. Is it ready to fold? What would we ever do?

July 3

Place: North Bay
Distance: 14.5 km
Wildlife: shadflies, shadflies, shadflies!!! perennial gardens on the waterfront

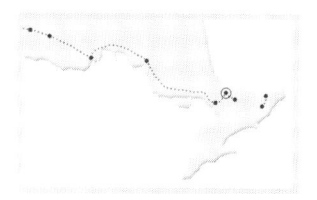

The alarm jolts me awake at 5:45 A.M. It feels like I haven't slept at all. Slowly, I drag myself out of bed and in to wash my face. I have an interview with CBC and have to be ready at 6:30. I convince the lady at the front desk to let me into one of the little apartments so I can have some privacy for my "on the air" interview. I reach CBC and the call comes back. I listen to the introduction and hope I won't have some kind of mental block when the questions start. First question, " How are your feet?" Then questions about our family and the railway unfold. When the interview is over, I get some coffee and return to our room. It is now after seven and everyone else is still sleeping. Today, Billy has agreed to take the van to a garage to have the brakes checked. I am nervous about the prognosis and the prospect of spending our precious cache of money on an unexpected repair job.

(from Shirley-Dale's diary)
We are in North Bay. Years ago, the Belmores came to work in the gold mines in Northern Ontario. My great uncle Sam's family stayed on. Our father, Bernie Belmore, moved back to Nova Scotia and spent the rest of his life planning to bring us back to visit. We helped him pack many times for the trip, rubbing his felt hat with hard bread, ironing his suit and finding his 'little jumper' and his white shirts. One of his dreams was to have us all sing for the Ontario relatives. Although he never realized his dream, here we are. Today, Juanita (Belmore) Campbell makes a luncheon for us and invites as many relatives as can make it. We scurry around finding wrinkled skirts and dresses balled up into a mess at the bottom of our packs, then drive over. The long-lost relatives arrive, little by little. They are: Peter Bowman; Juanita's sister, Ella; Ella's son and his wife, Judy; Juanita's son, Jeff Campbell, his wife Ginny their son Clint; Juanita's niece, Sheila, and her husband, Dave. We sing and dance for them and they sing with us. Nora plays the fiddle and Marcy makes her singing debut with Scott. It is good to hear our kids behind us making a chorus. We really do miss our sister Betty and our brother Roddy. This is a great reunion.

We then prepare to hike. After a hunt to find a campground, we get on the trail, with Clint Campbell and his girlfriend, Katie, in the lead. It was already 7:00 p.m. We hike on a rollerblading trail, the Kate Pace Walkway, to the tune of trains shunting around on the tracks behind us. The old station that Dad and all the other relatives would have been in is still here, but not in use.

We are united with our Belmore relatives in North Bay, Ontario.

Scott and Nora rollerblade. Clint and Katie walk with us, one by one or two by two, telling us bits of history and North Bay lore. We come to the beautiful shores of Lake Nipissing, dotted with islands and skirted with beaches. The sun is going down over the water, little boats rocking on the waves. We pick up Mom at Juanita's and walk with her to the marina for dinner.

Then the shadflies arrive, sticking on the windows, the odd one landing and squirming on the table, their last flight before death. As it gets darker, they arrive in droves, herds, gaggles…in our drinks, plastered on the ship walls, on our backs…and we don't shut up about them for the rest of the evening. We exclaim, we shriek, we laugh, we point at them, we feel sorry for them, and we are alternately in horror and in awe. We are lucky to be here during shadfly mating season, as I understand it is a phenomenon of North Bay only and happens one week of the year. They tell us that this is one of the most ancient insect groups and they spend up to three years as nymphs at the bottom of the lake. After mating, the shadflies make this one last flight and live only 48 hours.

We walk with Clint and Kate back to the campground, cracking shadflies under our feet. The cars passing on the street crack the billions of shadfly bodies lying in their path. The shadflies swarm the lights, cling to white buildings turning them brown, lie in piles in the gutters and on sidewalks—their last hoorah. At 11:45 p.m., we walk into an ice cream shop. Clint has been promising us an ice cream since we started and he holds true to his word. Then on to the tenting ground and good byes to our new long-lost cousin Clint and Katie. Belmore blood is strong after all these years.

Billy, who has been attending to the van all day as brake repairs are being done, has missed out on the luncheon, the walk and supper with the masses of shadflies. I am sure he will hear about it in the morning.

July 4

North Bay to Goulais River
Driving day
Wildlife: raccoon

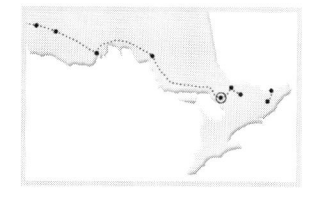

By 10:00 A.M. we are ready to leave North Bay. Marcy and Scott will return

home today and we linger our goodbyes. Then, we pile into our familiar seats in the van and head for Goulais River, near Sault Ste. Marie. We circle North Bay before leaving and again the talk returns to shadflies. I have become so touched by this creature that I have written a poem, which I share with the others as the van twists away from the bay and onto the highway.

Shad Flies of North Bay
Enwrapped in the comfort of my cocoon
Awaiting that day of freedom and death
Anticipation…of rising…of flight
Shedding the growth of three years
Like a cloak at dusk
Rising…silvery wings unfolding
Shining in the luminous glow of
The street lamps and windows
He feels my closeness and I join him
Our hearts beating fast in the passionate night
Then, tired, we unfold, exhausted
From birth and our union
We lie still, only sporadic slight movements
Reaching once more for each other
Our lifeless frail bodies sink back to the
Earth in silent death

Today, Dianne will drive Mum and Juanita to Timmins and Larder Lake where Mum and Dad lived when they were first married. It is exactly 60 years since our mother left Timmins, pregnant with her first child.

(from Dolly's diary)
It is late afternoon when we first sight the old Granger Hotel in Larder Lake. It was 1939 when Bernie and I rented a room here on the third floor. We only intended to stay until we found an apartment but we were here that whole long summer. Then, everything was new; streets and sidewalks were mud, most buildings were boarding houses with only one company store. The town was filled with miners looking for work. It was a booming place in those days. Now, I walk

the main street looking for anything I will remember or someone to talk to that might remember how it was, but all is quiet. The streets are empty, nothing but abandoned buildings, windows boarded up, the old Granger Hotel in ruins, the theatre only a shell. It is a forsaken town.

Kirkland Lake, our next stop, was Bernie's hometown for 15 years. Other industries have taken the place of the gold mines that drew miners here in the thirties. Wright Hargreaves mine is now a shopping mall. A memorial statue recognizing miners who lost their lives in the mine and a museum are the only reminders that this was once a thriving mining town. Here, Juanita finds a tree she planted the day her boyfriend left for overseas at the beginning of World War Two. He was killed shortly after.

Our last place to visit is Timmins. A lump comes in my throat when I see the weathered head frame of the Pamour mine looming in front of us. The name has letters faded, some missing, but it is unmistakably the mine where Bernie worked as a shift boss for four years. Now, the gates are locked and great slag heaps line the highway. In the city, I begin my search for our first home. I'm excited to find Bannerman Avenue, but there is no number 22 and no little brown house with a gate. As I go back to the car, I remember walking up this street every day to meet the bus coming from the mine. Later, when our trip is over, I find myself recalling things I'd not thought about for years. Even though I knew things would have changed, I was hoping to find a familiar place or an old friend. I have found neither, but coming back has fulfilled a dream I have had for many years. No matter how I felt when I found places in ruins, in my memory, Larder Lake, Kirkland Lake and Timmins will remain as they were when we were young and life held so much promise.

(from Julie's diary)

My journal entry today starts with an image...all of us sitting on the ground in the parking lot of the A&P Grocery Store in Sturgeon Falls, Ontario, watching the van being towed off into the distance. Welcome to Hike 2000! Needless to say, this is not a planned stop. We stopped for gas and smoke started pouring out of the engine. Talk about panic getting out of the van as we all had images of the van exploding. Luckily it was only a hose that burst. Yet another day at the garage for Billy.

Kathy will go with Billy today. Bonnie, Glenda, Heike, Nicholas, Nora, Maria, Mum [Shirley-Dale] and I spend a lovely afternoon shopping at the bargain store across the street. Four of us even buy some "very expensive" sandals. Three hours later we all pile back into the van and I find myself once again staring at the back of eight beautiful heads as the startling Ontario scenery whizzes by. Next on the agenda is a long wait in construction, only a minor setback. We are all still in

Ontario

good spirits. So, after an 11-hour drive for a five-hour trip we finally pull into a grocery store in Sault Ste. Marie. A friendly Nova Scotian woman who told us about the Blueberry Hill campground just outside of the city greets us. Things are looking up. We pick out our site and settle in for the night. Then it happens...someone reads a sign on the bathroom wall warning of black bears in the area. That is all it takes to set us off. We've spent the last two days obsessing about shad flies and now we can not stop talking about bears—bear stories, and bear bait, a bear's favourite food, and who the bear would eat first. We talk about bear maulings and Billy tells us about recent reports of bear killings. We talk about all of the bear safety rules we have ever heard (most of them wrong), who has a whistle, whether the cooking pot smells like food, who sleeps in the van, the route we should take to evacuate the tents, who blows the whistle first, who is sleeping on the outside in the tent, polar bear habits, and if we will take turns watching the fire. Glenda even tells us a scary story about a bear that gets his head caught in a honey jar, later realizing that it was Winnie the Pooh she was thinking of. We start the night by making plans for 'if' the bear comes, then, as our imaginations go wild, our plans change to when the bear attacks us all in the middle of the night. You certainly realize what everyone would really do in a crisis. A raccoon comes out of the bushes and everyone practically jumps up to run toward the van, each person for themselves. After we work ourselves into a total frenzy, we are off to bed and such is our night at the Blueberry Hill campground. Quite a thrill.

July 5

Goulais River
Distance: 21.5 km
Wildlife: black bear

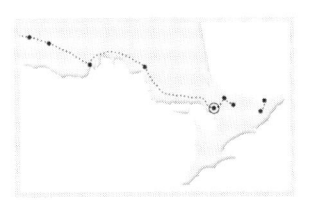

(from Glenda's diary)
I wake up several times in the night, listening to every creek and movement outside. All I can hear around me was the rhythmical snoring of someone in the next tent. It is cold; I feel damp and the wall of the tent is clammy and wet. What are we doing here in the heart of bear country, unprotected? I hear the clank of the trailer door and the muffled voices of Billy and Kathy going about their early

morning chores before the hubbub of the day begins. Billy has made coffee and has the fire crackling again. What a welcome sound. By the way, there was a bear in the dumpster last night, but it didn't make it to our campsite, thank God. Kathy makes blueberry pancakes, here at our campsite on Blueberry Hill. How appropriate. Kathy's camera drops in the dishwater—whoops! Another incident to add to the frustration. Yesterday the radiator hose cost $139. It sure eats up the gas money when there is an unexpected problem.

Bonnie is sketching the trees with the sun coming through the leaves, Shirley-Dale, Julie and Glenda are writing in their journals, Nicholas is playing the guitar, and Heike, Nora and Maria are drawing. It is a peaceful morning after last night's frenzy about bears. I call Gail Philips from the Ontario Trans Canada Trail Council to get details on the Voyageur Trail, which we will hike today. She explains that the trail begins at the top of one-mile hill, on the left, just beyond the gate marked "no trespassing." This should have been enough of a warning for what is to come. Nora, Heike and Nicholas decide to stay back with Billy today. Nora is not feeling well and since we are not confident about the length or condition of this trail, we decide it is best for her to rest. It is a good decision.

(from Glenda's diary)
We find our starting point along Highway 17. A little white sign says Voyageur Trail, so we know it is the right one. Kathy is told to follow the white trail markers, not any other colour. It is a good thing we know this, because it's all we have to go by. The trail is very over grown and in places completely washed out. We have to pick our way down a huge gully and up over the other side. We follow each other in single file, holding back raspberry and blackberry bushes, all the while blowing our whistles, talking as loudly as possible and banging rocks together to scare away any predators that just might venture onto our path. Near the end of the trail we come upon a huge beaver dam, which we have to make our way around. It is wet and boggy and there is no way through except plunging right in and forging ahead. It looks as though we are the first ones to use this trail for a very long time. When we finally make it across the swamp, we come to a big, grassy field. This must have been an old homestead. There is a wooden structure built into the hill with a cement block inside. What is it? An old mining site? A cellar? Most likely a bear's den! After we've walked 10.5 kilometres, we come back onto the logging road. Which way do we go? It is funny how the way you think you should go is the wrong

Ontario

way. While eating our lunch on the side of the road, a car comes by. It was Don McCrea, who lives near the road we've just hiked. He tells us to get in and drive with him. When we say we have to walk, he laughs really hard and says 'what for?' Why do you have to walk? It is hard to explain why you have to walk across Canada. He drives us out to the main highway. We walk almost eight kilometres up the highway and back to the Blueberry Campground where Billy is waiting. Nora, feeling better, has decided to go for a run. On her way up the highway she sees a black bear in the ditch. We head for Wawa.

Lake Superior is on our left the whole drive. It is magnificent. Lake Superior is the largest expanse of fresh water in the world and it makes up ten per cent of the earth's fresh water. Amazing! Since early times, native people have traveled the waters of Lake Superior in birch bark canoes to hunt, fish and trade with neighbouring bands. Hundreds of years later, brigades of voyageurs crossed the waters in a commercial version of a birch bark canoe. By 1700, the first schooners traveled the lake. The North West Company and the Hudson Bay Company used schooners to supply fir trading posts at Batchawana and Michipicoten. The railway was completed by 1914 and the use of the steamers was phased out.

We arrive at out campsite at Wawa RV campground at 9:05 p.m., same arrival time as last night. Time to get the fire going with last night's wood and the tents set up. We have our drinks around the fire, tell our best events of the day, sing and eat Maria and Heike's goulash, which is made with hot dogs. We are very relaxed and confident about the bears tonight. I even take my whistle off my neck and put it in the pocket of the tent, along with the flashlight. After reading the park literature, we put our toothbrushes and toothpaste in the van so as not to attract the bears. More than prepared I'd say.

We are camping in Wawa. The name Wawa was given to the Canada Goose by the Ojibway Indians. This noble bird, returning to the north each year, brings the renewed promise of spring. A large 27-inch-high goose statue, weighing 150,000 pounds, stands as a symbol of the Michipicoten area and Wawa. Once a miniature Klondike, Wawa was a bustle of activity in the early 1900s with nearby mining bringing settlers and businesses to the area. With the closure of the mines came an exodus of the residents, leaving the empty shells of the buildings behind. Once a booming town, by 1908, it was deserted, except for some stray horses that wandered through the wasted buildings seeking refuge from the flies and summer heat. With renewed interest in the mines, Wawa began to be resettled in the late forties and

Glenda, Shirley-Dale, Don McCrae and Kathy. Don McCrae spies us emerging from the Voyageur Trail and offers us a drive. He can hardly believe we have found our way on this obscure trail.

early fifties. Now, with a busy main street boasting businesses, stores and banks, there is little sign of the ghost town that once stood silent in the northern wilderness.

July 6

Place: Tremblay to Michipicoten Harbour
Distance: 23 km
Wildlife: 2 snakes, 3 ruffed grouse with chicks, chipmunk and bear at our campsite.

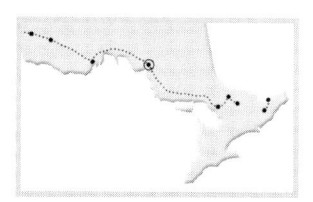

(from Nora's diary)
We wake up early this morning so we can start hiking earlier, which doesn't exactly happen. Billy is so patient. After Mum's French toast, we drive to our anticipated starting point for the day. We leave all the tents set up and the contents of the bins strewn over the campground for Billy to pack up. We tumble out of the van where the trail should have begun. One look around tells us we will never find the trail. We pile back into the van and drive to the Wawa Information Centre. The people at the tourist centre tell us we'll never find the trail, it is so over grown. People who make the trail maps must never walk them. But it is fortunate for us that we didn't find our original trail or we would never have met Jim Hoffman, who redirects us to an abandoned railway line that has not yet been derailed. This line runs from Tremblay to Michipicoten Harbour.

Wild flowers now grow between the ties on the line: tall daisies, yellow Indian paintbrush, flax and columbines wave in the warm breeze. The sun is beautiful but the wind keeps us cool. Holding hands and balancing on the rails, we could be in the movie "Stand By Me." Daisies, Indian paintbrush and clover growing over and between the tracks whisk our legs as we walk past. Small step, small step, small step...big step; the ties are either too close or too far apart to maintain a normal pace. How many men have been over these tracks, laying the rails, heaving the ties and pounding the stakes? Where were their families? We stop to explore an old railway building then continue up the rail stopping only to exclaim over the brilliant collection of wildflowers along the track.

At the ghost town of Bryant, we walk up the road apiece then return to the train tracks. About two kilometres further we come to some small, abandoned, windowless houses nestled between two ridges forming a valley. The train tracks diverge in three directions. We chose to go where the bottom route leads, then stand in awe. Reaching this spot completely by accident, we are in paradise. Long, silvery grasses, mottled with wildflowers, cover the bank leading to a sandy beach. In between the rocky, shoreline cliffs is water so blue, quietly lapping against two uninhabited majestic islands. Jim Hoffman later tells Mum that the Clergues lived on one of the islands called the Wigwam and had a swing bridge between the mainland and home. The swing bridge was guarded by two bears, chained to the end of the bridge. Now, a sailboat sways in the warm wind. To our right, we can see the ruins of a long wooden wharf. When the railway was running it transported iron ore here to be shipped to far away places. We are all alone in the ghost town rich with history.

Michipicoten Harbour was once a busy fur-trading post. Later, when the Helen Mine was opened, the harbour was used to ship the ore to other centres in Ontario. A 12-mile railway linked Michipicoten Harbour to the mine, where five large locomotives, one hundred steel cars and one passenger car occupied this Algoma line. By 1900, a 750-foot trestle had been built along with a 275-foot wooden dock and warehouse. A sawmill, company store, hotel and cabins for the residents had been built. Helen Mine had more than five hundred men working there and the influx of the families demanded a school. Francis Hector Clergue had founded the many industries in the area. His two sisters enjoyed the summer home on the tiny island called Wigwam. Other family members who frequently came to Michipicoten in the summer stayed at the three-storey Algoma Hotel, with its dance floor—the scene of bustling skirts and young, raucous mining men.

When the Helen Mine closed in 1918, the harbour became deserted, leaving only the carcasses of buildings and herds of moose and packs of wolves to wander through this once lively community. In 1924, a forest fire raged through the area, leaving only charred remains of this abandoned port. It wasn't until the fifties that activity at the mine once more brought people to the harbour, but the excitement and thrill of that first community was gone.

Now, a long, gray wharf leans out into the harbour bending like an old man with missing teeth. We climb down the bank that is growing with beach peas onto the soft warm sand. Our boots come off, our damp socks are laid out on the warm stones and we dip our feet in the cool water. Stretching our legs on the warm sand, we eat our lunch. Nicholas decides the water is much too inviting not to swim. I watch his long, colt-like, brown legs wade into the water and think how fast he is growing. He loves to swim and takes advantage of every opportunity, if only for a moment. Holding his arms high above his head, he winces as the cold water enters his shorts. The temptation overcomes Maria who strips to her shorts and joins him. Heike puts on her trim black bathing suit and also goes for a dip. I lay back, spread eagle on the sand, and look up at the cloudless sky. It is a perfect feeling. At 2:30 p.m., we slowly brush the sand from our feet, shake out our socks and tie up our hiking boots.

We return on the same rail bed that we came on. As we come to a small house with a tidy lawn, an older man opens the gate and ducks under the wires he has put up above his fence. "What's going on?" he asks, questioning our presence. We tell him we are walking up the line, which seems to ease his fears of our invasion. He tells me that his name is Leonard Ziggelman and that he worked in the iron ore mine and moved here in 1985. He says the train stopped running about two years ago. "When the train rolled by, the cups would fall right out of my cupboard" he explains. I ask him how many trains went by a day and he replies, "one." "Why didn't you hang onto your cup when you knew the train was coming?" I tease. He shoots a second glance, then grins, realizing that I am joking with him. His blue eyes sparkle and his smile flashes a mouth of missing teeth. He tells us how some young people in the nearby community pick on him and how he ended up in jail two years ago. I gather by his stories that he enjoys having a drink, which may have gotten him in trouble a few times. He tells us only

To our delight, the trail ends at a beach in Michipocten Harbour.

four people live in Michipicoten Harbour now. Just today, the power company cut the power to the houses that were owned by the mines. He counts us and disappears into his house. He reappears with a pen with his address on it for each of us, and a Polaroid camera. How special to receive a gift from this man, living all alone by this beautiful, peaceful beach, far from any other town. We would never have met him if we had tried to follow the Voyageur trail maps.

On the way back, we spook another ruffed grouse. We have already seen two on the way, one of which acted very strange on the side of the track, flapping around. Then we noticed a small chick trying to run up the hill beside us. The mother was trying to act hurt to lure us away. I felt very touched by her bravery.

We walk back along the line, two abreast, singing rounds and marching tunes. Back with Billy, we walk up to the graveyard where workers who died building the railway were buried. How sad. They had all died between 1889 and 1900. Only two of the graves have names on them. The rest are stolid, white, nameless crosses. Once again, my mind jumbles with questions. Who were these men? Why had they died? Overexertion from backbreaking work? Influenza?

We arrive at our campsite at 8:30—earlier than usual. It is still light outside. Our camping spot, at Neys, is tucked into a densely wooded area where no sunlight filters through. I am disappointed that I can't see the water of Lake Superior. There is virtually no room between our little tents and the thick woods. Other campers sit in their large campers, with full electricity, the blue light from their TV's glaring through the windows. Shirley-Dale and Julie prepare a supper of Mexican quesadilla, as the rest of us hurry to set up the tents before nightfall. Billy starts our evening campfire. Nicholas has nicknamed him "Billy the beaver," due to his wood-gathering skills.

As supper is being made, I walk along the campground road that curves onto the beach. I walk up the beach to scrounge some firewood. When I return, the park staff is at our campsite to warn us that a bear was at a nearby campsite where they are cooking fish. The park rangers look, in horror, at our six bins lying on the ground around the campsite. "Is there food in all of those coolers?" they ask. We simply say, "No." How could we begin to explain? We eat late then scramble to get rid of every hint of food. We drive dishes, garbage, food, toothpaste, towels and clothes into a pile in the back of the trailer and ram the door shut. With metal pot covers and spoons, whistles and flashlights to ward away the bears, we retreat to our tents.

July 7

Neys, Thunder Bay
Distance: 21.5 km
Wildlife: bear, 2 squirrels, chipmunk

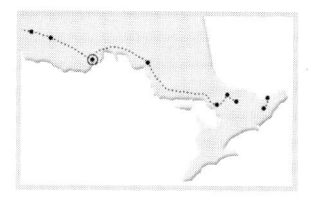

It is 3:00 A.M. I awaken to a thump on the trailer door. I am lying on the side of the tent that is tied to the trailer. I think Billy must be getting up but when I look at my watch, I know differently. I listen intently. I can feel the presence of something very close to our tent. Then, I can hear it…breaths coming in short grunts and snorts, like a pig. There is no question. We have a visitor—the bear. For about 20 minutes, I listen, hoping I am imagining this sound. The sound gets closer and louder. I wake Nora and Maria. Do I make a noise? I roll over to sit up. Oh no! I have been sleeping on my arm. It is asleep and I don't have enough strength to grip the spoon to bang the pot cover. I squeeze my hand, trying to quickly pump some feeling into my hand. Weakly, I tap the pot cover, afraid that if the sound is too loud, it might startle the bear and he might lunge at the tent. "Go away," I say in a 'not too convincing' voice. After all, I don't want to upset him! We have discussed for two nights what to do if a bear comes in the night, and now, here he is, not two feet away. We lie still, listening to every sound, then fall asleep.

It is 4:30 A.M. No mistake this time. It is light enough that I can see his shadow on the tent wall beside me. I am separated from the

June 18 - July 9 — Central Canada

Quebec - (Below) Maria strolls by Chute Fraser in Malbaie.

(Lower left) The trail bordering Lake Temiscouta is perfect.

(Lower right) An array of flowers lines the trail to Eastman.

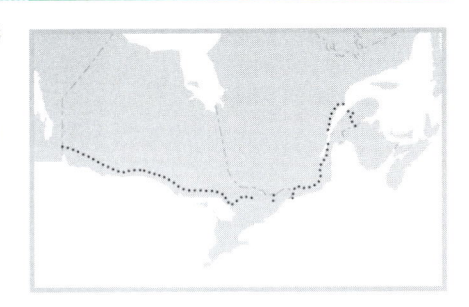

Hiking the Dream

Quebec - (Right) We walk next to the rail line and beach on the shore of the St. Lawrence River.

Maria and Nora. A time for cooling off and relaxing in the waters of Cabano.

Hiking the Dream

Quebec - Tonight we watch the sun set on the St. Lawrence River at Rivière-du-Loup. Tomorrow we will venture down the other side of the river.

(Inset) Kathy hikes through the bathers on the waterfront of Magog.

Hiking the Dream

Quebec - Heike and Kathy navigate their way along the powerline leading to Highway 241, Waterloo.

(Right) Nelson Dubé escorts us across the Lake Temiscouta to join the Trans Canada Trail.

(Bottom) La Malbaie, a bustling village with a wonderful pub.

Hiking the Dream

Ontario - (Right) We hang our drenched clothes on the parliament fence to dry.

(Below) Nicholas before the rain.

(Bottom) Warm water rushes down the street as we jump in the puddles. Our clothing clings wet to our bodies but it doesn't really matter—it's Canada Day!

Hiking the Dream

Ontario - Magnetewan. We stand in the old graveyards looking at headstones bearing the names of young children, whole families, whole communities that died of a strange illness in just days. We can only imagine their grief.

(Inset) Nicholas, Kathy and Bonnie on the ghost road in the pouring rain.

Hiking the Dream

Ontario - (Right) Voyageur Trail, Goulais River. Maria tries to skirt the swamp. White trail markers on trees indicate the way.

(Bottom right) Shad flies invade our supper table in North Bay.

Maria and Kathy climb down a large gully on the Voyageur Trail. This is only the beginning!

Hiking the Dream

Ontario - (Right) Kim Harrison's parrot, Gringo, 'chats me up' in the local giftshop, Ignace.

(Inset) Nora in the old watch station, Tremblay.

(Bottom) The old rail line from Tremblay to Michipicoten is adorned with wildflowers.

bear by the thin nylon of the tent wall. Again, I shake Nora and Maria awake and alert the other tent where my sisters and Julie are sleeping. Billy and Nicholas are sleeping in the van tonight to make more room. The snorting outside is distinct and the strong scent of the bear wafts through the tent. God, how I pray for morning. I blow my whistle and chatter starts up in both tents. The bear prowls the grounds searching for a morsel of food that may have been left. I fall asleep, unable to concentrate on listening for his advance.

It is 8:00 A.M. Everyone is up and babbling about last night's intruder.

(from Nicholas' diary)
I laugh at the picture of Mom tapping at the pot with a plastic spoon. Breakfast is scrambled eggs and chocolate milk for me. Nora can't find the showers and she gets so frustrated that she shaves her legs right in the parking lot. I laugh again. I go for a walk along the beach.

As I walk to the showers, which are located two kilometres from our tents, I can see remnants of garbage that the bear has been able to find in the night. The trouble sometimes with people who camp in their protective campers is that they aren't always as careful to clean up after their meal outside. I am told that they caught the bear this morning by putting a jelly doughnut in a live trap. Imagine bears liking jelly doughnuts!

Before leaving, we take a walk on the beach. Lake Superior is more like an ocean than a lake. The soft sand on its shore is strewn with white, bleached driftwood. Bonnie, Shirley-Dale and I walk to the end of the beach and crawl up on a rock. It is smooth and warm. After a sleepless night, I think how I could spend the day sprawled on its surface, listening to the water lapping at its base. Neys campground was formerly a prison camp for five hundred Germans during World War Two. It is a chilling thought. I would love to explore this place, but again, our time is limited.

Once in the van, almost everyone falls asleep. It is a long drive to Thunder Bay. We pass hundreds of acres of desolate, burned wasteland, where fires have raged. I can't imagine that anyone will ever be able to build trail through this area and I wonder how this whole Trans Canada Trail will ever connect. There are so many huge expanses like

Nora and Glenda prepare "bear and snake" shish kabobs in the light of the campfire in Thunder Bay.

this. Who will ever have the energy to plow through the thick undergrowth that twists around the burned remains of forest? And who will travel the trail in this area if it is built? It is a section of massive destruction. I think about the animals that must have frantically tried to reach safety in the roar of the fire.

I notice Billy getting a little sleepy. We stop for a stretch, then drive a short distance. The quietness of the van brings drowsiness again. This time we stop for a coffee, and continue on to Thunder Bay. We travel straight to the campground on the outskirts of the city. We choose a flat spot under some big trees with the water tumbling over Trowbridge Falls beside us. We quickly set up our tents and drive to the laundromat in Thunder Bay. It will serve a dual purpose: Internet access and washing facility.

(from Nicholas' diary)
I stay in the van and wait patiently, if I must say so myself. Then Billy, Glenda, Julie, Nora and I leave the others to hike. We are going to make supper. I am a great help. (Sarcasm). Julie plays music for Billy while I play with a soccer ball and try to break my previous record of hacks. Glenda and Nora make 'bear and snake' shish kabobs, rice and salad.

Bonnie, Shirley-Dale, Heike, Maria and I decide to hike back to the campsite. The intention is to hike through Centennial Park and up to the Trowbridge Falls campground. The sun is setting, sending a pink glow over the falls and the 'sleeping giant' in the bay.

(from Nicholas' diary)
Glenda and Nora get dressed for supper and wait until dark for the others to come. It is past 12:00 by the time supper is ready, since they are making it over an open fire and the others don't return until very late. We have a good time eating by flashlight. Nora and Glenda are in tears because of the smoke in their eyes, consider-

ing they have to stay in one spot over the fire holding the flashlight while Mom rotates the meat. It was so dark by the time they are washing dishes that they wash the melon in the dishwater and dry it. When we get in bed, we wonder if the storm clouds will open with rain.

After a very late supper, Billy spreads his sleeping bag on the second seat of the van. I promise not to disturb him with rummaging for things after he has gone to sleep. We retire to our little sleeping spots in the tents. With the threat of bears seemingly remote and the sound of the falls lulling me to sleep, I fall asleep quite quickly. Suddenly, thunder crashes and the tent brightens with a lightening flash. How appropriate that we would have a thunderstorm in Thunder Bay. Suddenly, Glenda appears in the door of the tent. "Get out, Kathy, we aren't safe under these trees in the thunderstorm." I assure her that we'll be okay. She leaves and I lie back on my pillow. "What ifs" begin to fill my head. I unzip the tent and peer into the night. The sky appears pink and the forms of the trees stand out with the frequent flashes of lightening. I dart across the wet ground to Glenda, Bonnie, Shirley-Dale and Julie's tent, unzip the door and jump in, out of the rain, to assess the situation with them. To my surprise, they are gone!

I hurry back to our tent and arouse the sleepers. Confused and a bit frightened, they hustle from the tent, the flashlight beam streaking across the trees, then the ground, the trees, the ground, as we run for the van. We open the door of the van where Billy is still sleeping. Glenda, Bonnie, Shirley-Dale and Julie are squeezed into the two front seats like wet rats seeking shelter in a sewer hole, peering out at the night. We crawl in. Poor Billy. We wait. Nine faces stare out the window at the black night, illuminated repeatedly with the passing lightening storm. I can hear Nicholas behind me…one one thousand, two one thousand, as he counts between the crashes of thunder and the flash of lightening, determining the distance of the storm centre from us. As the thunder fades, we return to our tents, pausing briefly in a huddle in the campsite to laugh at our second night of unrest.

Hiking the Dream

July 8

Place: Ignace
Distance: 16 km
Wildlife: deer, loons

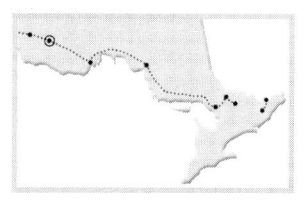

(from Heike's diary)
After yet another exciting night—I thought that experiencing a thunder storm while camping in Thunder Bay is rather appropriate—we pack up our wet stuff to head west into yet another time zone. Leaving, we find out that Thunder Bay is quite a bit bigger then we thought from what we saw the day before. Soon after we start, we have our first wildlife viewing for the day: a deer standing in the middle of the road, apparently unable to make up its mind about where to go next. It finally lopes off to the right, leaping effortlessly over the guard rail. After that, I keep my eyes peeled for more wildlife, and I think that I see a bear at one point, but it might have been wishful thinking, it might have been nothing but a tree stump, or a moose. The road goes ever on and on. When I'm not straining my eyes for wildlife, I am busy writing letters and reading James and the Giant Peach, one of my exploits from the great second-hand bookstore in North Bay.

In Upsala, we stop for coffee and other refreshments since none of us are feeling too perky after last night's interrupted sleep. They have a stuffed wild boar's head on the wall. I learn that it hadn't been caught locally, but imported from Texas. I have a nice cool bottle of cranberry juice. Although Upsala is in the central time zone, they stick with standard eastern. We'll soon have to adjust our watches, or the way we look at them anyway. Thus fortified, we continue our journey to Ignace, where we intend to hike the White Otter Trail. When we arrive there, Kathy goes to a souvenir shop to inquire about the whereabouts of the trail. Kim Harrison, who works in the shop, tells her, "You're on it." And, sure enough, there are signs for the Trans Canada trail on all the lampposts along the Trans Canada Highway in Ignace. We decide to have our base at West Beach on Agimak Lake, where Billy and I can hang out, dry the tents, write letters and have a snooze. All the others take off in the direction we came from.

We slowly drag on our boots. It is very humid and hot and my heart just isn't in it, knowing much of this hike will be on a sidewalk. Ignace is a small town with tiny shops on its main street, a railway running on one side and a deep flowing creek on the other. At 2.5 kilometres, we run out of marked trail and deviate onto a road that says 'Pickle Lake.' We think, 'Great, we can hike to the lake and have a swim." To our dismay, we read the sign more closely, "Pickle Lake, 263 km." We circle back to meet the main drag, where a truck stops. It is here we meet Hugh Broughton, who takes us back to his body mechanics shop to call the trail coordinator, Dennis Smyk. As we walk with Hugh, he tells us how some of the homes along the railway are made from old boxcars. Finding that Dennis isn't home, I leave him a note and we continue on. We stop at the gift shop to find Kim, the man we met earlier. He has Gringo, his pet parrot, on his shoulder. What a great bird! It grabs grapes from Kim, peels them with its tongue, spits the skin on the floor and eats the rest.

Hugh Broughton escorts us through Ignace, filling us with local stories on the way.

To return to West Beach, we choose an alternate route by the creek. We walk along in the heat passing the water airport, and finally reach the road that will take us to the beach. Back at the beach, we kick off our boots and wade into the cool water.

(from Heike's diary)
I must say that, apart from being pestered by insect bites, I spend a most agreeable afternoon, sitting in the sun and watching bush planes take off and land on the lake, which I later learn functions as an airport. I also see and hear loons and some kids frolicking in the water. There is an overall Sunday afternoon feel in the air, which I think is due to the sound of lawnmowers from the nearby cottages. Julie and Nicholas come back before the others and start doing what I'm doing, only Nicholas is energetic enough for a swim. The others soon join us. Kim shows up on his motorbike after work. While people are finishing their 'after hike' beers, Maria, who really is a sucker for motorbikes, goes with Kim to make sure he doesn't take too long changing into his volleyball gear. We then have a match on the beach volleyball court…the hags (aunts), Billy and Kim versus the haglets (cousins and me). We win. Then we bid our farewells to Kim and head for Dinorwic.

Hiking the Dream

When we arrive at the Viking Restaurant in Dinorwic, I phone our second cousin Jim Bowman, (Juanita's nephew). We have never met this cousin though, I have only spoken to him on the phone since we began hiking. He has been following our progress on the Internet, and is anxious to meet us. He and his wife, Toots, have offered us a place to stay for the night. I can hardly imagine what they think they are in for with this crew. He arrives to escort us to his house. I drive with Jim down the long winding lane that leads to their home. When we finally arrive there, the beauty of the place leaves us almost speechless. The house is located on a spit of land jutting out into Dinorwic Lake, so that you can see the lake from almost every window. The house seems to be growing directly out of the bedrock. Toots and their two golden retrievers, Rosy and little Daisy, greet us. Daisy just moved in the day before. Louis Belmore is the only one on my father's side of the family that I have met before coming to northern Ontario. Jim brings out some old tapes that Louis sent him years ago. They are the same songs that Louis sang on the tapes he sent us. He has since died in a train/car collision, so it is sad to hear his voice now on these tapes.

Soon, it is time for supper. Toots has prepared the most delicious meal: strawberry spinach salad, green beans, potato gratin, ham and for dessert, a drumstick cake. We lie back on the big comfortable chairs in their living room. It is such a relaxing house. Late into the night, Nora, Maria, Nicholas, Heike and I go to the little cottage on the lake and tuck into our cozy beds. I hear a loon cry out far off the shore of the lake. From even farther away, I hear an answer.

July 9

Place: Dinorwic, Kenora
Distance: 26 km
Wildlife: loons, dragonflies

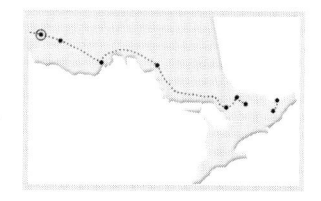

My peaceful sleep in the little cabin overlooking Dinorwic Lake is abruptly disturbed. Billy's subtle 'power saw' alarm clock under my window is a reminder that it is morning and time to begin what will be our last hiking day in Ontario. The sun sparkles on the lake as I walk across the dew-covered grass to the house above us on the big bedrock slab. Jim and Toots have a wonderful breakfast spread of coffee, fruit salad, ham and cheese strata, and bagels. Heike and Toots have gone for a swim and Jim is pouring the coffee. Showers and beds have put everyone in a relaxed mood, and no one is hurrying to leave this haven. We sit on the bedrock patio, enjoying breakfast and the company of our new found cousin, Jim Bowman and his kind, friendly wife, Carolyn (Toots). After breakfast, Nora, Maria and I decide to paddle our way up the lake in the paddleboat. Rosie swims after us in desperation to join us as we paddle away from shore. As we make our way along the rocky shoreline, the wind comes up and the waves slash over the sides of our boat. We struggle to keep ourselves on course. It is a beautiful sunny day and the waves dance around us. We retreat to the dock and change for our drive to Kenora.

After hours of waiting patiently, Billy gives us the 'All Aboard' call and we reluctantly pull ourselves into the van. We are on our way to Kenora to find the 'Lake of the Wood' trail. I certainly hope it is easier to locate this one than the others we have tried to find in Ontario. On route to Kenora, we meet the infamous water relay that has just left town. A long line of bikers, with shiny new support jeeps in tow, winds its way from the city. This is the entourage, similar to the one in St. John's, Newfoundland that is making its way to Hull from the west, carrying water drawn from the Pacific Ocean. We honk our greetings and drive on to Kenora where celebrations are still going on to mark the passage of the water from the Pacific and the Arctic through their town. The trail coordinators are excited about our ventures and quickly locate TV reporters to interview me. A couple of bikers who have just arrived from the west coast listen to my interview then we chat about the trail on each end of this country.

Jim and Carolyn (Toots) Bowman and their dog Rosie in Dinorwic. We are still raving about the food we were served here!

Kathy, Maria and Nora add some kilometres by water in the paddleboat. Jim and Rosie give the official send-off.

Nora, Maria and Julie decide to take advantage of the crowd at the waterfront and do some busking. With fiddle and guitar, they park themselves on the waterfront and entertain. Bonnie, Shirley-Dale, Glenda and I search out the Lake of the Woods trail while Heike and Billy go to set up the tent. Nicholas opts to stay with the buskers.

The trail leads around the waterfront and onto Highway 17. It is a very hot day and a late start. I have come to the conclusion that Ontario is way too big! The vastness of this province with its endless kilometres of wilderness amazes me. The combination of long drives, trail that is along highways, and two van breakdowns has left us 15.5 kilometres short of our goal.

After hiking, we meet the girls in the German pub, Christoph's Kneipe. Busking has been a success. We have a cold beer then head for the campground for supper. Bonnie, Nora, Glenda, Maria, Heike and Julie sing around the fire as I make vegetable soup from the leftovers. Shirley-Dale is cleaning out the food bins and making a list of all the meals we can make with the vittles. Billy sits by the fire, enjoying the singing and Nicholas stows away to the tent for a little reading before supper. Later, Nora makes us some chamomile tea and we devour the squares that Toots has given us. With no fear of bears or thunderstorms tonight, we leave the campground strewn with dishes, leftovers and clothing as we tumble off to bed.

Manitoba

July 10 - July 21

Nicholas, Kathy, Nora, Heike, Shirley-Dale, Julie, Bonnie, and Glenda at West Hawk Lake.

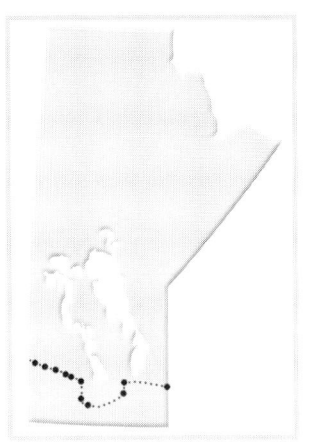

July 10

West Hawk Lake to Falcon Lake
Distance: 20 km
Wildlife: bear, deer, many mosquitoes, ravens, one single western red lily, purple gentian, woodpeckers, yarrow, mugwort, vetch

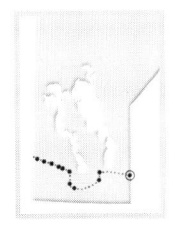

(from Shirley-Dale's diary)
We leave Kenora before noon, heading west for Manitoba. Lake of the Woods looks as though it has been poured into the woods from above, seeping in and around the trees. We cross the border before too long and climb up to the "Welcome to Manitoba" sign. Another province, fresh and new. We give a hoot and a holler and push onward, westward. At the information centre we meet a family from PEI traveling across Canada in a van. We drive to West Hawk Lake, Manitoba, and immediately begin our hike to Falcon Lake. We walk through long, high spruce and poplar trees towering over the well-marked trail. A deer runs in front of us as we start the hike, bounding onto the main road and into the woods. The flowers seem bigger and brighter here. We eat lunch in a little ice-fishing shack along the trail.

At 14.5 kilometres, we come out to Falcon Lake, a part of the major lake system in this part of the country. Our tent site is near the lake, a sandy beach and wharf. There are bear warning signs again. After supper, we go for a walk on the beach. Errol, Bonnie's partner, has warned us that 'mosquitoes are as big as crows in Manitoba.' The frogs are louder here. The echo of the woodpeckers in the trees carries through the campsite. We go to bed and listen to the night sounds: mosquitoes, other campers' voices and the rustling of the willows by the water. I begin thinking in the night about this trip and how Kathy really is a voyageur as she leads this troop across Canada. This truly is an historical trek and these daily journals are actually chronicling the progress of the Trans Canada Trail for the first time.

July 11

Birds Hill Park
Distance: 10 km
Wildlife: prairie dogs, 4 white-tailed deer, 2 fawns, squirrels, chipmunk, bunnies, wild turkeys, red-winged black birds, fields of yellow canola, blue flax

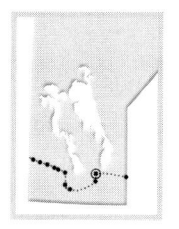

(from Bonnie and Glenda's diary)
This morning Kathy makes porridge with dates in it and we remember a saying of David Estey's, a friend in New Brunswick: 'You can cope with anything in the day if you have porridge for breakfast.' After a swim at Falcon Lake Beach (and the fright upon learning that there is swimmer's itch in the water), we pack up our van and head out to Winnipeg. Just outside of St. Anne, we have our first glimpse of the prairies. Heike says the landscape is much like where she grew up in Northern Germany. Nicholas remarks that this must be the home of the world's best hide-and-seek players.

We arrived at Birds Hill Park in the rain. The trail winds through fields, red pine plantations and marshlands. Long ago, Birds Hill Park was the bottom of a lake. Interpretive panels inform us that mastodons and woolly mammoth once roamed these parts in great numbers, and that Birds Hill Park was a favorite spot of author Gabrielle Roy. The rain brings the mosquitoes out in droves.

After the hike, we drive into the city of Winnipeg. Kathy meets up with one of her field hockey friends, Carolyn (Burfoot) Fedorowich, from the Canada/USA women's field hockey game. We (Shirley-Dale, Glenda, Bonnie and Julie) make arrangements for our 33-hour bus ride back to Ottawa. We drive over to Brian and Janet Forbes' place for drinks and a great meal. We meet Cleber, a gymnast from

Manitoba

Equador, who is living with them for the summer. Janet and Brian are good friends of Kathy. After supper, Janet gives us a whirlwind tour of Winnipeg on our way to catch the old Greyhound bus back to Ottawa. The four of us begin to backtrack the same route we journeyed over the past ten days. We are sad to be heading east—the opposite direction of Hike 2000.

July 12

Place: Winnipeg
Distance: 6.5 km

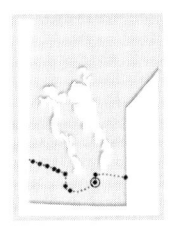

(from Maria's diary)
I awake to the sound of Nicholas' voice, "Maria, how do you like your eggs?" I crawl out of my cocoon of sleep and walk upstairs to a wonderful breakfast cooked by Heike. Heat pours in through the open windows and even the shade of the basement still brings beads of sweat to our brows. Uncomfortable and without relief, I bring out the computer to write diary entries I missed in PEI. I accidentally erase one of the days and spend the rest of my time on the computer trying to find the missing file anywhere....but, no luck.

Carolyn (Burf) offers to drive me to see her mom and dad. I haven't seen them since my field hockey days in the eighties. I came to Winnipeg on various trips both with the Nova Scotia team and the Canadian team, and I always had a special room in their house where I was welcome anytime. I came out for Carolyn's wedding and spent a week with her folks. I can't wait to see them again. They have moved into a senior's apartment and are anxiously waiting for us by their door. It is remarkable that they haven't changed a bit. Carolyn's petite mom welcomes me like a daughter, her

Evelyn and Bob Burfoot in Winnipeg, unchanged since we met in the early seventies.

eyes bright and twinkling with life. She is dressed in a neat blouse and cardigan. Her husband, Bob, jokes and pokes fun at Carolyn as we sit down for a cup of tea. He begins to tell me of 'The Moonlight,' a special train that ran from Winnipeg to Grand Beach when he was young:

"Grand Beach is about a hundred miles due north of us here on Lake Winnipeg. We traveled on 'The Moonlight' for about 75 cents return. We went to the dance hall, which had a live orchestra. 'The Moonlight' came in every night, left the city at six and was down there at 7:45 so we could dance at 8:00. It left there at 10:30 at night and had us back in the city before midnight.

A number of years ago, the only way into Grand Beach was by train. When we went in by car in 1933, it took us two and a half hours. Later, they put a highway through and you could get there in just about an hour. In 1934, my brother and I bought a camp in 'Campsite.' That's in the government property. At one time you rented the property from the railroad but since the government has taken it over the taxes have gone up. In about 1960, they stopped that train. The freight train goes down to Iron Falls but doesn't come into the beach."

We chat for an hour, reminiscing about the good times we had in previous visits. I fill them in on my family and they tell me about theirs.

Carolyn drives me back to her house with a quick visit to the train station on the way. It is a beautiful old station, with a high oval ceiling, stained glass and carved pillars. We talk briefly with the station agent, then drive home. The air is hot and we find a cool spot in the shade of the backyard. Carolyn has to go to work for a while, so leaves. The rest of the day we work on laundry, the web site and generally putter around preparing for our start in the morning.

(from Maria's diary)
Mom makes pork chops and salad, then we get ready to go on a sight-seeing tour with Brian Forbes. Heike, Mom, Nora, Nicholas and I pile into the van where Cleber, Brian, his daughter, Gill, son Robert and friend Eric wait. We drive to the Winnipeg Forks where the Assiniboine and Red rivers meet. The water has risen due to the rain in the last month, and the water flow covers the walking path to the top of the gates, which are along the park. A solitary man sings songs near the square, which is flooded for skating in the winter.

As we walk through the streets, we occasionally stop to view historical sights of forts and legislative buildings. Music can be heard from tents in an

Brian and Janet Forbes welcomed us into their home.

enclosed park area. Brian asks, "Where would you like to go?" We all look at the tents and swarms of people, then back at Brian, "It's up to you, you're the guide." To the tents. A live band plays, and cooks from restaurants serve their most famous dishes to the people meandering outside. We stop to have beverages and stand talking and laughing in a circle, doing our famous dances: the lawn mower, the bus driver and the shopper. Then, we head back to the parking lot where we have chicken fights with Mom on Brian's shoulders, and Nora on mine. The sun sinks behind the buildings, casting a golden glow on the edge of the cumulus clouds. Cleber demonstrates his superior handstand ability.

Back at Burf's house, the younger adults, Nora and I, get ready to join Cleber and Jill at Boogie Nights. We dress up in the same hiking clothes we have been wearing for the last three days, put on some deodorant for others' sake and are off for a night on the town. We arrive at Boogie Nights Bar, where eighties music is pumping hard. We try to bring life to the dance floor, but the band, with its side strip show, highly outclasses our moves. We see Wade Lake, a friend from home, who we have plans to meet while we're in Winnipeg. Wade really wants to join us on our trip. The lights come on at one o'clock, so we chat with the bouncer, then leave for our vehicle. We drop Wade off, promising to see him on the trip, then sadly say goodbye to our new friends Jill and Cleber.

Carolyn has invited friends over tonight, some of whom I have not seen since my field hockey days. Manitoba and Nova Scotia always were the friendliest teams at the tournament and when we came together at nationals, in our free time, we were like one big happy team. Now, they are here for the USA/Canada game. I think back to '74 and '76 when I was playing for Canada and stopped in Winnipeg on our cross-Canada tour with England and Scotland. Tonight I will see Madge Johnson, Manitoba's former goalie, who played for Canada when I left, Jeannie MacDonald, Janice Butcher, and new friends of Carolyn. We tell stories and laugh well beyond midnight. It is so great to be back among these friends.

July 13

Place: Spirit Sands Desert
Distance: Spirit Sands: 15 km, Spruce Woods Park: 5 km
Wildlife: Fox, grass snakes, beetles, chipmunks, and grasshoppers

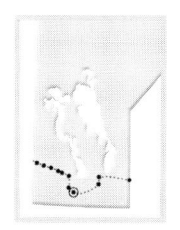

I am up early to see Carolyn's husband, Jim, before he goes to work. It is a beautiful morning. At eight o'clock we are packed up and ready to leave Winnipeg. We say our goodbyes to Carolyn and head to Robin's Donuts for breakfast. We are soon on a country road, rolling along prairie farmland. Stretching before us, there are fields of golden canola (rape seed) and blue flax as far as we can see. The contrast of the colours leaves us exclaiming and jumping in and out of the van for an "even better" picture. We make a quick pit stop in the village of Elie. Here, we find a garage with a welder. He agrees to fix the broken hinge on our trailer door. Payment? "Have a good day." What great guys. They are so friendly. As the door is being fixed, Nora and I wander around the tiny neighbourhood. Children play in the front yard and have dinosaurs drawn all over the road in front of their house. There is no traffic and the houses remind us of the television show, 'Little House on the Prairie.' We drive to Spruce Woods Park and set up our campsite. We quickly eat our lunch and Billy drops us off at the entry to Spirit Sands Desert.

It is very hot and we are to hike in one of the few desert regions in North America. We carry only cameras and water with us. The hike into the sand dunes is much like walking on a beach path and our boots slide back with every step in the loose sand. As we near the high sand dunes, the ground becomes more arid and plants become more and more typical of a desert environment. On the dunes, temperatures soar to 30°C, and the desert sand to 55°C. Needless to say, we stop often for water and hike slowly. Sweat pours from the brims of our hats and we muse at the dry salt collecting around our mouths. Occasionally, we come across water pumps where we replenish our water supply and pour some over our heads.

Carolyn (Burf) and Jim Fedorowich. For two days, we camped in their basement, ate all their food, then left. Thanks guys!

These sands were once the sacred grounds of the natives, who believed that the moving sands would also move and rejuvenate their spirits. As we walk through the waves of heat and drifted dunes, we can imagine a covered wagon making its way along this trail, or natives appearing high above us on their painted horses. Kiche Manitou, as the area is called, denotes this spiritual meeting place. We hike into what is called Devil's Punch Bowl. Adding the six-kilometre return hike seems much further, as the heat not only pours from the sky, but is also reflected back from the sands three fold. At this point, a bowl-shaped depression, 45 meters deep, holding an eerie pool of green water appears before us. Underground streams from the Assiniboine River create these ever-moving pools in this dry sea of sand.

We hike back to the campground and strip, trading our salty, wet clothing for bathing suits. We walk along another path, another kilometre, to a lake. There, we immerse our stinging bodies into the cool water—what a relief!

Back at the campsite, I make sausages, sauerkraut, and potatoes. Maria makes a salad and we gorge ourselves. The sun has sapped our energy and we are aching to lie down. Before retiring, Maria and I take a short walk around the park to finish off the kilometres. The moon shines brightly in the sky, and to our delight, no mosquitoes! Our campsite is situated in a cozy circle of trees, protecting it from the hot sun in the day and giving privacy at night. The fire pit that sits in the centre of the plot is the focal point for us. It has a perfect grill for cooking and a swing grate for loading the

Billy, always up early to start the fire.

wood and keeping the food warm. Tonight, the tents face the open hearth and our chairs, pulled close together, give us a sense of security. What would we do without each other? Despite the peacefulness of this night, I feel lonely for home. It is so hard to believe we have made it this far... and to believe we are in this little oasis of trees in the prairies.

July 14

Place: Carberry to Wellwood
Distance: 20 km
Wildlife: Black and yellow snake, squirrel, and deer

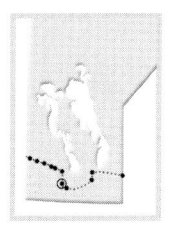

It is another hot day. Thankfully, we are tenting in a shaded spot and have protection from the sun while we pack our tent. For the first time this trip, our van won't start and we envisage a long wait for help to arrive. One of the park staff who just happens by has jumper cables and we are soon on our way to Carberry, the starting point for the day. We have been warned about tornadoes on the prairies, especially with such heat. It is a new threat and we scan the sky for 'funnel' clouds before stepping from the van onto the dusty grid road to Wellwood.

Maria and I are the only two to hike this morning. Nora is feeling ill and Heike and Nicholas have decided it is just too hot. We watch the van drive ahead of us, kicking up rolls of dust that float away over the flat blocks of yellow canola fields. We watch the van as it grows smaller then comes to a stop. There is not a bend in the road, and it is the first time we can see the van at the five-kilometre mark ahead. As Nicholas says, "You can see your dog run away for three days." Maria and I walk along, passing the occasional farmhouse and long stretches of brilliant, yellow canola. We snap pictures of ourselves in the chest-high plants, ducking deep into their stalks upon hearing approaching vehicles. With faces next to the plants, I am surprised at how much they smell and resemble broccoli that has gone to seed.

A long irrigation pivot resembling an overgrown 'Orville Wright' plane is situated in the middle of the field. We crawl back up onto the road and continue walking as a four-wheeler rolls along beside us. It is Brace and Myles Olmstead. This father and son are going out to move the irrigation pivot. Brace talks to us about this 'canola' business and we chat about our trek. The young boy, brown-faced and bright-eyed, flashes us a wide smile as he jumps off the four-wheeler, grabbing a pair of pliers to help with the task. As we walk farther up the road, we see a monument to the Olmstead settlers who first came to this area to farm.

(from Nora's diary)
I join Maria and Mom for the trek in the heat. I love Manitoba. It is so different from anything we have seen so far. For as far as you can see, it is flat. To the left and right of us are fields upon fields of yellow canola, blue flax and silvery wheat. We can't stop taking pictures. We even dare to crawl through the canola to get a few pictures, only to dive flat as tractors drive by. When we get out, yellow flecks cover our clothes. It isn't hard to tell who made those big flattened indents in the field.

Another thing about Manitoba, the people sure are friendly. Every car, truck, tractor, you name it, stops and the people wave, interested to know what we are doing. Once, a man named John Hoffer, stops us. "What is this, Hike 2000?" he asks. We talk for almost an hour on this dusty farm road. Billy drives up beside us and John borrows his mouth organ and plays us a tune. With the yellow fields waving in the warm wind behind him, it is a perfect sight. He is absolutely amazing on this instrument. We learn that he lives on a Hutterite colony, where all goods are common. Each person has his or her own role, and the leaders of the colony are voted into their positions. Hutterites marry other Hutterites. There are many, many colonies throughout the world. Once they are married, they cannot divorce for any reason at all. John tells us about his colony where he is head and watches over the farming aspect of their society. I am very interested in everything he tells us and would love to visit their colony.

Later down the road, we are stopped by two cousins, Mark (23) and Travis (19), who offer us a ride to where we are going. Instead, Travis gets out of his truck

Cousins Mark and Travis from the nearby Hutterite community. On this open stretch of prairie land, we exhchange views on our very different ways of life. It was a warm, heartfelt meeting.

and walks with us as Mark drives the truck beside us, swerving precariously close to the ditch as he tries to keep a conversation going with the rest of us. They are also from the Hutterite community and were looking for the supper that John is supposed to bring them after a long day of clearing fields. They are just like us, even though their lives are so different. They stay in the same community all their lives, don't really travel or become involved with the outside society. But, they seem happy and satisfied with less. They are such good sports, trading spots with each other to walk with us, laughing and joking the whole time.

We get to the van at 20 kilometres, then drove to Neepawa campground where we get a very 'warm' welcome from the 'happy' guy at the campground. He cautiously gives out the code to the washroom. We set up our tent, then drive to the Garden Path Bed and Breakfast, owned by Joe and Glenda MacPhee, who were our neighbours in West Gore when they lived in Nova Scotia. The old Victorian style house is surrounded by an intricate design of beautiful gardens. Glenda is very gifted at gardening and even has the honour (and stress) of being the head gardener for the Neepawa Lily Festival. Neepawa is the lily capital of the world. Glenda and Joe have a whole table set up with cold cuts and salads for us. Then comes strawberry shortcake, a first this summer. It is well after midnight when we finish eating. With offers to come back for breakfast, we crawl into the van and are off to the 'friendly' campground.

July 15

Place: Wellwood to Neepawa
Distance: 22 km
Wildlife: Flock of pelicans, deer tracks, snakes, dragonflies, crayfish, first ripe raspberries.

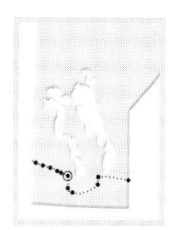

(from Maria's diary)
After a filling breakfast of fruit salad and muffins at the Garden Path, we pile into the van and are led through the back roads to Wellwood, where we'll begin our hike. Mom, Nora, Nicholas, and I set off over the dusty road to Neepawa, the lily capital of the world. Heike decides to stay and explore the town for the day.

The road is bordered with tall poplar trees and raspberry bushes that hang with ripe fruit. Our boots make imprints on the soft gray silt, as we make our way through the small hills and expansive fields. We stop to check out the corral where cattle have probably been branded and given shots. We then make our way into the canola field for another picture. We pass herds of horses, branded to their homestead, grazing in tall grasses. We line the barbed-wire fence to get a closer look, and the stallion first whinnies and comes to check us out. His hair is a glistening copper, and his muscles ripple under the sheen of his coat. After finding we are not a threat, the mares venture over to the fence to have a look. Sixteen mares, thirteen foals and one stallion line one side of the fence, and four hikers line the opposite side—both sides interested and inspecting each other. What beautiful horses.

We pull ourselves away to continue walking only to be interrupted by the wild honking of our van, which is coming down the road behind us. We've missed our turn and are about two kilometres out of our way. Joe is with Billy, and has wonderful sandwiches, lemonade and cinnamon buns for our lunch. Nicholas stays behind so Mom, Nora and I continue on.

The road seems long as we hike through the fields, making up songs along the way. We laugh at our lyrics, but begin to feel a bit scared that we are going crazy when we spot pterodactyl flocks in the sky. We later find out they were pelicans, which still seems odd to us. The sky becomes dark as we reach the highway on our last leg to the campground. Thankfully, we reach the van before the rain or lightning, grab our gear and quickly head for the Garden Path. Wade Lake, from Walton, Nova Scotia, now living in Winnipeg, has arrived on the afternoon bus, ready for the big adventure of hiking.

After warm showers, Joe and Glenda treat us to supper. After dinner we play crokinole as the lightning and thunder crash outside and water pours from the sky. Thankfully, we are not yet in our tents. Glenda and I try on dresses that will be used for the open house the next day. After another long visit, we are driven home to crawl into our tents, which, surprisingly are dry. We quickly fall asleep.

July 16

Place: Neepawa to Clanwilliam
Distance: 22 km
Wildlife: 2 deer (a buck and a doe), hawk, gopher

We waken to Billy's disgruntled voice, "Anybody up in there? Coffee's on. That would be nice." His sarcasm sets us all into a burst of laughter from inside our wet tents. There are no fire pits at this campground (so, no chance to make coffee), the owner is very unfriendly and the rain has left the ground spongy and full of puddles around our tent; definitely not the nicest thing to wake up to. The stream running behind the tent is full and pours over the cement platform before curving away from us. Wade Lake is sleeping in the little tent beside ours. This is his first day with us and I am sure he must be a little apprehensive about the journey ahead. He is a friend of Nora's from high school days and his new enthusiasm and dry wit give us a lift.

(from Wade's diary)
Today is my first day on the hike, and what a fine day it is. The six of us are unloaded on the outskirts of Neepawa, Manitoba. After a short-lived problem with the pedometer, we head up the trail. I say up, because we are within sight of hills, a rare occurrence in prairie Manitoba.

There isn't a whole lot of action until we see the deer, or it sees us, and bolts for the sanctuary of the woods. I get my first picture taken in a canola field. After that, there are more canola fields, one of which is rather big (the biggest I've ever seen), and split by our trail, which makes for a nice picture.

Not much to report until our halfway point. Then, we get a big surprise. Billy has made friends with the locals in Bethany, who turn out to be amazingly nice people. Ed Rourke is a bit of a comedian who steals the words out of Billy's mouth. Isabel, his wife, has juice and coffee ready for us, which absolutely makes our day. Before we leave, they give a tour in their pick-up truck of their quaint little town of 25 people. If you ever have a chance to be in Bethany, stop in and say hi, because they will really enjoy it. Tell them Hike 2000 sent you.

Following our tour, we are back on the trail. Maria and Nicholas opt to stay with Billy and catch up on some much needed sleep. To be honest, they don't really miss much on the trail. The four of us meander our way up to Clanwilliam, where we meet our second set of hospitable people. Walter and Shirley Syslak treat us to a snack and some refreshments. Walter has a lot to tell about the railroad, since he has lived in Clanwilliam throughout his life.

Maria and Glenda model dresses to be worn at the Garden Path's open house.

"I was born in Clanwilliam, Manitoba, in 1933. The railroad would have come through Clanwilliam just about the turn of the century. My grandparents came to this area in 1893 and they came up on the CPR, which came to Minnedosa. When the CNR came to Clanwilliam in 1893, it wasn't a town yet. The town came into conception sometime just after the turn of the century, because of the railroad. The trains came through here on a regular basis Monday, Wednesday, Friday, and went north from Winnipeg. The train came back on Tuesday, Thursday and Saturday. My Dad was a cattle buyer and we used to bring our cattle here into the stockyard and load the cattle. He would drive the freight trains to Winnipeg with the cattle. It would take him a day to get there, a day in the stockyard there and a day to come back. He'd be back the evening of the third day. My mum was always saying, 'How'd you make out, Dad?'

The passenger train came through on Monday, Wednesday and Friday. When the bell rang at four o'clock at school, we ran all the way across town to the railroad station that was on this corner and met the train at 4:30. The old train came puffing in and there were always passengers and, of course, the freight came off. We would just go watch them taking off the freight. The newspapers came in from the city and once and a while somebody would get off the train and they'd ask, 'Do you know so and so, and where do they live?' We were sort of the local authorities. We'd even offer to carry their stuff for them.

My Dad left Norway when he was 16 years old. He came to Clanwilliam because there was a Norwegian farmer here that took boys from Norway to work for him. Then, my father eventually got his own farm. When he arrived, he had a trunk and ten dollars. He came all the way from Norway, rode all the way across Canada from Halifax to Neepawa. When he got to Neepawa, he had to change trains to come to Clanwilliam. He saw some very nice buns in the window of a bakery and he decided he was going to break his ten-dollar bill, so he bought himself a bun. He always told that story.

In winter there was a lot of snow. They used to put up railway fences to keep the railroad open and there would be just tons of snow. We used to go over there and dig in that snow and dig tunnels. I swear, the snow banks would be 20 feet high."

Shirley gives me a tour of her house and shows me their collection of antiques, the main things being their old oil lamps. Shirley gives us the use of her crokinole board, much to the appreciation of Heike. Before leaving, I am given wine glasses from their collection. This has been such a surprise meeting. We feel totally at home here with these complete strangers. We thank them, then make our way to Minnedosa.

When we reach Minnedosa, we are welcomed wholeheartedly, and are given a great deal by the kind people running the Minnedosa campground. We set up shop and head for shelter as the rain is upon us again. While we're cooking supper, Ed and Isabel arrive, which is a wonderful treat! They come bearing gifts of food. The party ends following a little music and a 'lotta bug flingin,' as Wade would say. Glenda and Joe MacPhee, from Neepawa, show up bearing gifts of strawberries as well. With everyone beat from a most adventurous day, we head off to bed. "If this is any indication of how the rest of the trip will be, then I will thoroughly enjoy my time with the hike," Wade remarks, as he crawls into his tent after another day on the trail.

July 17

Place: Erikson to Sandy Lake
Distance: 26 km
Wildlife: 'Mock hawk,' snakes, herd of dragonflies, and a large bear.

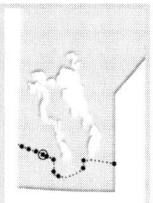

We are blessed with sunshine this morning and the freshness of a 'fall' day. The facilities at this campground in Minnedosa get a 'ten' on our rating scale, with hot showers, big fire pits and sheltered picnic spots. I treat the gang to a breakfast of pancakes and strawberries covered in warm syrup.

As I finish my phone calls to Mum and John, Ed Rourke, the friend we made in Bethany, arrives. He has new potatoes for us. Billy hinted yesterday that he would crawl over a mile of broken glass for a new potato. I guess his small hint worked. Ed and Isabel have showered us with gifts since we met them on the trail in Bethany. If only we could bring them with us.

Soon we are on our way to Erikson to begin our day's journey. It is twenty to two in the afternoon. A late start, but we really don't care. The air is fresh and cool and who's looking at a watch, anyway. The trail begins along a golf course in Erikson, then winds away from the village, through shrubs, borders, and fields of rye and wheat. The path, for the most part, resembles the road down to 'the little house' in Caribou. This is the old railway line which once had two trains a day picking up grain from the storage bins. Another train carried passengers and, at times, cattle were carried to the market place.

Nora, Maria, and I chat about life as we hike along. When you have five hours a day to walk together, there is not a lot you leave out. Nicholas and Wade walk along behind, discussing music. Heike is spending the day catching up on some letter writing in the van with Billy. I am amazed at the number of florescent blue dragonflies along the trail, and also by the snakes that scuttle into the tall grass as we pass. At the 13.5-kilometre mark, we spot our beloved van. Billy and Heike are there waiting. It is five o'clock. We climb into the van and enjoy a gourmet lunch of rye bread, salami, dill pickles, and cheese. This has to be the best trail lunch we have made ourselves in a while.

Back on the trail, we are off to Sandy Lake. Billy, Heike and Nicholas go ahead to set up camp and begin preparations for supper. It is here that the journey becomes interesting. No sooner are we on the trail, than we hear a horse whinny. No sign of horses here! We discover where the noise comes from—a hawk circling overhead. I whinny back, it copies...I laugh...it copies...I whinny...it copies....I laugh uncontrollably...it copies my laugh to a 'T.' This, I must say, is the closest I come to wetting myself on the trail during the whole trip. I name it the 'mock hawk.'

On we go, past lakes and fields. At Rackham, we meet a man on his way home from the berry field. He tells us that we are standing right where the old station used to be. There was also a post office, two grain elevators, and a two-room schoolhouse with 60 students. The grain elevator burned. The only sign of a village here is one abandoned house, now grown over with bushes. The man who has lived here all of his life is Ukrainian. His parents were homesteaders, coming here before the roads.

At the 20-kilometre mark, we begin to tire. I invent a game to occupy our minds; we will think of songs starting with every letter of the alphabet. We come to the letter "V." Nora belts out, "V...A...C...A...T...I...O...N." Maria and I join her in our loudest voices. It's so great that no one can hear you along the trail. So, on with the song... "V...A...C...A...T..." STOP! A bear! The song suddenly ends. A huge black bear stands on the track in front of us, staring. Impulse? Run! No, we shouldn't run. We back up slowly, questions flying...Is it male or female? Does she have cubs? Is she lactating? The bear moves off to the right. Do black bears circle like polar bears? Do we have food? On and on…Next move. Do we wait and go by, or do we detour?

I go back to check out the detour route. Nora, Maria, and Wade join me. There is no question what to do now, as they hear a cry in the bushes. Wade throws rocks to test the wetness ahead of us. They splash and sink. It doesn't matter; we have to go. Down over the steep bank through bushes and through the swamp we scramble. We crawl up onto the highway on the other side of the swamp. We are soaking wet, but relieved that we are not being followed. We are wearing our bear whistles and have been tooting them but I wouldn't want to depend on them as a life-saving device. When we feel it is reasonably safe, we divert back to the railway line. It is after 8:00 and the sun is low in the sky. Along the trail we meet the Millers, a couple out for an evening bike ride. She tells us we are the first hikers they have seen on this trail.

Billy is waiting for us at the 26-kilometre mark. We are relieved, as usual, to see the van. Back at the campsite Heike is starting supper and Chris Milne has arrived for a visit. He is the trail coordinator for the Rossburn Subdivision trail. Chris is a tall, blonde, soft-spoken man who is more than willing to please us. Before leaving, he invites us for breakfast at the home of his parents. There are two things we never turn down: a place to sleep and food. We will certainly take Chris up on this generous offer. The temperature tonight has dropped to about 5°C. Brrr—back into my Newfoundland long johns. Before going to bed, we go over to the old toilet that is falling down. The usual one is too far to go in the dark. It is so spooky to go into this decrepit building. Not only do I think of bats finding a home here, but the thought of a snake or even the intrusion of a bear hurries my visit.

July 18

Place: Sandy Lake to Elphinstone
Distance: 13 km
Wildlife: another pterodactyl (ok, pelican..), loons, garter snake

(from Heike's diary)
Waking up today is a journey in itself. I have to come back

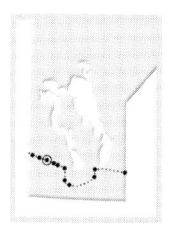

Earl Symonds and I, dressed in our identical train clothes, visit his train room at his home in Sandy Lake, Manitoba.

from some far away place and take a while arriving in the real world. Decamping and packing is a relatively swift affair with the prospect of breakfast at Chris' parents' cabin. There, we meet Chris' parents, Rita and George Milne, Jim and Beryl, who are visiting from England, aunt Elizabeth and Uncle Boyd and their children, Rachel and Matthew. Nicholas and Matthew soon find that they have a lot of interests in common: kicking balls and strumming guitars. Apart from all of these new people, there are Newfoundland superdogs Annie, Ceilidh and Bridie as well as "Cockerpoo" Rusty. The breakfast is delicious and plentiful.

Chris has promised to take me to Earl Symonds, a former railway man. We drive to his home. He is waiting and jibes me for being late. Being a station agent he tells me, when a train is arriving at ten, it arrives at ten, not one minute before or two minutes after. I'm not sure, in the beginning, how to take this man, but soon warm to his humour and we spend hours talking about the railway. He is a tall man, wearing a railroad t-shirt and hat. He throws me a similar outfit to wear for my visit. He has re-constructed his entire basement into a world of trains. Trains run under mountains, up and down valleys, over bridges and in and out of stations. With a flick of the switch, he delights in the switchovers and flashing railway crossings as trains pass in perfect timing. Off handedly, I ask him if he is married. He says, "I had a wife, but when I suggested I put just one train line up through the floor to the living room and back down, she left me." He is a George A. Crawford and Garnet Buell kind of guy. He loves trains. He shows me into his train library where we spend time leafing through the many books on the prairie railway. He talks about his life and the railway:

"I came from a little place about a thousand feet down the hill from the station in Sandy Lake. When I was 14 years old, I walked up the hill to the station and that's where I spent another 18 years of my life. And where you stayed in the campground, that was where I grew up, in that station. Where the CN Park is, is where the station was located. There was a water tank here. My dad was the station agent here for 30 years. The station, in those days, was the focal point of the community. The roads were almost non-existant, especially in the wintertime. When snow would block the roads on the flats, there would be no transportation in or out. In fact, farms around here in the wintertime used to get snowdrifts 20 feet deep. Today, the snow just keeps on blowing, but in those days, it just kept piling up. I could show you pictures of snow banks 15 feet high, right around the station.

Everything came to the station, the telegraph, parcels, the mail came by train; that was the only way to get in and out of town, by train. Very few people had cars then. In the forties, cars started to come. Going back in the books to 1908, there are sections that are just blank about the Sandy Lake station and nobody seems to know.

When I started railroading, I started in Grand Beach as an assistant agent. Whenever anybody asked me what I was going to do when I grew up it was, 'be a station agent like my daddy.' I always said that ever since I was two feet high. I just loved the railroad; there was nothing else in my life.

And even my subjects at school, if you look, they all seem to come from the railroad thing…geography, arithmetic; I was never good in spelling. On the telegraph, you used a different kind of language. When I was 18 years old (they say you have to be old enough to hang because you had to be responsible for the handling of trains), I was a telegrapher, like the middleman between the dispatcher and the train crews. The dispatcher would give train orders and I would give them to the train crews—sometimes on the fly, it all depended on the type of order. I don't think that they ever hanged anybody in Canada for a train wreck but they certainly put a few people in jail.

One accident was the McDougal wreck. The Number Four passenger train going east was stopped at McDougal station, coming in to the double track. The rule says that you deliver the meat order to all trains that arrive from one direction when there are two trains involved. When Number Four came in, he gave it the order, so it was standing at the station, and then he gave the counter special a green light. The counter special had already received the order previously, so, when he saw the green light, he figured that he was going to be able to be advanced against Number Four, so he just opened up his engine and they hit at 60 miles an hour and killed 30 people. The Canoe River wreck out in B.C. they blamed on the operator, and he sued the Winnipeg Tribune because he was actually innocent. It was during the Korean War and Arthurton was the operator at Red Pass junction. He made an error in the train order, and because of that error, the two trains hit. That's where John Diefenbaker got his start. John Diefenbakerbaker was a lawyer in Prince Albert, and he defended Arthurton and got him off.

Diefenbaker was a smart man. He said, what if Arthurton was repeating his order and a bird sat on the wire and shorted out the line? Anyway, that's the story.

Eventually, I got to Rivers as a terminal operator. That was in the sixties. I was promoted and then it was my job to close the stations, which was a sad job but I was one of the people picked to do it. I came to Sandy Lake here on a Wednesday. Closing the station was very political. I stayed right in this house. Wednesday morning I called my office and I was told we got the order to start closing stations and the first one on the list was Sandy Lake. I was right here. This was the first one I did. Of course, my dad had been retired for 10 or 15 years. When we closed it, we stood on the platform here and cried."

It is well beyond lunchtime when I leave Earl's house. I am wearing my new train t-shirt and have brought along two railway books which I will treasure as part of my own collection. Back at the Milnes' cottage, lunch of pizza, lasagna and salad has been served. The hike 2000 crew are relaxing by the fire. It is pouring rain outside and the Milnes offer us a place to stay for the night. As much as we would love to stay in the comfort of this cottage and enjoy their company, we cannot get behind in our already tight schedule.

(from Heike's diary)
We get going eventually, with flashlights in our packs, just in case. Chris hikes with us, too, which is yet another one in a series of highlights. Without him, we wouldn't know we were crossing a buried rail bridge just after the start of our hike. Chris also points out a pioneers' cemetery a bit off on our right-hand side, dating from the late 1800s. The trail takes us through undulating farmland interspersed with small lakes and boggy areas. We see (and hear!) a pair of loons and another pelican, and cross two trestles altogether. It was a very satisfactory day for me personally. Just before the end of today's hike, after the crossing of a trestle, within view of the van, I find a snakeskin. When I pick it up we catch a glimpse of a little garter snake slithering away into the grass.

It is at the end of our 21 kilometres, in Elphinstone, that we meet the Kiliwniks. Billy is waiting in the little park and informs us there is no campground here. However, a lady by the name of Anne, who was walking her dog and spied our van, has gone to check on the Lions Club Hall as a spot for us to take refuge. We wait for her return. With a positive answer, we load into the van and follow Anne to the hall.

Susan and her mother, Anne Kiliwnik. Until tonight, "Elphinstone" was only a name on a map. Here, in the arms of its people, we feel as if we've come home.

Waiting to greet us there are Anne's husband, Walter, their daughter, Susan, granddaughter Sarah, and Sarah's friend, Desiree. Susan snatches up all of our wet towels and hurries off to wash and dry them. Walter and the young girls stick around to watch us go through our supper-making routine. It is a treat to have an oven and two helpers, Sarah and Desiree, to help me make a cherry pie and hot biscuits. They are so enthralled with the success, they try making them again when they go home. Walter puts on a pot of coffee and we sit and chat until supper is ready.

Nora lifts the fiddle from its case and Maria joins me on the guitar. Soon we are singing and pulling our new friends from their chairs to dance with us. Anne and Susan arrive back with not only clean but folded towels, the likes of which we haven't seen in months.

As we finish supper, we are delighted to have Chris Milne drop by to see how we're doing. We talk late into the night before Chris drives back to Sandy Lake. The Kiliwniks invite us to breakfast at the Elphinstone Hotel. The hospitality in this small town is overwhelming. As I crawl into my sleeping bag on the floor of the hall, I think about this place, 'Elphinstone,' that was only a name on the map until tonight, and here, in the arms of its people we feel as if we are coming home.

July 19

Place: Elphinstone to Oakburn
Distance: 21 km
Wildlife: Many snakes, ducks and ducklings

(from Nora's diary)
I am having the most amazing day today. From start to finish, it is fantastic, all because of the friendliness of the Manitoban

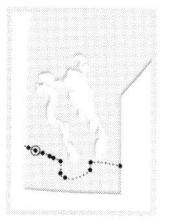

people. We start our day in the Elphinstone Hotel, where we are treated to breakfast of eggs, sausage, bacon, toast, and drinks. In return, we decide to get the whole hotel involved in a dance and sing along. Mom and I have been invited to see Nestor's grain business (which is great) and he returns with his fiddle. I play a tune, then Nestor, Jack, and John all take turns, enticing us to bounce around the restaurant, inviting people drinking coffee we have never seen before to dance. Mom and I grabbed a lady who was sitting at the bar and circle around, only later realizing she is the hotel manager. She must be having fun, though, because she gives us all souvenirs to take with us. Jack ends up bringing his guitar over to the spontaneous party.

We have a great time, and stall leaving as long as possible. We must have hugged everyone goodbye at least 50 times. As we leave, more and more people start walking with us. At first there is Silvia (a fantastic lady with a wonderful sense of humour), and Dennis (also friendly and very knowledgeable about the hiking trail). Then Jack runs up with his friend Joe (they had plans to practice their music today) and walks with us for a bit, then turns around part way. From the distance we can see adventurous Susan (who now feels like a sister) running down the hill, her long blond hair bouncing behind her. 'Pick me up in a hour,' we hear her yell to Walter, who was our Lions Club host for the hall the night before. The mood on the trail is excellent.

As we walk through a green valley, with a river over-flowing beneath us, there comes Chris Milne, bounding over the hill to our right, who joins us for the rest of the walk. Before our halfway point, Anne, with Sarah, and Desiree, meet up with us and walk to where the road joins the trail. In a cloud of dust, Nestor pulls up in his huge grain truck, opening the levers to spill grain into our cupped, waiting hands. The grain, like confetti, is thrown into the air, and we let it fall on our heads. We are so happy.

We continue on to Menzie, our halfway point, by ourselves, as the others have to work. What a pleasure it is to have them walk with us.

The clouds are hanging low in the sky and we keep up a constant chatter about where there might be a culvert to crawl into in this long stretch of prairie land should a tornado touch down. We have been given all the precautions about the warning fluorescent colour of the sky and the fast-moving swirl of clouds. Our eyes are trained now on this moving mass of clouds that seems within reach of our hands. I believe that here on the prairie, we can see so much of the sky that we are more aware of its constant changes.

(from Nora's diary)

As we walked along the trail, we could see two people standing on the trail, pulling chairs out of the trunk of their car. 'Who were they?' we wondered. Our new fright is twisters and tornadoes, so, naturally, they must be twister-chasers. Coming closer, the most amazing sound hits our ears. Perfectly in sync, Jack and Joe are welcoming us into Menzie with a fiddle and accordion tune. They are super! Mom and I take hands and spin around the road, then break apart, grabbing the others for a dance. What a welcome!!

After our break, we continue down the track, then stop abruptly. There, on the trail, scratched into the dirt with a railway stake, are the words, 'Welcome to Menzie, Hike 2000.' The goodness of the people here never ends! And the goodness just keeps coming. To our surprise, Anne and Walter, who have cherries and juice for us, meet us in Menzie. They had called ahead to Oakburn and set up a place for us to stay—an ice-rink—definitely a first!

When we reach Oakburn, people are scurrying around inside the rink, preparing for their upcoming homecoming. Before going out to supper in Oakburn, we stop into Shirley and Peter's antique shop. They have an amazing collection of old radios, furniture, shoes, bottles—everything. Shirley even gives us some squares for dessert. While eating supper at the Oakburn Restaurant, who should show up but Chris Milne. He is going to join us at some point of our trip, we hope.

Walter Kiliwnik

Back at our ice rink, Walter, Anne, Susan, Desiree, and Sarah from Elphinstone all show up with strawberry daiquiris. We sit back and relax as the people from Oakburn string Christmas lights over the dance floor. This place will look amazing for the big party. Saying goodbye to the Elphinstone people is so sad. They are so humble, giving and kind. We are left alone in the rink. Mom, Maria, Heike, Wade and I sneak into the rink with Chris. There, in the solemn darkness, Chris walks back and forth playing his bagpipes. I can't get the lump out of my throat.

We all go outside to see Chris off and I have another first—I have now seen the northern lights. The sky glimmers and dances like a curtain around us, all of the strands of light originating from directly above us, to enclose us like a lampshade. We huddle together in the crisp, cool air, watching in wonder.

From start to finish, this day has been amazing, and there will never be another one like it. The generosity of the people today has been overwhelming. I am already sad at the prospect of leaving.

July 20

Place: Vista to Birdtail
Distance: 22.5 km
Wildlife: Many snakes, gopher, fox

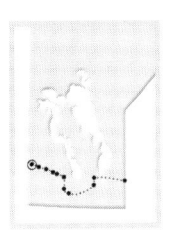

It is five to eight and Billy is itching to go. We are in the trophy room of the Oakburn rink, and have been invited to breakfast at the local tavern. We slowly drag ourselves from our sleeping bags and dress for breakfast. Peter, the schoolteacher, Janet and Albert are waiting for us. A man who could be the twin of George Matthews of the West Gore Hardware store is also there. Nicholas is too young to sit in the tavern, so Wade, Nora and Maria join him in a small side room. We are served eggs and sausage, toast and home fries, and all the coffee we can drink.

The talk turns to rattlesnakes and whether we should worry about them on the trail. The general feeling is that there will be rattlesnakes and to guard against them; we should get some stovepipes to wear on our legs so we won't get bitten. This idea sends us into a frenzy of questions and gales of laughter. The thought of hiking 20 kilometres with stovepipes on our legs is too much. I suggest I will have to get an elbow so I can at least bend my knees. Not knowing whether these people are serious or not, I plan a stop at the next hardware store just to see if I can, in fact, fit my leg into a stovepipe.

Chris Milne arrives to show us the trailhead in Vista. He is more than happy to direct us as I drive along with him in his car, the Hike 2000 van in pursuit. I get the feeling from Chris that he is disgruntled with his job and I sincerely invite him to join us if he can. We stop at a little general store in Vista where the owner comes out to greet us in a big straw hat. This could be the setting of any Western movie. The store, with its wide wooden planked floor, has barrels of dry goods, large jars of candy sticks, boots, and kettles. There is a true feeling of the old west in this town.

Just before noon, we are on the trail, which parallels the road to Rossburn. The trail is overgrown with white and yellow sweet clover that reaches over our heads. Dark blue clover covers the dry ground and, sometimes, the woody stems wind around our boots, tripping us. Snakes slide into the tall grass occasionally. Suddenly, a gopher is running straight down the path toward me. It jumps up on my boot, clunking its head on my leg. I am not sure who is more surprised, the gopher or me, but we race off in opposite directions. It is a little déjà vu of the partridge that pursued me in northern New Brunswick. We later learn that a lot of animals are rabid in this area, a comforting thought.

We meet Billy in Rossburn for lunch. Chris joins us and escorts me to the local hardware shop. I have become paranoid at the prospect of an encounter with a rattlesnake on the trail and go in to check out the stovepipes. The store clerk tells me that coils for dryers will work better. I have no idea if they are telling the truth or can tell a sucker when they see one. In any case, I'm not giving them the satisfaction of watching me try those clothes dryer coils on my legs, and decide to check for something in Silverton.

As I return toward the van, there is our angel, standing on the corner with a parcel of food for us. Walter has driven all the way from Elphinstone with a Caesar salad and strawberries. Anne couldn't come with him but has prepared the food for us. We are so happy to see him again. His clear, blue eyes are the most beautiful I have ever seen and his smile you can see from down the street. The kindness of these people never stops.

After lunch we head for Birdtail, on the far side of the Waywayseecappo Reserve. The trail bed changes to rough gravel and we scour it for collectibles. There are amber and coal black stones which we tuck into the pockets of our packs. We pass fields of cows. A deep gorge on out right appears lush and green in contrast to the dryness of the trail. As we reach the grain elevator in Birdtail, we can hear people talking and children laughing.

(from Nicholas' diary)
When we got to the end of the road, we see Billy, Wade and five other people taking pictures at the end of our trail. Their names are Cody, who is five years old, Kayla, who is going into grade five, their mother Pat, and their grandmother, June. The woman taking the pictures is actually the mayor of Rossburn. We walk along the bridge and everyone is nervous about Cody being along the edge of it so we walk together. Pat tells us that she isn't giving us a choice; we are going to eat supper at her house. Needless to say, we eat supper at her house.

Wade Lake with Pat, Kayla and Cody in Birdtail.

June brings out some cold Kokanee beer when we return from the trestle bridge. Soon, Kayla calls to us to come to the picnic table. She puts a white tablecloth over it and brings out cheese, crackers, spaghetti, meatballs and garlic bread. June brings out some whiskey that she shares with Heike. The rest of us are given more cold beer and all the supper we can eat.

(from Nicholas' diary)
Later Cody and I go to his room to play '64' for a while. After that, I get on their trampoline and pull some flips off on it. It is pretty fun. Billy also shows us some stunts on the trampoline.

We find out that Pat has a hair cutting kit and decide to cut my hair. She cuts it pretty short, and it feels much better after that. Then Heike gets her hair cut the same as mine. Then Nora, Wade, Kayla and I play soccer. When I'm hackeying, I set a record of 60. After a while of talking, we have to say our goodbyes. It is so strange. If we had come a different way, we would never have met these people. The only reason we meet them is because Wade had to use their washroom.

The setting sun warms our shoulders as we sit in the yard with these wonderful people on the edge of the Waywayseekapo Reserve. As we were hiking, Cody had tapped on the van door where Billy was sitting. Billy, concerned for him, asked, "Where's your Daddy?" Little Cody points to heaven. For Billy, it was a touching moment.

After supper, Nora, Maria and I offer to help with dishes. We begin discussing Pat's husband, whom we know has died. She tells us that he was a hemophiliac and had received tainted blood. He was HIV positive when they married 11 years before. It was a miracle that she didn't become positive and that they have two children who are AIDS free. As her husband became ill, Pat continued to look after him, sharing his bed and holding him at night. Pat relates, 'He lost his mind first, and lost control of his functions, then went into a coma a week before he died.'

We listen to her story, sitting on the bed beside her, that same bed they had shared and where he had died. The room is airy and cool, curtains floating slightly in the small breeze. Her photo albums lie across the bed open to his pictures, as she pours out her story. Tears brim in our eyes, and fall down our already wet cheeks. She is such a beautiful, strong person. The love she had for this man is unequaled and somewhere God had to be taking that into consideration when he delivered them two healthy babies.

As I enter June's kitchen to say goodbye, I meet her friend, a former railway man. He is an investor, has clients in Siberia and speaks perfect Russian. He tells me Mel Weaver, my railway contact in Rainy River, is dying with a brain tumor. This is so sad. I have spoken with Mel several times and we planned to meet when he was better.

We hug them all goodbye. This has been such a chance meeting. We originally planned to hike from Angesville to Russell, but Chris suggested this hike, and we are so glad he did.

Back in Rossburn, there is a crowd waiting for us. As we get out of the van, feeling a bit guilty, a big burly man standing on the front step says, "Where were you? In Kennetcook or some God damn place?" He, of course, is joking with us. Formerly a police officer in Nova Scotia, serving both Windsor and Stewiacke areas, he knows our small community in West Gore and my home, Caribou. He bought groceries at Dan McLeod's store in Upper Musquodoboit, the same store that delivered our groceries every Friday night when we were kids.

The group in the hall is waiting with strawberry shortcake, shortbread cookies and coffee. Once again, some of the friendliest people on earth treat us. We eat, talk and sing for them. Billy steals a little dance with Marie in the kitchen before they pack up. We are given permission to use the local rink for a shower. We take our turns in one of the big team room shower stalls. The ice is no longer in and the centre resembles a big paddock. There are no lights and we feel our way back to the hall. Chris kindly offers his office as a sleeping spot. We strategically arrange our sleeping bags around the desk and boxes of papers in his office. What a kind guy!

July 21

Place: Russell to Lake of the Prairies Provincial Park
Distance: 16.5 km
Wildlife: bear, gophers, Saskatoon berries

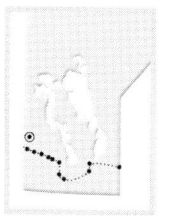

Billy is shocked that he has slept until 8:00 A.M. Chris' office is dark and quiet and everyone is tired from yesterday's hike. The Lions Club invites us to breakfast at the little restaurant in town and we hustle to get ready. Miraculously, by 9:00 P.M. we are completely packed and ready for breakfast. Chris arrives with his bagpipes to pipe us to the restaurant. Now, we feel like true celebrities. As we walk single file behind Chris, I feel a strong sadness come over me. It is our last day in Manitoba, and the people here have showered us with their hospitality. I concentrate now on little things so I won't cry... the little flowers on the sidewalk, the buildings, the back of Billy's legs, marching in time to the piper. Ron Burt and the mayor are waiting. A buffet breakfast has been prepared for us. We fill our plates with eggs, sausages and home fries. We talk about out travels and about the kindness of the Lions Club.

After breakfast, we climb into the van and make one last circle in the U-turn spot of town. There is June, driving in her truck, with little Cody and Kayla. They have driven from Birdtail to find us. If they had been one minute later, they would have missed us. We spill from the van and give them big hugs. We promise to write and invite them to visit us in Nova Scotia. They throw their arms around our necks and hold tight, their little faces pressed against ours. It is hard to imagine that we have known these children less than 24 hours, yet we feel so close to them. Finally, we are on the road, heading out of Manitoba. We look back at the long stretches of grain and long dusty roads and think how blessed we have been to meet such warm and giving people. They will always be special to us.

In Silverton, we stop at the little upholstery shop. I want to find leather to make gaters to guard against snakes. I have a plan in my head what they should look like. We are told a leather worker in Lake of the Prairie may be able to help us. After 11 kilometres down a side dirt road, we reach Lake of the Prairie. As per directions, we find Ernie Thickett working on a saddle in his shop. I tell him my wish and give him the description of the 'snake gators' that I have in my head. He doesn't laugh. That is encouraging. We discuss how high they should be and he measures our legs from the floor to our knees. As he chooses the leather, we watch with great interest. Moose, buffalo, elk, and deer hides are tossed onto the workbench. We discuss which hide would best withstand the clamp of a rattler's jaw. Just the thought of it makes me shudder. He cuts, turns and sews the first one, carefully gluing the seams and placing a drawstring at the top. It is perfect. Now, he will make six pairs as we prepare to hike the wilderness trail that leads directly from behind his workshop.

The trail begins among blackberry bushes, then dissects a large field, which stretches down to the lake and dances with dragonflies, darting in and out of the tall sweet clover. There are hundreds of them! A hawk soars overhead as Nora remarks, 'What a perfect day'. The trail then heads up into the dense bushes. We are aware of snakes and Ernie has also mentioned sighting a bear last week. For me, there is a feeling of pending doom. I can't explain the feeling except that I feel our passage through this area is forbidden. The trail winds out to a road that will take us to another trail to the cliff that Ernie has mentioned. He has seen a bed of snakes there, tells us it will be interesting. The thought of snakes twisting and turning over each other certainly doesn't enthrall me. My fears are soon realized. Directly in front of us appears a very large black bear. He doesn't notice us, and I quietly command, "Back up, don't run." We walk backwards until we are well below the crest of the hill, and then quickly retrace our steps back to the workshop. Maria sits up at the bench and helps glue the final gators. Ernie's dog races into the bushes after stones the size of his head. Tireless, he brings the stone and teases us to throw it again.

We pay for our new gators, and head off to find Spruce Woods Provincial Park. We reach the Saskatchewan border. I look around me at the van of sleeping bodies. I had always imagined the excitement of crossing each border, but now the pull of sleep is much too strong. Maria opens her eyes long enough to pass me her camera.

I climb from the van and take a ceremonial picture of the sign. At Spruce Woods Provincial Park, we chose one of the two remaining campsites. We feast on perogies and Caesar salad from Anne and grilled chicken over an open fire. Strawberry shortcake rounds out the feast. After supper, Nora, Wade, Nicholas, and I go for a walk along the lakeshore and around the cottages and campsites. I never imagined sleeping in such a forested park in Saskatchewan.

July 22 - July 30 — Saskatchewan

Joe Milligan, with his wife Lynn, their baby, Jane, and friend Donna Lyn, leads us along the Trans Canada Trail in Lumsden, Saskatchewan.

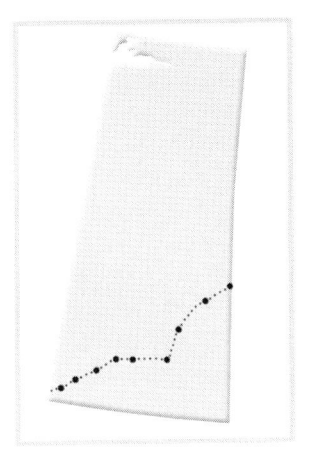

July 22

Place: Good Spirit Lake
Distance: 18.5 km
Wildlife: deer, gopher, dead fox, porcupine

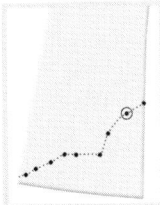

It is still dark and I am lying awake. Far off in the distance, I can hear the howl of coyotes. It seems to be a mother and her pups. Sometimes the sound is of little yelps, then a long, distinct howl. It is my first night to hear them. The sound is what I imagined it would be, here on the prairies.

It is late as I sit in the "queen's seat" watching Billy make his morning toast and coffee. Slowly, I drag myself to the shower line-up. When I return to our campsite, everyone is up and making breakfast. I cook the last egg for Nicholas and prepare a toasted tomato sandwich for myself. The flurry of attention in Manitoba has changed to a very quiet "on our own" feeling.

Billy is teasing Maria about the neatness and compactness of the tent she is folding as she challenges him to do better. It is the typical start to our day—some friendly banter, a recounting of the previous day's activities and a bit of a plan for the day to come. If anyone is out of sorts as they crawl from the tent, the group brings them out of it quickly with a few good laughs. We are so fortunate to be this easy going, with no hang-ups or grumpy moods to deal with all day. With everyone pitching in to make things work, we have become a true team.

Today, I feel sadness for the mountains. Each year, I return to Switzerland to guide hiking tours and now, as we enter Canada's flat lands, I feel a longing for the mountains. How strange!

We drive to Good Spirit Lake, where Donald Gunn was the first white settler. He set up a trading post here in the late 1800s. Our campsite is far from the main entrance, in the quiet tenting area of this park. We select a flat site with a hint of shade, a place to hang our clothesline and a spot relatively close to the waterspout. Today's lunch is Havarti dill cheese with rye bread. Variety, of course, is the spice of life. After lunch, we prepare to hike. The Trans Canada Trail is supposed to be here. We will have to see.

It is extremely hot and our pace is slow. We walk the trail, which borders Good Spirit Lake then winds through the campground. Large trees provide some shade in the afternoon sun. The Trans Canada portion of the trail is a disappointing one-mile stretch that runs along the road to the path gate. The brochure for the trail speaks of wildlife and an extensive trail system. The land here is extremely dry and the threat of grass fires is evident. Back from our hike, we pull on our bathing suits and walk back down the road to the lake. The shore of the lake resembles Little Lake in Caribou Gold Mines, Nova Scotia. The sand is hard packed and very slippery to walk on. Reeds grow in clumps on its surface. We search to find a dry patch of sand to lay our towels on.

The pale blue water is inviting and we walk in. The water is warm and shallow for another half kilometre off shore. Farther out, motorboats buzz back and forth. We lie back in the shallow water, giving up on a deep-water swim. Puffs of cloud float above us. It is a wonderful feeling, lying in this warm water, lazily watching the sky.

Finally, I make the long walk to shore and open my journal. As I think of how it must have been for Donald Gunn as he opened his trading post here, this poem falls from my pen.

Good Spirit Lake
To sit on your shore
Gazing at the pale blue of your waters
I wonder how it was for you, Donald Gunn,
The first white settler here.
Was it this peaceful?
This shallow water over warm sands?
Did you come to this spot
and also gaze at white clouds
Mounding like heaps of cotton balls on the far horizon?
Did Natives slip quietly through these waters
In canoes laden with furs for your trading post?
Did your children also walk barefoot
Where my footprints now lie?
The strong presence of the past hits me on these shores
Does your spirit still stand here
Watching out over this opaqueness?
I feel your quiet eyes watching for the approach of the canoe
Your keen ears listening for the lap of the paddles as they approach,
Perhaps in the light of a pale moon.
I can't imagine harshness here,
Only a strong and steady man
With a heart for his work and a passion for his land and family
If there are spirits, I have been moved by yours
On the shores of your "Good Spirit" Lake
—*July 22nd*

Billy returns to the campsite as Wade, Nora, Maria, Heike and Nicholas and I stretch out on our towels. The sun is lower now, its warmth welcome on our wet bodies.

There is an advertisement for an open air dance tonight by the path entrance. We return to our campsite with intentions of making the long walk to try it out. Unfortunately, when you walk all day, swim, then eat a nice supper, there is an overwhelming need to sleep. We renege on the dancing and go to bed. Long into the night, we hear people returning to their campers, some in "good spirits" others in too many spirits.

We fall asleep to the chorus of a coyote mum and her pups howling in harmony somewhere in the distance.

July 23

Place: Melville
Distance: 17 km
Wildlife: dead skunk, fiberglass buffalo, giant lilies

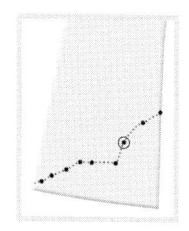

(from Heike's diary)
With last night's coyote concert still ringing in my ears, I psyche myself up for another day on the road. "It's going to be another scorcher," Billy predicts reassuringly. And sure enough, he is right. On the road, I see a dead skunk and a sign warning against the spread of Dutch Elm Disease: "STOP! Do not transport elm firewood." We pass an alfalfa field dotted with little round orange and white tents housing legions of leafcutter bees hired for pollination work. Grain elevators mark the locations of settlements like church steeples.

Again the Trans Canada Trail has put on evasive airs. No positive information to be had as to whether it is possible to hike from Yorktown to Melville along the trail. Apparently this section hasn't left its planning stage yet. So, we decide to move straight on to Melville, set up camp there and see what we can find. Once we negotiate the long and winding access road, we set up camp in a nice spot at a campground run on a trust basis. Firewood is supplied for free, and a ball game is in progress on one of the nearby diamonds.

I decide to take time out due to the effects the heat is having on my system. Nicholas, Maria, Nora and Kathy head out for a hike around the town. Billy, Wade and I soon bump into them again at the superstore, where we are stocking up on ingredients for the "almost shepherd's pie" Billy has promised to make for supper. On leaving the store, Maria suddenly notices she is without the far-traveled and newly shod hiking stick that Iain brought her from the Philippines. Fortunately, it later turns out to have been left behind at the tourist information centre. I feel a sudden yen for Skittles and can't find any, though I search the entire store. The commercial over-stimulation is obviously too much to handle after such a long time in the wild. The air conditioning is cool, and we could hang out here for the rest of the afternoon. But, after a wee spin of the downtown area, it is back to the camp.

Sleeping outside in the shade is out of the question since Saskatchewan bugs like me just as much as any of my Canadian counterparts. So, I have no choice but to conk out in the tent. Between fitful bouts of sleep, I keep waking up drenched in sweat. When I'm finally able to pick myself up and crawl out of the tent, I scrounge an 'apple' from Billy. After my unrest and dehydrating siesta, its effect trebles. Since the preparations for the almost shepherd's pie are under control, there is nothing left for me to do but wake up. Soon, a somewhat sapped looking Wade struggles out of the boys' tent. I know how he feels. We then don't have to wait long for the return of the hikers who met some railroad people on their walk.

We approach the golf course. A group of former railway men are enjoying a cold beer and swapping yarns. I am interested in their railway stories and they invite me to join them. Versions of the same tale overlap as they fill me in on railway history, controversial accidents and life on the train. They tell me that Melville was built around the railroad. First, I talk to Ed Shanks.

"I worked 38 years. I hired on in '49. I used to sell tickets. Melville is one of the larger centres. Population-wise, it is strictly railroad people. We used to have our own ten-passenger trains that worked out of Melville, east and west, north and south. When they started to reduce wages and jobs, they added new equipment. Instead of running a 40-car train, they started running a hundred-car train. We used to live on First Avenue and my mother used to give the hobos food. When I was just a little kid, we lived on the main line and hobos were always there. They would jump off the train down the road and roll into the ditch. There were a lot of them 'riding the rails' we used to call it. The first time I ever rode on the front end of an engine was from Rivers to Melville. I was on a course then and teaching computers to the trackmen. I've seen some derailments that were bad."

Ed's friend Nick Slobojan chimes in.

"I used to like to go out on the road and copy train orders. One train is superior to another. They had one car right next to the cook car, an auxiliary. Being next to the cook car was great. Did you know that even numbers go east and odd

Hiking the Dream

numbers go west? That's with the passenger trains. East trains are superior to the ones running west. Even numbers are superior to odd. If they are both fourth-class trains, the east trains have superiority."

The next table soon fills with railway men just in from their last shift. They invite me to join them on the run to Bigger the next day. How I would love to. They all have a story to tell as they pull up their chairs and pass around the pitchers of beer. Lawrence Kosedy begins to tell me of a railway accident.

Lawrence Kosedy - "The worst one I was on was Boxing Day. On Christmas eve, we made a quick trip to Kenora and coming back, we were on time, so I could go visit family, open presents with the kids and so on. I lined the switch to where it normally went not realizing they had changed it around and I lined it into a bunch of tank cars. I gave the engineer the go ahead and went right into the tank cars with the long nose. When I got into the unit, I just sat down and I looked and it was all black. We hit this tank car and I found out three days later that it had a double wall. We went through the first one, but we didn't go through the second one. It was a tank of gasoline, three of them in a row. If we had gone through that other wall, it would have been around the world in 80 days! I would never be back to tell about it."

Curtis Payment tells me he has been working as an engineer for 23 years.

Curtis Payment - "Trains are up to ten or eleven thousand feet and you only have five minutes at a crossing. That's all you have. When you pull out of a town, you haven't time to get that long train over the crossing. Some day it's going to kill somebody's child. Trains are now running four thousand feet longer than they should be. He tells me about a head-on collision between a freight train and a passenger train. The two guys in the front end of the freight train were killed. They figure that they fell asleep.

There are situations where the train is just too big and too fast. It's not the stopping so much but you want to make sure you don't pull apart. Sometimes

Glen MacLean and Mark Lockholzer offer me a ride on their freight train to Bigger.

you're carrying a mile and three quarters of a train. That's a lot of cars. You have to be very careful that the train will fit in the siding when meeting another train. Now, the siding is 6400 feet. If you're pulling a train that's 6300, that's okay, but if your train is outside the siding, you get a penalty."

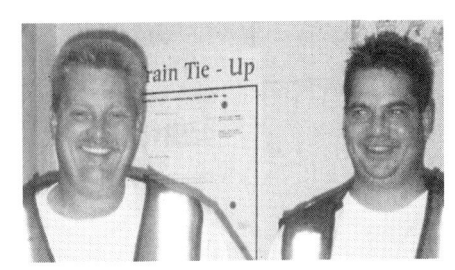

On our way back to the campsite we stop at the railway station to take a few pictures. Glen MacLean and Mark Lockholzer are preparing for their run to Bigger. They tell me if I get to the overpass, they'll pick me up and I can ride on to Bigger, and be back tomorrow. It is such a temptation. I explain to them why I can't take time out from hiking, as much as it is a very generous, exciting offer. Someday, I will ride on a freight train. Glen tells me a bit about his involvement with the trains.

"I am a locomotive engineer for the CN Rail and I operate locomotives to Bigger; that's where I'm going right now. I've been to Winnipeg, Kenora and as far north as Churchill. There are a thousand million stories, you know. In the winter there's all kinds of snow. The rails are so well traveled that the snow never really stays around that much. In Melville now there's 20 east-bounds and 51 west-bounds a day. There are no abandoned rails in this area of Saskatchewan."

Glen's partner, Mark, tells me about a harrowing experience he has had on the train.

"I was going over a switch and I was only going about five or six miles an hour but it shook me right out of the seat when we hit the ties. You run over a frog, that is where the train goes to a different track, over a switch that turns the rails this way or that way. Where these two tracks come together there's a frog. It's a big steel contraption. It cracked and then it let go. These engines are pretty heavy and it hit the ground and I started to jump like this. So that's my own personal experience with cars."

(from Heike's diary)
From one of the railway men, Kathy learns about Violet Cameron, who made a tape of trains. After a superb supper, Billy, Kathy and myself set out to meet Violet, while everybody else engaged in relaxing activities and quests for hygiene facilities. John and Violet Cameron meet us at their beautiful home. Violet has a copy of her tape ready to give to Kathy, and we are treated to a tour of the premises into the bargain. A lily patch in full bloom is reminiscent of Neepawa, now hundreds of miles down the road. We admire Violet's inventive interior design and John's woodcarvings and beautiful furniture, all made from cedar wood. We then view excerpts of some of the videos Violet makes and so catch glimpses of our next destination, the Qu'Appelle Valley.

Violet Cameron is a small, white-haired, bright-eyed woman with an amazing affection for life. She shows me the flowers, crafts and videos she has done. She offers me her tape of railway history and entertains us with her homemade videos of life in the prairies. She has done an excellent job of filming and has added appropriate music for every scene. She and John have an extensive library of music and have organized a regular studio for putting the videos together.

(from Heike's diary)
After we get back to the base, everyone is bundled up into the van for a tour to the Foothill Creamery Ice Cream Shop. I particularly enjoyed Saskatoon pie, a flavor made from Saskatoon berries. Some of us who walk back are treated to a spectacular display of lightning. Land of the living skies!

July 24

Place: Crooked Lake
Distance: 17.5 km
Wildlife: gophers, snakes, horses

It is hot already and the sky looks threatening. We are on our way to Crooked Lake in the Qu'Appelle Valley. Violet has given us a hint of the beauty of this valley in her video but what falls before us as we drop down from the plain is totally unexpected.

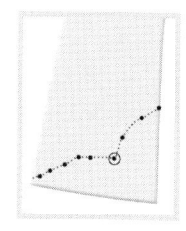

The Trans Canada Highway cuts a trough through the flat lands and we are amazed at the dryness of the prairie grasses. We turn off the highway and head south toward the Qu'Appelle Valley. Suddenly, the flat dry land drops into a long valley. The hills roll back from the valley floor, giving a feeling that we are sitting in a canyon. We travel east a bit, exclaiming about how different the scenery is here. Tall grasses wave in the hot wind that sweeps up the valley and dark clouds build in the distance. On the crest of a hill, horses appear as if on cue in a staged movie taping.

(from Wade's diary)
The valley is surrounded by seemingly never ending rolling hills. After taking pictures, including one of a small herd of horses grazing on one of the bigger hills, we proceed to find one of our nicest campsites yet. We are at the bottom of the Qu'Appelle Valley and right on the lake.

We set up camp in the small field beside the lake. We seem to be alone here and again it is an "honest pay" system. We decide to start out quickly with our hike, which is on the marked Trans Canada Trail. The trail begins in the shade of big trees and then leads out of the park, bordering the secondary road. We hike along in pairs, Wade and Nicholas, Heike and Nora, Maria and I. Crooked Lake is the home to many vacationers who have built along its shore. To our left and on our right, the hills rise abruptly. We come across the following passage, written on a plaque, on our hike:

> AGOOSE
> Agoose, a member of the Sakimay Band,
> was a renowned runner of the late 19th century.
> His Father and his son, Paul, were also runners.
> One of his feats was immortalized by Duncan Campbell Scott in the lines
> "..... Akoose, Fleet of Foot, who in his prime, a herd of antelope
> From sunrise, with our rest
> A hundred miles
> drove through rank prairie
> Coping like a wolf
> Tired them and slew them
> Ere the sun went down...."

The road drops from the flat prairie land to the rolling Qu'Appelle Valley.

Heike, Nora, Maria and I climb to the ridge of one of the hills for a better view of the lake. Heike walks on the crest to see what lies beyond. Nicholas and Wade wait for us at the bottom of the hill. They see no point in making an already hot and tiresome hike any longer. The enclosing clouds and distant roll of thunder warn us to hurry back to our campsite. We are hiking without rain gear today. It is extremely hot and lightening our packs was a risk we decided to take by leaving rain gear behind.

Back at the campsite, Heike is in charge of supper. The rain begins as she sets up the camp stove and puts on the famous lentils as a soup base. Nora and I retreat to the solid washhouse for shelter and to work on the website. Rain pours from the sky and thunder cracks and shakes the building. I peek out of the door to see if everyone is protected. Nicholas and Wade are running for the washhouse on the men's side. Lightning forks through the purple sky and thunder claps around us. Billy, Heike and Maria have found shelter in the van as Nora and I and a little girl huddle on the floor of the washroom. We have been warned of tornadoes following a bad thunderstorm and I wonder just how solid this brick building really is.

For more than 30 minutes we seem to be in the worst of the storm with no time to count between the flashes of lightening and the deafening thunder. I play word games with the five-year old girl cuddled next to me. Her mom must be frantically wondering where she is. I think of the parents who would have rushed to the bomb shelters during the war, clutching children that are not their own. And the children, holding tight to the parents they have never known. The ground would lie above them, void of life, after the bombing. How frightening it must have been. Here, next to this little girl, I pray that the storm doesn't develop into a twister that will tear the roof off our hiding place.

As the noise outside subsides, the washroom door opens and two teenage girls come in. The little girl flies into their arms. They have obviously been caring for her and are relieved to see her safe and dry. The torrents of rain have not yet sunk into the parched ground and little streams run down the hill to our campsite. Heike is out in her full rain gear faithfully cooking our soup, which she has dubbed, 'rain soup.' Puddles have formed on the ground around her feet and raindrops bounce in and out of the pot. She is determined to see it through, as we watch her from the shelter of the van. The rain subsides long enough for us to eat and to clean up our campsite. We retreat to our tent, hoping that this storm won't make a full circle in the night.

July 25

Place: Katepwa, Labret
Distance: 23 km
Wildlife: gophers, chipmunk, dead snakes

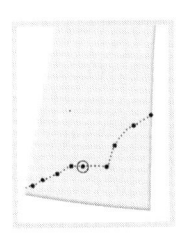

The ground is spongy wet from last night's downpour. I want to put in a few kilometres before the rest get up. Billy joins me on a walk across the grassy campground lawn and along a path leading out of the campground and up the shore of the lake. It is a short walk as mosquitoes chew at our legs, making us uncomfortable and annoyed at their persistence. We give up on this irritating walk and I decide to go pay John a phone call. An annoying woman insists I should get off the pay phone, even though I was here first and haven't been speaking more than three minutes. It is my third encounter with a "phone hog" since entering the province. We are heading west today, farther along the Qu'Appelle Valley. It is a glorious day. We drive by Wolseley, the home of Dr. Ballard and Beaver Lumber. I think of how absurd it is to have the home of Beaver Lumber here on the prairies.

We drive to Indian Head, then head up toward Katepwa Beach. We spy an old abandoned house in a field. We have been looking at the many abandoned houses on the prairie as we drive along, wishing

Little abandoned house on the prairie, one of the many we have been itching to explore.

we had time to explore. We can imagine the trials and excitement of the pioneering families who homesteaded so far from their nearest neighbour. We convince Billy to stop at this house. We have to get this bug out of our system. Maria walks along in front of us, poking the grass with her hiking stick to alert any sleeping snakes. As we approach the house, a flock of pigeons wafts through the paneless windows. In the old kitchen, a large nest clings to the boards on the walls, where perhaps a clock once hung. Little eyes peek over the rim of the packed mud, tiny pigeons, too young to fly. They are probably scared to death with our intrusion. I look out the windows at the stretch of fields and wonder about the family that lived here. Perhaps there was a mother watching her children through this same window.

Heike, Billy, Wade and Nicholas sit patiently in the van on the side of the road. Our constant wish to explore an old prairie homestead is realized.

(from Nora's diary)
Two golf courses surround us in our new, quaint little campsite in Katepwa, which is also at the bottom of a valley. After lunch Maria, Nicholas, Mom and I set out on the Trans Canada Trail over the ridge. Billy and Wade take up their golf challenge on the course adjacent to our campsite. Heike has decided to explore the nearby village. It is very, very warm, and our water is hot in our bottles as well. Yuck!

We walk six kilometres out of our campground and back, then Billy, Wade, Heike and the rest of us jump into the van to go to Labret. Once parked, we grab our hiking sticks and climb (scramble) our way up a steep hill, past 13 crosses, to a small, red and white church overlooking the entire valley. I can not get over the amazing view of rounded, sloping hills, giving way to a large, winding lake.

We walk by a sign reading, 'Who Calls.' Legend has it that long ago a native man left his home village to travel up river. Days later, on his return, he heard his name being called, the voice sounding like that

July 10 - July 30 | **Prairies**

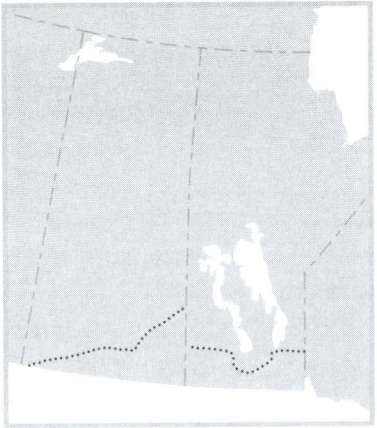

Manitoba - Nora, Maria and Nicholas climb the sand dunes on the Spirit Sands Desert, where the sand reaches a temperature of +55 °C.

Protected against the mosquitoes, Heike entertains us with flute music at Falcon Lake.

Hiking the Dream

Manitoba - Those amazing canola fields.

(Inset right) Nora in a canola field.

(Inset bottom) Field of flax.

Hiking the Dream

Manitoba - (Above) On the trail from Erikson to Sandy Lake we cut through a swamp to escape a black bear and her cub.

(Left) The hot sun at Spirit Sands Desert radiates off the sand, caking our cheeks and mouths in dry, white salt.

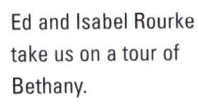

Ed and Isabel Rourke take us on a tour of Bethany.

Hiking the Dream

Manitoba - (Above) Nestor, a grain farmer, takes time to entertain us on the fiddle while we eat breakfast at the hotel.

(Inset) Our hearts were captured by the people of Elphinstone.

Jack and Joe meet us on the trail and welcome us to Menzie with fiddle and accordion.

Hiking the Dream

Saskatchewan - (Below) Violet Cameron, pictured in her garden in Melville.

(Right) The little church at Labret.

On the Trans Canada Trail to Gravelbourg, Nora peers at tracks left by the van the night before as it bumped and lunged its way through the wheat field.

Hiking the Dream

Saskatchewan - Undulating farmland stretches to the horizon 360°. This is the path we navigate to Gravelbourg, van wheel tracks our only clue.

(Inset right) Heike, Kathy and Maria, overlooking the prairie marsh at Buffalo Pound.

(Inset bottom) Little grain storage sheds standing in a row…a familiar sight on the endless prairie.

Hiking the Dream

Saskatchewan - Sunset on the border between Saskatchewan and Alberta.

(Inset) "The Hiker" created from railway spikes by Walter Slater.

Hiking the Dream

Saskatchewan - We bump over a Texas cattle grate on a dirt road and we're in Alberta.

(Inset) Walking down the middle of the road for four kilometres, the setting sun warms our faces. "I can't remember feeling this free in a long time," says Nora.

of his wife. He would answer, "Who calls?" When he returned to his village, he learned that his wife had died two days before. It is said her spirit is still here and sometimes her voice can be heard on the river.

(from Nora's diary)
Back at the campground, a Corona slips easily down my throat, then comes the three-minute shower, and I step into my skirt and blouse. It is a rare night out to a restaurant. However, our exact plans are not to be. All of the doors to the restaurant are locked, but a lady came to the door and gruffly (some may even venture rudely) tells us they are closed because not enough people are there. Instead, a friendly lady at the bar serves us excellent meals—they are great! We chat with a man with a lot of tattoos for a while, then watch him peel away on his motorbike. Some of us head home for bed but, for me, it is an 'interesting' night still in the men's toilet.

There I am, sitting in the men's washroom with Wade, camping chairs set up in a locked stall, electrical cord for the connection to the computer plugged under the door. Other than the drawback that I shouldn't be in here, it is a haven away from the flies. Speaking of flies, someone just came in and is having a huge old poo, and does it ever stink. And here I am, not able to leave because someone else is using the urinal. How awkward. I'm taking the first chance I can to get out of here.

July 26

Place: Lumsden
Distance: 23 km
Wildlife: pocket gophers, choke cherries, yellow coneflowers, sunflowers

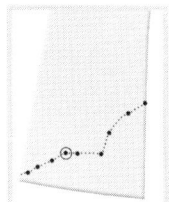

Today we will meet Joe Milligan from the Saskatchewan Trans Canada Trail Council. He has promised to hike with us from Lumsden, then out of town down the Qu'Appelle Valley. The driving is slow as Billy veers the van and trailer around the potholes on the gravel road leading to Lumsden.

Joe, his wife, Lynn, and their baby, Jane, are waiting with their friend Donnalynn. Joe is a young, ambitious sort of guy, anxious to get going. He has arranged for us to download some of our information onto the web in his office, and that must be done first. Nora and I meet Chris Elexes and work on our web page as the rest wait patiently for us in the van. Once finished we have a quick lunch, then lace up our hiking boots. Just as we are all about to leave, a reporter from the local newspaper arrives to interview us and take pictures. Half an hour and we are ready.

The trail begins in Lumsden, winds through some back streets, then emerges onto a dyke. The trail is well marked in town but as it heads out to the farmland, there is not much indication of a trail except some scruffed-up surfaces running alongside a fence bordering a wheat field. The trail is full of tall thistles and weeds, which makes walking very uncomfortable. Joe walks along in front, with little Jane sleeping peacefully in the carrier in front. We talk about the Trans Canada Trail and the common difficulties each province is having in developing it. We talk about the water relay and how plans for the fountain, which was to be built in Hull to celebrate the trail opening, have been cancelled. We have common views of this project, which has cost a major amount of money already.

We stop occasionally for water. There is no wind and it is extremely hot. We are walking on the floor of the Qu'Appelle Valley and the heat feels trapped between its walls. The valley was carved centuries ago by torrents of glacier water. It is hard to imagine glacier water as we struggle along in temperatures soaring over one hundred degrees.

(from Nicholas' diary)
After hiking sometime along the road, the day only promises to get hotter, as the buzzards keel over in the field, probably waiting too long for us to die.

Billy is waiting at the five-kilometre mark as planned. Our Lumsden friends will leave us at this point; we must continue along the fence line, then up on a long,

Warren Pletz, recognizing our exhaustion in the heat of the Qu'Appelle Valley, returns with popsicles and water for us.

dusty road. It is unbearably hot and we choke from the need for water. Suddenly a truck rolls up beside us in a cloud of dust. Warren Pletz, the driver, offers us a place to camp and a fresh water supply. He tells us he is a teacher in Lumsden and owns two aces of land farther along the trail. He has worked on the Trans Canada Trail in the area. He is a friendly man, genuinely interested in our venture. We must stand out; four women, one young man and a boy making their way along this hot valley floor in temperatures soaring above 36°C.

We join the trail again as it splices between two large grain fields. The earth is baked and cracked from the summer heat. Our pace is slow as the heat drains our energy. We focus on reserving our water supply until we spy the van, small in the distance. It is now safe to dump our remaining water down our throats, letting the overflow drip over our shirts and trickle down our salty necks. Warren has given Billy a fresh supply of water and we pour it into us when we reach the van. It is only 15 kilometres but it feels like 25. Feeling dizzy from the heat, I sit in the shade of the van. I feel I can't continue on this shadeless trail.

(from Nicholas' diary)
They are going to walk more kilometres—for what reason I can not guess.

We decide to hike three kilometres more but with no packs on. We shed our packs and cameras and fill our water bottles. We are ready to start off when Warren Pletz's truck pulls in beside us. He has freezies for us. We are overjoyed. There couldn't have been a better treat in this sweltering valley. So, with a bit of rejuvenation, we walk back along the dry valley. Billy is waiting at the three-kilometre mark to drive us back to Lumsden. We decide to camp right in town as we are in desperate need of a laundromat and we want to use the library computers to answer e-mail.

(from Nicholas' diary)
When they go to do laundry, I sit at the picnic table, drawing. After that, Wade and I play hackey sack with the volleyball for a while—we don't beat our record. We have pork chops for supper, and after supper we do what we always do—sleep.

The stars are bright in the sky as I crawl into the tent. Tonight we are leaving only the screens up on the tent. We are camping by a stream on the edge of a ball diamond. A cool breeze passes over us. What a relief.

July 27

Place: Buffalo Pound Provincial Park
Distance: 14.5 km
Wildlife: buffalo, doe, fawn, waterfowl, gophers

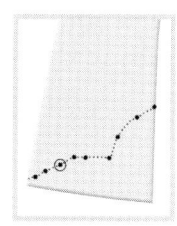

(from Maria's diary)
A slight breeze blows through the open tent flaps early this morning. No crows wake us; a pleasant change. Mom and Nora leave with Nicholas' laundry and to do some computer uploading. Heike and I are allowed to use Elizabeth Yaskowich's computer to check e-mail.

I am sitting in the laundromat listening to the lady next to me chatter about tornadoes and how today seems to be perfect for one. How comforting!

(from Maria's diary)
The sky is troubled with low clouds, threatening rain. As we drive down the highway, a dark cloud in front of us reaches down to touch the ground. "It's just rain, right?" I ask hopefully. Mom searches for culverts in case of twisters. The clouds are bubbled like the ocean and the lighting is that of dusk, not early morning, as it should be.

We talk incessantly about what the colour of the sky means, an endless evaluation of whether it is pink or purple, fluorescent and funneling, or not. Our little van is alone on this flat stretch of highway, with the 360-degree horizon around us, as far away as the eye can see.

(from Maria's diary)
We stop near Moose Jaw for gas and groceries then drive on to Buffalo Pound Provincial Park. We drop down into the lush valley where we set up camp, then head off on our hike. Billy drives Heike, Mom, Nora and me to the bison range where we

begin. Fortunately, we are able to see the bison before they head into the open range. They are such ancient-looking creatures—straight from a western movie.

Our hike takes us through grassy hills and down into a dark thicket of trees. We can see out over the grassy flats of the valley, which are the breeding grounds for waterfowl. The marshes of the prairies supply 80 per cent of North America's waterfowl with breeding grounds. We walk to the Nicolle homestead, where broad-armed trees surround the old brick house, casting shade over the front lawn. Teams of horses collected the rocks, left by glaciers, from the valley. However, construction of the T-shaped barn ceased in 1906-1907 when the harsh winter killed four hundred RCMP horses that were being raised on the farm. This left the family deep in debt, which the young son worked until death to repay, unsuccessfully. I can imagine owning this many horses but can't imagine dealing with the death of the entire herd and preparing for their burial. Such a sad loss. I can imagine these beautiful shiny-coated creatures appearing on the hill above us, giving a shrill whinny then turning with a snort to run in the other direction. I can feel their presence and wish just once we could step back in time.

(from Maria's diary)
We make our way back to the meeting spot for Billy and travel to our campsite. With the great chopping help of Heike, Nora and I make a supper of sautéed vegetables and chicken with alfredo over lemon pepper fettuccini and a lovely salad. After supper Mom, Nora and I brush our teeth together in the washroom and give the surrounding crowd a quick song. One lady quickly tells us off and goes on her merry way. It's good to know everyone is having so much fun.

July 28

Place: Shamrock Regional Park
Distance: 0

It is already hot when I emerge from the tent shortly after 6:00 A.M. I head to the showers to beat the crowd. The water feels great and relieves me for a short time from the heat. Steven McCrum, a railroad engineer on a much-deserved holiday, is camping next to us and we have made plans to talk over a coffee by our morning campfire. Steve comes over as planned and sits down in one of the camp chairs by the fire. He immediately begins to share his stories:

"I drive freight trains. The trains are over 10,000 feet. We had a car on a crossing that we could see about three quarters of a mile away. We started blowing the whistle but it wasn't moving. I put the brakes into emergency. We only had a short train with mostly empties. If I'd had a long train we would never got stopped before the crossing. It was just kids playing a game. As soon as we got close, they started the car and moved off. I've had it happen about a dozen times in 20 years."

Steve also mentions suicides on the tracks. It is such a scary situation to be in as the train engineer. There is such responsibility and so often these multi-car freight trains just keep pushing on long after the brakes have been applied. Steve returns to his camping spot and we begin to pack up.

Billy throws bacon in the pan as Nicholas and Wade keep up the challenge to up their "hacks" with the volleyball. This is a nice campground, shaded with big trees. One bonus is its clean washrooms. We give it a 'ten.' The little prairie graveyard on the boundary of Buffalo Pound Park is the resting place of Charles and Catherine Nicolle. Adjacent to the church, acres of blue flax nod under a cloudless sky. It is quiet here and dragonflies dive in the still air.

We're back in the van, driving to Moose Jaw. My intention was to hike at Old Wives Lake, but I have been told the trail is non-existent there, so I opt for Mossbank as a better bet. We stop at the library in Moose Jaw where Nora registers for her fourth year at Acadia University. While in the library, I learn that Al Capone built a maze of tunnels under Moose Jaw in the rum-running years. In the roaring twenties, Moose Jaw was a hub of activity, dubbed, 'the New Orleans of the North.'

On our way out of Moose Jaw, we make an amazing discovery. The old railway station is now a liquor store. How perfect! The ticket office holds the beer as the ticket agent rings in our purchase. The old marble pillars reflect the specialties, as electric trains chug around the containers. The baggage area stores the extra spirits. As I snap photos of

Saskatchewan

this unique station, a former train engineer is next to me. He tells me he worked on the line for 30 years.

We head to Mossbank, crawling out of the Qu'Appelle Valley onto the flats. The mercury rises to 115°F and the hot sultry air wafts through the van windows. We travel miles between flat, endless fields, heat radiating in a blur off the baked prairie floor. At Mossbank, we stop at the local co-op to ask about the trail. The young man in the store tells me to inquire at the museum. He takes me outside to show me where the museum is located. "It is the house by the tree," he says. There is no mistaking it. We have driven 45 minutes without a trace of a tree, person or animal, only crimewatch signs. We joke about the possibility of committing a crime in an area where people could see you for miles. And what would you harm? There are no buildings, fences or animals, let alone people, in that long stretch of prairie.

I enter the cool of the museum and discuss trail options with the young man in charge. We decide it would be suicidal to head into the prairie in this heat. There is absolutely no shade or water source for miles. As I come out of the museum, I find the Hike 2000 crew lying under the small tree in the yard, panting for a breath of air. Our thermometer has soared over 45°C and we contemplate the possibility of frying our last egg on the hood of the van. If it weren't for the lovely paint job, I would have. We literally crawl back into the van and reach for our water bottles. They now contain hot water. But water is water and I instruct everyone to drink it anyway. The young boy in the museum told us of a campsite at Shamrock Park where we can spend the night. The van bumps along the long dirt road for more than an hour. I turn around and watch sweat beaded on the faces of the five people behind me. We have no clue where we are going and I suddenly feel hysterical laughter building in my throat. It is the same feeling I had on our first morning in St. John's, Newfoundland. These trusting souls sit behind me in the agonizing heat waiting for our next move. It is too much. I laugh uncontrollably. Billy's big hands on the wheel guide us in and out of potholes as farm vehicles pass, choking us with dust. Those beaded faces in the van watch for the dust to settle and stare out at the same rolling, moon-like surface stretching on forever. Whether it is my own delirium, the heat or just the thought of us bouncing across this dry prairie, I find it hilarious and laugh until tears streak down my cheeks.

Finally, we reach Shamrock Park, a small prairie oasis where we set up camp for the night. We soon learn that the campground has experienced severe flooding recently and the entire area where we are camping has been underwater. Now, with the silt of the flood layering the ground, it is a perfect breeding spot for mosquitoes. We load ourselves with repellent as we race to set up our tents under the trees. Billy learns about a moonlight golf tournament and urges Wade to join him. We refresh ourselves in the small campground swimming pool and opt to buy burgers at their little take-out. It is much too hot to cook and no one can stand still long enough with the swarms of mosquitoes attacking. To our delight, Ray Lizee, my contact for Gravelbourg, has arrived with cool refreshments. We talk until dark, swatting mosquitoes constantly. Ray offers to show Billy and I where the trail begins for tomorrow's hike.

We get in the van, Ray in the front passenger seat and me directly behind him. Billy drives out of the campground, expecting a short trip to the trailhead. We pass the golf course and Ray tells Billy to turn onto a farm path leading into a wheat field. The deep ruts ahead of us have obviously been made with a large farm vehicle. We drive on, Ray looking as though he is going on a Sunday drive, Billy, as if he is driving in a snowstorm. This farm road ends in a slough (water hole). Here Billy is instructed to cut through the farmer's field of freshly plowed black earth. By now, Billy is not amused. Ray gets out of the van, assesses the situation, then tells Billy to head straight through the wheat field. For two more kilometres we drive on, the van rocking in and out of badger holes. Occasionally, it hits a large stone, lunges on its side and bumps back into position. I move to the high side of the van and tighten my seat belt. Billy clings to the wheel, face bent low, trying to see what is ahead in the wheat that swishes back and forth above windshield level. As the van parts the tall stalks, the headlights on the waving wheat send an eerie glow in front of us. "Lord luva flying duck," Billy exclaims as Ray gets out, looking a bit perplexed in the middle of the field. He climbs back in and tells Billy he's doing fine. "Just follow the road," he says. "Is that a road?" Billy asks sarcastically. "Yes," returns Ray. "Could have fooled me," Billy replies. Finally. we reach a cross-over road and return to the campground. We have driven ten kilometres in a wheat field in the pitch dark. How will I ever find this tomorrow?

After the trail search, I order a burger at the campground takeout. Wade, Heike, Nicholas, Nora and Maria have joined me. A car pulls up, shining its lights in our faces. It is Mitch Wilcox, Nora and Maria's friend from Walton. He is working in Saskatchewan and has decided to join us. Unfortunately, our web itinerary states that we will be in Old Wives Lake tonight and Mitch has spent six hours looking for us in that unpopulated area. We are excited to see him and catch up on all his news since he moved west.

Back at our campsite, we crawl into our tents out of the mosquitoes. Next to us, a group of young teenagers has arrived for an all-night party. They spin cars around the campground, smash beer bottles, yell and scream, fight over girlfriends and party hard until 6:00 A.M.

July 29

Place: Shamrock Regional Park to Gravelbourg
Distance: 27.8 km
Wildlife: ducks, deer, frogs, gophers, one coyote stalking us...

I have been awake most of the night. The rowdy group in the next tent continued cursing and yelling until well after daybreak. Maria, who was sick in the night, exited the tent several times. It has been a horrible night for her and I decide to let her sleep now. Nora, Heike and I will leave early for Gravelbourg on the famous trail that Bill and I previewed last night with Ray.

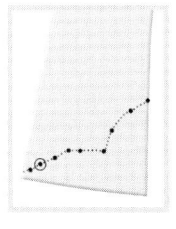

(from Heike's diary)
Nobody feels too rested after last night's overdose of a local teenage tenting party, but at least this way it is easier to get going and leave the place. Our 16-year-old neighbours in the next tent spent the night getting drunk, piling into a truck and then reinforcing the booze effect by driving around and around in circles well into the wee hours, which isn't exactly my idea of splendid Friday night entertainment...

So Kathy, Nora and myself are on the trail at 7:00 A.M. tracing the van's "hike" from last night. Doused in fly dope, we savor the long-distance vista without sweating like some hens hauling hay. Undulating farmland, dotted sparsely with farms and interspersed with only the occasional saw blades of Lombardi popular for wind shelter, stretch as far as the horizon. The Gravelbourg water tower and grain elevator are visible virtually every step of the way. Nick and Maria man the support crew to catch up on some sleep and help Billy pack up. Wade and Mitch, our new arrival for the weekend, decide to spend the day in Moose Jaw.

Early into our hike, Kathy twists one of her ankles in a badger hole. Apart from the gazillions of mosquitoes, it is very peaceful and quiet. All we can hear is the occasional bird, the wheat swishing in the breeze, and the sound of our footsteps. The soft wheat brushes our arms, helping to keep the onslaught of mosquitoes at bay. We soon reach the Wood River. The effects of the recent flooding are still evident. Vegetation debris lines the riverbed above the normal watermark, and upriver, the water is almost level with the road surface, the culverts underneath just barely coping with the run-off. Little frogs jump from their sunbathing spots, and large shells have been washed up on the banks. Looking back, I notice a tractor working a field on the slope behind us.

It is a glorious morning with the sun bright in a cloudless sky. I delight in the freedom from threat of tornadoes today. I have been told there are no rattlesnakes in this area and I expect bears don't travel in wheat fields. We begin singing "Oh, What a Beautiful Morning" at the top of our lungs.

(from Heike's diary)
Shortly, we see the first human being since leaving camp. A woman is driving toward us then past us in a red minivan. Soon, the van returns and stops alongside us, now with a man in the passenger seat. The couple introduce themselves as the LaRochelles. "Do you know that you are being stalked by a coyote?" they ask. Apparently, it has been tailing us as closely as 50 to 100 feet! Reno LaRochelle had been watching us from the vantage point of the hill where he was working with the tractor I saw. At first he thought we had a dog with us! What an eerie experience. The things we don't see on our hikes....

We soon reach our first potential pit stop. Since there is no van in sight yet, Kathy leaves a juice bottle as a marker for Billy to see that we've passed this point. At the next junction, we again meet Reno, who is going back to his field in a truck. He advises us to turn left instead of carrying on straight and helps us put up a marker for the support crew. He has all the necessary tools and materials on the flatbed of his truck: cardboard, a pointed stake, and a hammer. But this time, the cool of the morning has worn off, giving way to the scorching midday heat. Luckily, the van arrives soon with fresh water and some bread and cheese.

Thus fortified, we carry on, casting occasional furtive glances back over our shoulders, but the only escort we get is from some bored farm dogs with nothing better to do than run after us and bark in the sweltering heat. Another pit stop is welcome.

As Billy drives away, we watch our precious Hike 2000 van moving farther away between the hay bales until it is only a speck in the distance.

The restoring effects of the pit stop wear off again in no time, which delights a farmer who is making hay in an air-conditioned tractor. He comes out, initially to tease us, but it turns out that he is Janet MacKenzie's cousin, Byron Richmond. What a coincidence! Kathy has been trying (unsuccessfully) to get in touch with them over the past few days. Had she been successful, we could have camped at Joan's (Byron's mother), beautiful farm and gone horseback riding instead of enduring others' Friday night fun. But, it is a good thing that we end up meeting after all. We are all treated to a ride on Byron's truck, Nora and I on the flatbed. We first go to Byron's house to meet his wife, then on to Joan's. While Kathy is chatting with Joan, Nora and I find that we could hang out on the porch all day.

We are then treated to a second ride in a truck, Joan's this time. She drives us back to the van. What a shame that we don't have more time to spend with these friendly folks!

Joan Richmond has recently been widowed and her family has gathered in the big farmhouse to help her with the horses and keep her company on this summer afternoon. When we arrive, they are just finishing their midday meal. A bowl of fresh beet greens is on the table. I could eat the whole bowl I am so hungry. Joan invites us to lunch, but we think of the others in the hot van on the side of the dusty road and decline. Joan drives us to meet the van in her truck. Billy, Maria and Nicholas are lying in the shade of the van. We drive within five kilometres of Gravelbourg, then Heike, Nora and I get out to finish off our hike. The temperature is now 100°F and the tar on the road, which is now melting, sticks to the soles of our boots. As Heike says, "I am still fascinated by the fact that here on the prairies, you can walk right on the centre line of a major road and get away with it. Anyway, the few cars that pass are visible well ahead."

After a few wrong turns, we reach our meeting spot—the shop of Ray Lizee. The entire map of the prairie land is laid on a grid so if you make a wrong turn, you know that you can just walk forward or back a square. It's really pretty simple. The grid roads are exactly straight, like the lines on graph paper. We are wet with sweat when we reach Ray's. It has been 27.5 kilometres in the hot sun and we yearn for cool shade. Ray escorts us to the Evergreen Motor Court, a former monastery, which is now being refurbished by Paul LaRochelle. A cloister of nuns lived here their entire lives, not even venturing out to the small village of Gravelbourg for groceries.

(from Heike's diary)
I immediately fall in love with the wild garden "on the edge of the prairie" and make a tent-and-breakfast arrangement with Paul, while everyone else stays indoors to get a proper night's sleep. In the hope of seeing some more northern lights and/or a prairie sunrise, I pitch my very own little cell in the old cloister garden.

I make a deal with Paul for a room inside the old monastery. The cool tile floors lead to cozy rooms with high ceilings. Wooden frames outlining the doors are inscribed with the quote "Vive la precious sang de Jesus." We choose a corner room with a small kitchen. There is a kneeling bench outside the door and a little place for a plant with a small light above. It is the perfect spot for prayer. We lie back on the comfortable beds, taking turns at the shower. It is such a relief to wash away the salt that stings our hot skin. I think how effective our suntan lotion must be since no one has suffered from sunburn in this merciless heat. We choose the local Chinese restaurant for supper. They serve us large homemade egg rolls, which are delicious. We eat in abundance. Two full pitchers of water still don't quench my thirst. After supper, we stop at the little ice cream shop for a treat.

Wade and Mitch have not returned from Moose Jaw, so Nora and I decide to take one last look for them. We dart back to the local ice cream shop to leave a message, should they arrive there. An onslaught of mosquitoes bombards us and we run like crazed animals for the nearby phone booth. It is amazing how you can find energy to run when mosquitoes are swarming you. With no luck in finding the boys, we return to the monastery. Paul has placed some fans in our room to help circulate the warm air.

Saskatchewan

July 30

Place: Thompson Lake Regional Park
Distance: 22.5 km
Wildlife: many antelope, deer, fawns, 2 weasels, jackrabbit, 3 hawks, pocket gophers

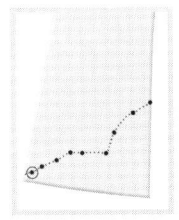

(from Nora's diary)
I guess my day really started at about 12:45 last night, when I opened my eyes to the figures of Mitch Wilcox and Wade Lake standing over my bed, looking down at me. I was more than relieved to see them. Yesterday morning, they left for Moose Jaw for the day, planning to join us by 6:00 at the latest that evening. We figured they'd find us just by driving around Gravelbourg; it couldn't be so big that they wouldn't see us, right? We started watching out for them at about 6:00; by 8:00 we got a bit concerned and went around to gas stations and pit stops to let workers know where Hike 2000 was staying should anyone come in to ask. By 9:00, mom and I tried to outrun the mosquitoes, hoping that by chance they'd drive along in Mitch's black charger so we could flag them down. No luck. We went to bed after 12:00, leaving a note on the van. We had no idea where they were or what would happen in the morning if they never found us. Well, they finally found us by asking a man with a shovel walking around in Gravelbourg at 12:00 P.M. where Ray Lizee lived. They then woke him for directions. What a nice man.

Together Mitch and Wade unravel the story of their day—including the shift in Mitch's car unhooking in second gear, how the repairs cost half as much as his car, why the gash in Wade's foot is gushing blood, and how Wade lost his mind and bought a mountain bike—his way back home to Winnipeg. After a restful night for us in Paul's beautiful bed and breakfast we are welcomed into the former praying room for a beautiful breakfast of juice, exotic fruit, bread, yogurt, and coffee. Yum.

Paul LaRochelle is a quiet, kind man. His idea of turning this old monastery into a bed and breakfast is a wonderful one. I sit for a while in the back garden, thinking of the toil that must have been spent here. A long, low building borders the garden and rows of clothesline remind me of the many sheets, towels and pieces of clothing that must have hung here at one time. Tall hollyhocks climb the old brick wall by the back door and traces of the former flowerbeds beckon to be renewed. How I would love to help restore this place.

We meet Ray Lizee as he heads off to the renowned Our Lady of the Assumption Roman Catholic Cathedral, built in 1919. Between 1921 and 1931, Monsignor Charles Maillard embellished the church with scenes from the Old and New testaments. The former bishop's chair is a Louis X1V Episcopal throne dated to 1780. The monstrous cathedral stands in the centre of this little town, as though it has been dropped there from the Renaissance in France.

Ray suggests I hike in the Thompson Park area today. It is a good idea, as there is a swimming pool, shade trees and a golf course for Billy. I put on my pedometer and tromp around the campground, the golf course, and the surrounding subdivision on my own. The others seek shade and spend some time in the park swimming pool. It is so hot my water reaches burning temperatures. The thermometer again climbs to 115°F as I wind around the camper trailers that sit baking in the sun. After 15 kilometres, I decide I've had enough. We will drive to Alberta's Cypress Hills. Wade and Mitch have to return to Mitch's home. It has been such a short stay for Mitch. As for Wade, we are so sad to see him go.

(from Nora's diary)
Then comes the hardest part of the day—saying good-bye to Mitch and especially Wade, who after two weeks of sore Achilles, NO whining, and the cleanest dirty clothes has become part of our group.

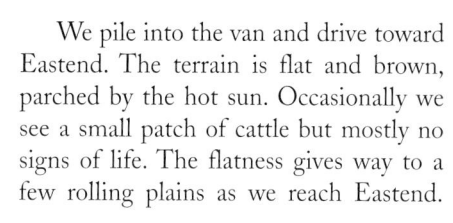

We pile into the van and drive toward Eastend. The terrain is flat and brown, parched by the hot sun. Occasionally we see a small patch of cattle but mostly no signs of life. The flatness gives way to a few rolling plains as we reach Eastend.

Our Lady of the Assumption Roman Catholic Cathedral, Gravelbourg, Saskatchewan.

Here, we stop for a coffee. Inside the local watering hole, a gentleman is chewing on a matchstick and enjoying his coffee. We strike up a conversation. He tells me he has always lived in this small prairie town. I ask him about rattlesnakes. "No, not here, it's too cold," he replies. The temperature on the outside wall reads 110°F. I wonder just how hot it needs to be for those snakes to migrate north. He continues, "there's some down there over the border in Montana, but they don't come up here." Outside, we joke about the American snakes that have no visas to pass the border. Nicholas gives us his rendition of the conversations among the snakes deciding whether to cross the border from Montana, which is only 15 kilometres away. The land, which stretches as far as the eye can see, resembles an African safari territory. It is hardly an area too cold for snakes.

We enjoy an ice cream and move on. Again, the dry landscape becomes totally flat with grasslands stretching to the hazy horizon. The small tarmac road runs like a strip of sticky licorice, its hot tar shining in the sun. As we reach the Alberta border, the sun is sinking low in the sky. Hills appear, a dramatic change from the flatlands. In the distance we can see three small peaks and, to our right, what must be the Cypress Hills. Fences border the land where large herds of buffalo and beef are grazing. Then the most awesome scene unfolds around us.

(from Nora's diary)
Entering Alberta is one of the most amazing feelings I have ever experienced. Imagine this—the provincial border is marked by a small sign saying "Alberta," overshadowed by a larger sign indicating that livestock are now free-range and to take caution. We bump over a Texas cattle grate, and there we are, in Alberta. Behind us lies the dry valleys of Saskatchewan. Ahead and to all sides—flat, dry, tufts of grass, no fences, and far off in the distance, the black forms of cattle standing together in the warmth. I can't remember feeling this free in a long time. Here, at the provincial border, we stand in the middle of the road (having only seen two cars in the last three hours) waving our arms over our heads in excitement. "Alberta!…Saskatchewan!!" we yell as we hop back and forth over the 'provincial line,' out of and back into Saskatchewan. Giddy, we could walk all night in the warm air as Billy drives slowly beside us and has an 'apple.'

There are no boundaries and no fences. I immediately think of the old song, 'Oh give me land, lots of land under starry skies above, don't fence me in.' With arms raised over our heads, we prance and bolt like wild animals given freedom after years of captivity. The glow of the setting sun illuminates our faces as we walk along the gravel road, Billy following in the van. We walk for four kilometres, the feeling of excitement and freedom pushing us onward.

(from Nora's diary)
It is dusk by now and getting darker. Back in the van and driving to Elkwater (our new destination), two new rules are formed: (1) No driving at night; (2) No 'apples' on the road (deemed 'road apples'). The darkness and curvy roads make it feel like we are going a lot faster than we are. Not only that, but Alberta is full of wildlife such as deer, antelope, rabbits, and weasels, all of which decide to cross the road as we round blind corners. "Billy—there is something on the road up there..." we say. "There is? Where? How far up? Between my glasses and the windshield (which is spattered with bugs), I can't see anything," he answers. "Billy!! Right in front of you!" we respond. The next morning the muscles in my arm are sore from gripping the back of Billy's seat and Maria's shoulder as we scanned the sides of the road for animals. Not exactly the most thought-out plan—putting mom with no eyes and Billy who doesn't like to drive in the haze of sundown in the front seats. Nonetheless he got us there, and safely, I'll add.

Finally, we make it to Elkwater, which promises to be picturesque tomorrow if the sun is shining. We can see the moon lighting up a strip of lakewater as we drive past it to our campground to set up our tent. The park ranger assures us there are no bears or rattlesnakes in the area. Perfect!

July 31 - August 10   Alberta

We hike along the canal through cattle country in Little Bow Lake, Alberta. Maria, Nora, Kathy, Nicholas and Heike.

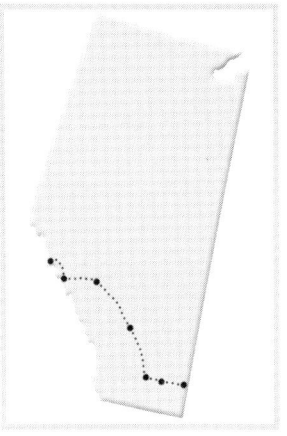

July 31

Place: Elkwater, Cypress Hills
Distance: 24.8 km
Wildlife: moose, deer, rabbit

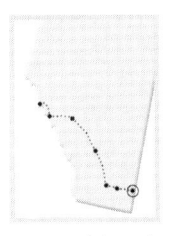

Cool air and clouds greet us in the early morning in Cypress Hills. The French fur traders named the area Cypress in the early 1800s. They mistook the lodgepole pines that grow here in the forest for the cypress or jack pines that grow in Eastern Canada. The hills are famous for the Cypress Hills Massacre, which occurred on June 1, 1873. The Assiniboine were camped in a beautiful valley along the north fork of the Milk River; their hope was to trade with the Americans who were wintering in the Cypress Hills. Ten angry wolf hunters arrived from Montana looking for 40 horses that they believed the Assiniboine had stolen. They attacked the encampment and shot the elderly as they tried to escape in the riverbed. Girls and women were raped, lodges burned and bodies dismembered. The Assiniboine tribe, already weak from their trek across the merciless prairie in winter, lost up to 80 men, women and children in the massacre. Canada was outraged by this attack. As a means to re-establish some kind of order and trust of the native tribes, Fort Walsh, an RCMP post, was developed.

Hiking the Dream

Today, 127 years later, we will walk through the same oasis of trees where that hopeful group of Assiniboine sought shelter, built camps and were later slaughtered like sheep.

Nora, Maria, Heike and I decide to hike at 6:30 A.M. to beat the heat. I quickly cook some oatmeal, then we walk down the hill to the campground entrance. We walk along the boardwalk that borders Elkwater Lake. Tall bulrush on the shoreline gives refuge to waterfowl. At the end of the boardwalk we cross the road and climb up the Beaver Trail. A low pond is home to a large beaver lodge. The trail winds through poplar and spruce forest and makes a loop that crosses a creek, becoming quite wet in some areas. This is enough of a pre-breakfast hike and we stop at the campground grocery store for lunch food.

Nicholas joins us for our second outing. Billy, in the meantime, packs the van and waits for our return in the nearby restaurant. Shortly up the trail we hear a snort. In the trees nearby is a mother moose. She is carefully removing leaves from each branch of a tree, running the branch through her mouth, cleaning the leaves off, one by one. Watching her, as if taking a lesson, is her young calf. They are oblivious to our approach. She is such a nice mother, quietly watching her offspring. We are so lucky to see this.

We continue on and reach an archaeological dig. A basement-sized hole has been carefully excavated, exposing layers of life, long forgotten. The basement reaches to seven thousand years before our time, uncovering a stove. The lady working on the site found an arrowhead this morning. Used before bow and arrows on a fling-type spear, arrowheads would have been strapped with leather to a rod made of sapwood that was pivoted by a racket and thrown. Apparently, natives who used this device were very accurate. There had been a volcano 3500 years ago, covering the hills with four inches of debris. This volcano had occurred in Montana and reached as far as Edmonton.

After our archaeological lesson, we walk up the trail that leads to the forest. Suddenly, a young deer bounds into the thicket, turning once to give us a quick glance. So graceful, she seems to hang in mid-air as she clears the shrub below. As we retreat to the van, a very stubby looking rabbit crosses our path and scrambles into the underbrush. We haven't expected to see this much wildlife on a trail so close to the campground. It is a treat.

Alberta

We meet Billy at the restaurant and go in for a cold drink. Deer from the nearby forest have strayed onto the lawn and one even becomes brave enough to approach the window. We are tempted by wiener schnitzel and pie. It is delicious.

On the outskirts of Medicine Hat, we detour to a campground on Craven Lake. It is high on a hill with little shelter. There is a threat of a thunderstorm and the owner warns us that the coyotes will start howling in three hours. It is not what I have in mind tonight and we decide to move on to Medicine Hat. It is already dark when we set up our tents in the town's campsite. The facilities here are excellent and we feel a little more secure against the impending storm.

August 1

Place: Medicine Hat
Distance: 16.5 km

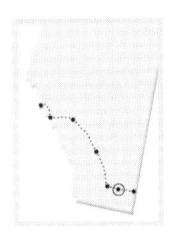

(from Nicholas' diary)
I wake up to Mom dragging me by the feet out of the tent. As I look up at the fully starred sky, I wonder what Mom is doing. Turns out that there is a storm, so she is dragging me out to the van. I don't object; it is early morning and there is not a cloud in sight. Mom apparently saw a flash of lightening and had promised Glenda to take us out of the tent at the first sign of a storm.

After sitting out in the van for some time, then going to sleep in the tent, I wake up again. The others have gone hiking, so I do all of the dishes (by command). I spend the rest of the day reading, drawing pictures and listening to Korn on my Discman. There is a water fight going on between a six year old and a ten year old at the campground. The ten year old's name is Tyler and we shoot pop cans with his water gun. Mom, Nora and Maria are at this time walking around Medicine Hat. When they come back, I'm kicking the volleyball around.

Today our goal is just to clock some distance in Medicine Hat. Heike will go off on her own today and Nora, Maria and I will explore the city on foot. We stop in at the old railway station, which is now a centre for family counseling. It is a hot day and we drift in and out of shops to avoid the sun. At a real western store, Maria decides on a knife for Iain's birthday.

I have been having a lot of discomfort lately and decide on the spur of the moment to drop in to the Medicine Hat clinic. I fear that a tick has burrowed its way under my skin. As I lie on the cool sheets of the examination table waiting for a doctor, I drift asleep in the quiet room. I honestly believe I am exhausted from our constant moving and that, given the right circumstances, I could probably sleep for a week. I am abruptly awakened by the doctor's voice. The examination of my pubic area is embarrassing enough but to be lying sound asleep, hiking gear still on, drooling on the pillow is a bit much. There are so many unexpected pleasures while hiking and diverting to the undergrowth while on the trail, ticks being just one of them.

We return to the campground where Billy is trying to keep himself cool with a bucket of water. There just doesn't seem to be any relief from this hot sun. We have an early supper, then go over to Rob Gardner's—my trails contact for Alberta. He has offered his computer hook-up for us to update our web pages. He welcomes us to his home and goes over trail maps with me for my plans in Alberta.

Tonight there is another threat of thunderstorms and, with it, perhaps a tornado. I call Jeanette Osborne, a friend from university. She lives in Castor and promises to travel to Calgary to see us there. She broke her back this winter coasting with her children, Michelle and Gregory, and husband, Kevin. I haven't seen her in years and can't wait to reunite with her in Calgary. I also learn of a devastating tornado south of Red Deer that has ripped through a campground, killing those in its path. Apparently, large campgrounds with their many recreational vehicles are prime targets for the frequent twisters, this one with fatal results. It is so frightening to think of this as we make our way across the prairies, which have had an uncommon frequency of tornadoes this summer.

Alberta

August 2

Place: Medicine Hat
Distance: 24.5 km
Wildlife: sagebrush, cottonwood trees, wild rose, three types of cacti, snake

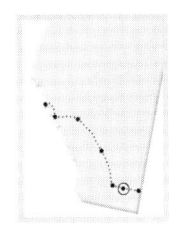

I get up at 6:30 to be ready to meet Rob Gardner at eight o'clock. It is overcast and suprisingly cool. After some eggs, we climb into the van to pick up Rob. The breeze is brisk as we start our walk along the city trail that begins by Highway 1. As we walk along, Rob points out different varieties of cacti. My preference is the pincushion cactus. It lies low to the ground and has tiny outgrowths of bright yellows, pinks and oranges. The ground is dry and parched as we walk above a deep gorge far below us. On the low, flat land below the cliff, Rob points out where large pits of buffalo bones have been found. Apparently, it is an area where large herds were forced over the cliff.

We walk on to the world's largest teepee, which was brought to Medicine Hat after the 1988 Olympics in Calgary. Inside the teepee, scenes of native life are depicted on large paintings. We walk on through the park and along Seven Person's Creek, where in very early times seven dead people were found. We walk past the Medalta pottery building, the site of the first industrial exports to the East. The pottery made in this factory was used on the trains in wartime and shipped to the

Largest teepee in the world, Medicine Hat, Alberta.

army overseas. We pass the old flourmill and stop to admire some of the broken pottery pieces, discarded years ago. We approach the railway yard where trains are chugging in and out of the station, hauling soy and wheat, the noise always in our presence.

We are grateful to Rob for having been our host and showing us this great city. As we climb the hill back to our campground, the sun comes out, reminding us of the heat we had been missing all morning. Billy has taken the tent down, as we have to move on. We say our good-byes to Rob and head for Enchant.

Our campsite in Enchant is a circle of trees, like a fairy ring around us, protecting us from the wind. I make chop-suey for supper as the sun drops behind us, sending a glow over the campground. Tomorrow we will hike on the canal leading to Little Bow Lake.

August 3

Place: Enchant (along Little Bow Lake Irrigation Canal)
Distance: 24.5 km
Wildlife: ducks, geese, unidentified wading birds, coyotes

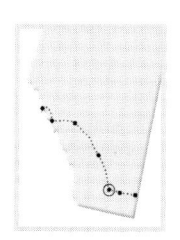

It is cool in the tent and there are no sounds from the outside. I crawl from the tent into the fresh air. A quick bathroom stop and I am ready for some journal writing. Billy is up by seven o'clock. It is hard to believe I am up first. My next move is to clean the van. It is amazing how much junk can collect in just a week.

I put together some grilled cheese sandwiches, then stroll over to see the campground manager to inquire about the trail. Rob Gardner has sent me to see him, especially because he is a trail supporter. I mention this fact to him and jump back at his reply. "That fucking goddamn son of a bitch. He's gonna get it from some of these ranchers. They don't want this trail and I know because my brother's in the municipality and all the ranchers are against it. There's no one supporting him or the trail." He turns to walk into his office without a word of good day or good luck. I ask, " Where are you going?" He replies, " I have work to do." Slam! The door bangs shut behind him.

Last evening I learned that we could walk along the Little Bow Lake Irrigation Canal, but that would be at our own risk. There are a number of anti-trail ranchers who have been known to 'plant' bulls in the fields to deter trespassers. With this in mind, we arrange for Billy to drive ahead on the canal trail and wait for us every two and one half kilometres. This will give us a chance to replenish our water supply and make for a good get away should we encounter any trail haters in this portion.

The right side of the trail is bordered by a fence, which holds back fields of cattle on the left. The canal runs cool and pale blue through the parched land, brown a metre past its banks. Ducks, geese and other birds dart from the bushes and into the water at our approach.

(from Heike's diary)
The hike on the dyke along the canal turns out to be really pleasant, and it isn't obvious to us what harm a few hikers could do on an already existing trail like this one. Admittedly we do startle some young ducks, one of which tries to escape in the wrong direction only to find us catching up with it again and again. It tries frantically to get airborne, eventually succeeding with a little help from the wind. When it gets too hot for me, I decide to take time out in the van. Billy, Nick and I watch coyotes through Billy's binoculars and I try my hand at drawing Nick's portrait.

Nora, Maria and I continue on, singing songs and talking about morals, sex and their futures. There are few topics we have not touched upon in the hours we have spent together on the trail. We pass rows of cows, staring at us. We are definitely an oddity here in this wide stretch of cattle country. One longhorn, then three bulls judge us with suspicion. Maria stops to take their picture as I urge her not to make eye contact and to hurry along.

The dyke along the Little Bow Lake irrigation canal pierces through cattle country.

Hiking the Dream

(from Heike's diary)
After a few pit stops, we find that our trail has come to an end, and there is a lot less than the desired 40 acres to turn the rig around in. Unhitching the trailer and getting everything sorted out separately accomplishes the tricky task. Off we are to our home for the next night. Finding the campground (six sites) in Arrowwood (population approximately 150) isn't quite as easy as one might expect. We finally reach the campground right next to the railway tracks—how appropriate! Kathy is gone to the museum across the street to find out about campsite procedures and the trail. The "museum" turns out to be a very interesting shop that stocks everything. We women folk go for just a look, only to be overcome by our whims and buy jewelry, dresses and arty prairie postcards. Since the only thing not to be had here is trail information, Kathy and I head across the street to the Centre Eatery to inquire. By and by, all patrons pipe in and try to help. Finally Ralph draws a map showing the best route to Carseland for Kathy—most important: turn sharp at Snakefoot's. The food that is getting cold on Ralph's plate looks so appealing that we decide to come back for breakfast. Back at camp we have a very scrumptious supper consisting of Kathy's potato salad, thyme carrots, sausages and salad. After supper, Billy, Kathy and I go for a little stroll through town.

August 4

Place: Arrowwood to Carseland
Distance: 28.5 km (22 km on hike, 6.5 in Okotok)
Wildlife: Canada Geese, gopher, 2 owls, hawks

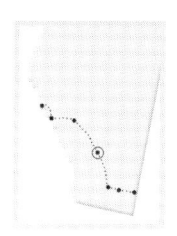

Heavy rain, thunder and lightening startle me awake. No, I am not going to wake everyone this time. I cover my head and wish for it to go away. Suddenly, I hear the shunting of a train on the tracks next to our camping spot. They told me at the little restaurant that trains only come by when the grain elevator is full. I am so lucky for this to be the night. It seems every night I see or hear a train. I feel it is a good omen. I love trains and am comforted tonight in this remote prairie village hearing the 'grain train' arrive.

This morning we will pack up early. We have planned to have breakfast at the Centre Eatery, here in Arrowwood. It is a 'sunshine breakfast' for everyone. Billy's breakfast is a layer of ham topped with home fries, topped with melted cheese with two fried eggs on top. This is sprinkled with croutons and baked. There is enough in a dish to feed a whole family.

It is good to get out and walk off our huge breakfast. It is still drizzling, so we pull on our rain gear. I am carrying Ralph's map in my hand and I tell Billy to wait for us at each turn so neither one of us will get lost.

(from Nora's diary)
Traveling along a complex puzzle of twists and having Billy wait for us is almost like a scavenger hunt. It also makes it possible for us to carry less and get a drink of water whenever we reach him. We pass by the houses of Casey Jones and Big Snake, which make for a lot of conversation. At one point, we walk over the Coulee Bridge startling two owls that are resting under the beams. They fly out from under the bridge, disturbed, only to land next to where hawks are resting. Like a snowball effect, the hawks rebut, trying to drive the owls away.

Three pickup trucks stop us to ask if we are all right and if our van has broken down. The first guy, Ed Taylor, is a former railway worker…maybe a relative? A farmer who insists that walking doesn't make sense drives the second truck. He thinks we are crazy—he'd rather chase cows for exercise. The third truck provides the most amusement for us. Inside are Jonathan the cowboy, ten-year-old Danny, and Chris, who wishes his name was Josh. They are all Hutterites. They are full of stories and friendly banter. We sing songs to each other, then ask questions about the others' lifestyles. It is very interesting.

They are a friendly group and ask us to sing. We decide on "Further Along." I think how true these words are as I watch them listening to us, their lives so different from ours.

> Further along we'll know all about it
> Further along we'll understand why
> Cheer up my brothers
> Live in the sunshine
> We'll understand it all by and by.

The little boy in the middle, Danny, is so cute, sitting with his brown and white long-sleeve shirt, buttoned right to his neck and tight at the wrists. I wonder about his life and what he is thinking. Back in the van, after 22 kilometres of hiking, we travel to Carseland. The campground here is one where the washrooms are a mile away and there is no one to ask about snakes or bears. There is something foreboding about this place and we decide to go on to Okotok.

(from Nora's diary)
At 22 kilometres, we get in the van with Billy and drive to a campsite in Okotok, outside Calgary. They are full, but give us a place to stay anyway. Our tent site isn't the best underfoot. It is very, very rocky with rosebushes springing up through the tent floor. The campground itself, though, is picturesque, sitting on a peninsula between two small bodies of water. It is half a kilometre to the washroom, which immediately means I have to go a lot during the night. Maria and I have an adventure with Billy trying to get into the parking lot of the grocery store. We make pita pizzas (ouch!) over an open fire, garlic potatoes and a salad. After cleaning up, then roasting a few marshmallows, we climb into the tent to sleep.

It is so nice to get some laundry done and have someone else make supper. I watch Nora and Maria make pizza over the open fire. They are such good sports and so determined to continue with their plan, despite the heat of the blaze. When it is ready, it is without a doubt the best pizza I have ever eaten.

As I walk back from the washroom for the last time, I notice a path of moonlight on the water, then five Canada geese lift and fly straight over this path of light. It is beautiful and lonely at the same time.

August 5

Place: Glenmore Park, Calgary
Distance: 19.5 km
Wildlife: gophers

(from Nicholas' diary)
Woke up with a rock in my spine. Luckily I am not paralyzed by this campsite. We have pancakes for breakfast then drive to Glenmore Park in Calgary. We walk the entire loop. Despite a

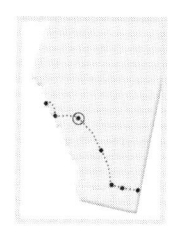

Alberta

Glenn McInnis and Julie Easley. Glenn's little home in Calgary is a cozy refuge from the threat of tornadoes.

sign saying, "Warning: bears frequent this area," we keep walking. It is starting to rain when we come to a sailor's club. It is times like this that I wish I was a sailor. Nonetheless, they give us some food, and after a bite or two, we go on again. We trek around the lake several times up and down the highway, looking for the trail. After visiting the washrooms, we go to the van. We have a picnic beside the van—bread, meat and cheese. After driving some time on the road, we get to Glenn McInnis' house.

Glenn, Julie's boyfriend, has offered us a place to stay while we regroup in Calgary. He is a newsman with a local TV station and shares a small house with Dan Reid and Kirk Stoodley, also in the TV business. Julie has flown from Fredericton to spend some time with Glenn and support Hike 2000. We haven't seen Glenn since he moved to Calgary more than a year ago. We are given a warm welcome and come in to the neat little house and make ourselves at home. Since Glenn has to go to work, the rest of us vegetate in front of his TV. It is so nice not to have to move. I cook up a batch of spaghetti as we sip on a bottle of Cote Du Rhone. Supper is late. Nora, Maria and I stumble upstairs to Kirk Stoodley's bed. I sure hope he doesn't arrive home tonight. He'll get quite a surprise to find three women in his bed.

August 6

Place: Elbow River Trail
Distance: 22 km
Wildlife: Canada geese, black squirrel

(from Nora's diary)
Mom and I are the only ones who go hiking today. Maria will

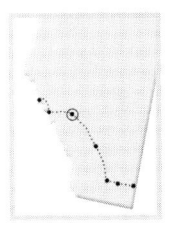

We bump into Scott Veinot, Nora's friend from Nova Scotia, on the street in Calgary.

go to the airport with Julie and Glenn to pick up Iain, who is flying in to join us for the rest of the trip. While they're at the airport, they see Valdi, the musician. Heike decides to go check out the theatre. Billy and Nicholas relax at home. It seems like any place we stop is called home. I called our tent home the other day.

We leave directly from Glenn's, traipsing off in the heat with our packs filled with water. We wander along the Elbow River, grateful for the occasional shade. We are feeling a bit woozy from the sun, some might even say a bit giddy. We pass by Stanley's Park, subdivisions of beautiful houses next to the river and the Calgary Stampede grounds. We emerge next to a church and train station turned into a boarding school and are given directions to 17th Street, which we just happen to be standing on. We are trying to find an Internet café, but without much luck.

Then, the weirdest thing happens. As we are crossing a crosswalk who should we meet but a friend of mine, Scott Veinot, from Nova Scotia. I'm not completely sure if it is him at first but I give him a hug anyway. Isn't this the craziest thing you have ever heard? Then it gets even weirder. While we're talking, I ask him if he has met anybody out here and he tells me about a 'going away' party last night for this guy named Kurt—'you remember, that guy who used to be on Breakfast Television?' This blows me away. This is the exact party Glenn and Julie had invited us to. Not only that, but Kurt is Glenn's roommate. It sounds so odd to say 'Well no, I don't know the guy, but I slept in his bed last night.'

We meet up with Heike, who continues looking around the city, then with Iain and Maria in the Internet café. It starts to get much cooler and gusts of wind start pushing through the tree branches. By the time we walk back to Glenn's, the temperature has dropped from over 30°C to 16°. Billy informs us that another tornado has already touched down outside Red Deer in Elnora, and that tornado warnings have been issued. As the sky turns dark gray to a pinky gray, we watch the weather channel and the 'A' channel, of course, where Glenn works. He calls to tell us to get under the steps in his basement if things get bad outside. He has spent the day sending out tornado warnings to various towns. While watching TV, we actually get to see Glenn sitting behind the anchor. He turns and looks straight at us. Yesterday he stuck a pen behind his ear, at our request.

Alberta

  It isn't too long afterward that the sky clears up and a rainbow emerges next to Glenn's house. The rest of our night is spent eating pizza and chatting. At 12:00, I finally have a shower and go to bed.

  Heike, who had been rushing to get home before the storm blows her away, walks in the door. We have been so worried that she might not be all right, but we have no way of getting in touch with her. Nicholas is the first to give her a big hug, followed by the rest of us. We have become very protective of each other now and are relieved that she has arrived home safely. We make plans for how we will pack ourselves under the steps should a tornado strike. Billy pulls the mattress that he is using in the basement under the steps for some added comfort should we have to stay there for long. It is amazing how we have started to take all warnings in stride, as though they have been part of our lives all along. We've never prepared for a tornado before but here we are peacefully making supper, watching the weather warnings and preparing for the touchdown without batting an eye. Thankfully, the storm passes without incident and we go off peacefully to bed, leaving Billy to sleep on the mattress under the stairs.

August 7

Place: Rest day in Calgary
Wildlife: rabbit

(from Maria's diary)
Today has been a day of much needed relaxation. We haven't had much opportunity to watch TV in our travels, so the 145 channels available are causing an overwhelming attraction for our idle minds. Thankfully, Jeanette and Kevin Osborne and their children, Gregory and Michelle, save us from our demise. Jeanette and Kevin are good friends who used to live in Nova Scotia. We sit around in a circle, catching up on news since we last saw each other almost five years ago. Then our second cousin, Jeff Luxton, whom we've never met before, arrives. A whole lifetime of

Jeanette, Kevin, Gregory, and Michelle Osborne, friends from Castor, drive all the way to Calgary to visit. We are so happy to see them!

249

news is needed, so we drill him with questions. As we talk, Heike, Nicholas, Gregory and Michelle occupy themselves with drawing. They are given quite the surprise as Ruth, Glenn's neighbour, comes over with a batch of cookies right from the oven. What a treat!

    Later in the day, Julie takes Mom to get her hair cut and Glenn and Billy go play golf. Those that are left behind read, sleep, play volleyball and watch TV. When Mom, Julie, Billy and Glenn arrive home, a cameraman from Glenn's TV station comes by to interview us. We stage the start of a normal hiking day—dirty socks and all. Later that evening we are able to see ourselves on TV. We try to tape it, but due to the complexity of the TV/VCR satellite combination we mess it up. The result is video with sound but no picture. That pretty much encompasses the rest of the day. It rains off and on, but later in the evening as Nora plays the fiddle for Ruth and Waldo, it pours harder, joined by lightening and thunder. The sky is an eerie colour, and the lightening is spectacular. After our wonderful supper of Glenn's mashed potatoes and Shake n' Bake chicken, we sit on the long couch and play songs. We have killer chocolate brownies, made by Ruth, before heading to bed.

Ruth and Waldo Hindle, Glenn's neighbours, invite us over for a chat. Nora and I sit in their comfortable living room as Waldo chooses some relaxing music. I feel so vulnerable and emotional tonight. As I listen to the favorites of Waldo, I try to swipe away the tears that are forming in my eyes. I can't explain why, but these people make me feel so comfortable that I could pour my soul out to them. Already, I am feeling the end of our journey drawing near and the thought of it saddens me. The peacefulness of this room, this couple and the melancholy music allow me to stop and think of what we are actually accomplishing. I think of the countless hours on the trail and the priceless nights together around Billy's campfire. The thought of it all ending so soon seems to flood over me and I just can't help but let go. Waldo recognizes my sadness and gives me a hug. I love this couple. They are

Waldo and Ruth Hindle of Calgary: the warmest people anyone would want to meet.

the warmest, loving people anyone would want to meet. Waldo gives me the tape, then Nora plays the fiddle for them.

So, as we sit around the living room enjoying the evening meal that has been carefully prepared by Glenn, we chant off our bests for the day.

> Glenn—having us all here.
> Julie—being here with Glenn and Hike 2000
> Billy—having played golf with Glenn
> Nora—seeing her friend from university
> Maria—having Iain arrive and being here with Julie and Glenn
> Nicholas—having a day to do whatever he pleased
> Kathy—being here with Glenn and Julie, meeting Waldo and Ruth
> Iain—being with us (Maria) again

It is our usual ritual to say our bests for the day, whether at home or on the trail.

August 8

Place: Canmore
Distance: 21 km

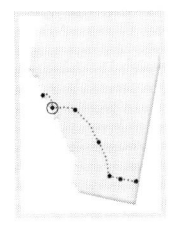

As I slept on the floor in Glenn's living room last night, I dreamed our hike was over. It is strange to wake up and know we must keep going. As we scurry to pack our van, I see Ruth next door, peacefully drinking her morning coffee by her back door. She brings over fresh muffins for our breakfast. She and Waldo are so genuinely thoughtful. We hug Julie and Glenn goodbye and beg Glenn to quit his job and come with us, if not for a few days then at least around the block. Julie and Glenn climb into the van with us, then we stop and pick up Ruth. Ah ha……kidnapped! Billy slowly circles the block as we threaten to keep going to Canmore. We circle back to the row of little houses on Glenn's street where Waldo is just returning home. We pick him up and make one more loop. In harmony, we all sing "We've been walking on the railroad." I turn to see Glenn's eyes welling up with tears. It is contagious. This time we have to say good-bye for real. This is so sad for us and for Glenn who lives so far from his home in Glace Bay, Nova Scotia. Finally, we wind our way through Calgary's streets and on to the 1A to Canmore.

The bald rock faces of the Rockies loom before us. It is at this point that I feel emotion squeezing my throat. We are here—it's just a climb over the Rockies and we will reach the Pacific Ocean. Our mission is almost over. Sad? Excited? Every emotion is present. The rolling foothills dotted with bales of hay contrast with the backdrop of the black mountains. Soon, we reach Canmore and the campground. Chris Milne from Manitoba is waiting for us and will hike the final trek through the Rockies. He has left his job as coordinator for the Rossburn Subdivision Trail in Manitoba to join us. We are either a very bad or a very good influence on him. Chris is a gentle, soft-spoken young man and this sudden decision to drop his normal life for a nomadic one is uncharacteristic of him. We are happy he has chosen to be 'one of us' and welcome him into our family of hobos.

We are given the most picturesque campsite at the campground, next to a mountain stream. I have received some trail maps from the campground office and make a plan for today's hike. The trail takes us over the river to the end of the village. From here, we crawl up the bank to the highway where all traffic is stopped and huge trailers are parked. Is there an accident? No, we have climbed directly into the set for a movie. We hustle out of the camera's view and find the continuance of our trail. The trail leads to Quarry Lake. The blue green of the water is inviting. First Nicholas and Iain shed their hiking boots for a dip, then the rest of us join them. The water is refreshing and we lie on our backs taking in the panorama around us. The mountains surrounding us resemble those in Switzerland. I think how rugged the landscape is compared to Switzerland's picture perfect farms with window boxes overflowing with flowers in the neat little chalets. We float and swim in the cool green water, then lie back on the bank to dry. Now, the warmth of the sun is welcoming as it dries our shirts stretched out on the rocks behind us.

We walk on to the ski and training centre, home to the 1988 Olympic Games. From the centre, we pick our way down the power

Our camping spot in Canmore was picture perfect.

line, which leads to the old railway trestles that carried coal trains long ago. They now lie abandoned, except for the odd biker or hiker making their way to the village of Canmore. Sometimes dubbed a 'yuppie town,' Canmore is nestled under the shadow of the Rockies. Crawling with visitors, it is a hubbub of activity. Markets with fresh fruit and vegetables spill onto the streets and open-air cafes invite the passersby. We are anxious to return to our campground to eat so we must push back the urge to drop everything and sit at one of the little pubs for the rest of the day.

Back at the campground, contents from our bins spill across our site. Our clothesline is strung for our wet clothing and guitars come from their cases. Everyone pitches in. Heike chops the onions while keeping harmony with Nora on "Angel from Montgomery." Maria chimes in as she minces the garlic. It is the best time of the day after a long walk to sit back, have a cold drink and prepare the evening meal. Tonight will be stroganoff. I think how far we have come and how fortunate we are to be so happy and healthy. As I return from the washroom, the moon appears above the peaks of the mountains sending a pale light over our campsite and to the stream beyond. It is a perfect night.

August 9

Place: Canmore to Banff
Distance: 28 km
Wildlife: Douglas fir, poplar trees, elk, and deer, bear claw marks on trees as well as raspberry-filled scat.

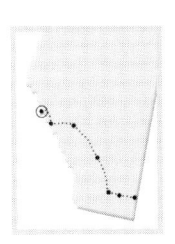

As the rest of the troupe cleans up from breakfast, I make a quick jaunt to Valhalla Pure Outfitters. This company has sponsored us with a tent, clothing and cooking utensils. I am on a search for protection from bears. I am informed that we will be in Grizzly country from now on and we must be cautious. Not a welcome thought. The warning signs are everywhere. Bears can react with speed and deadly force. Bears that have lost their wariness of people and associate human activity with food retain their violent unpredictability and can be extremely dangerous.

I purchase larger bear bells. We already have small ones given to us by my sister, Betty, back in Newfoundland. I also purchase a container of bear spray, which I hook onto my pack. This is only a last resort measure, as you have to be very close to the bear for it to have any effect. God help us all if the bear is close enough that I have to use it. I purchase a book on the Rocky Mountain trails and return to the campground.

(from Iain's diary)

We begin the day with the most beautiful scenery. Mountains tower above us in all directions and the sounds of the creek fill our ears. A simple breakfast is prepared and after a brief discussion on the day's hike, it is decided that we will hike from Canmore to Banff and meet Billy there. We start the hike right from the campground, walking through the town, passing a multitude of outdoor recreation stores, like wonderful Valhalla Pure Outfitters, restaurants and small cafes. I could definitely spend more than a few days in this area.

The trip from town to the Nordic Centre involves a steep climb. A long set of stairs leaves more than a few of us huffing and puffing, but that is only the beginning. By the time we get to the centre, it seems like it cannot possibly get any warmer. Then again, I guess I did miss some very warm days in Saskatchewan. After a brief bathroom break, we are on our way on the Banff trail. The centre seems to be sort of a mecca for bikers during the summer due to the many well-kept trails here.

A mountain biking class for beginners is just setting out as well, practicing braking while going downhill. I am very interested to see what they are being taught, so I watch intently. The instructor first shows the proper way to do it, then asks for a volunteer. Unfortunately, the student brakes a little too hard and is sent tumbling down the hill. Fortunately for her, the bike travels faster than its rider and misses landing on her. Although the Banff trail seems like a popular one, these are the last bikers we will see for quite some time.

Alberta

Tall, perfectly straight Douglas fir and poplar trees border the trail. Every once in a while there is a break in the trees that reveals a beautiful meadow surrounded by the vast mountains. The threat of bears is always on our minds. Bear scat and claw marks on the trees are ever-constant reminders that an encounter is possible at any moment. With all of our bear bells ringing, I'm sure that it would take a very deaf bear not to know that we are here. We don't take any chances. We don't open up any food until we are near a quickly flowing river that we can jump into if need be.

Although the trail is beautiful, it seems to go on forever. It eventually turns into a road but we aren't quite at our destination. We are originally told that it is 18 kilometres from the start of the trail to the Banff golf course where Billy is waiting. This is certainly not the case. After about three more kilometres of walking on this road we decide to stop and eat. Kathy won't hear of us removing food from our packs on the trail in case we entice a bear. We wave down a passing vehicle to ask how far it actually is to the golf course and find out that it is only about a ten-minute walk, so we gather our gear together and are off again. We quickly encounter the first couple of holes on the course and when we turn one corner we spot a herd of elk grazing on one of the tee-offs. We take picture after picture of these wonderful animals. We watch two avid golfers tee-off among them and wonder why they can't just skip the hole rather than endanger the elk. I am more than happy when we finally arrive at the clubhouse, because I am in dire need of the washroom. I must say that I have never been in such an extravagant washroom. There are even couches in it. At this point I think that we are all exhausted. Although the hike hasn't been much longer than a normal day, hiking in the mountains and on actual forest trails takes much more energy.

We originally plan to stay in one of the many campgrounds in Banff, but they seem very full and the hostel is quite expensive. (The vibes of Banff are off today.) After a brief stop in town for groceries, we drive on to Lake Louise. Unfortunately we have no more luck there, as both the primary campground and the overflow are completely full. Even the hostel has no rooms left. After Kathy explains our story and describes all of the places we have slept, we are able to secure the ping-pong room in the basement of the hostel. It is actually quite nice with real mattresses and pillows. Another advantage is that we have access to a large kitchen where Kathy, Maria and I prepare chicken with pineapple and green pepper, pasta, vegetables, rice with mushroom sauce, broccoli and a salad. The place has many added facilities as well, such as a sauna and Internet access. The sauna is perfect for my sore and tired muscles. Unfortunately, Kathy, Maria and Nora come back from checking email with news that a dear friend, Sandy Young, has passed away. Tears are shed in remembrance of what a wonderful man he was and how much they will miss him.

Sandy Young had been my professor at Dalhousie University and a close family friend. Tonight I feel like such a deserter to be so far from him when he died. I email our mutual friends, Ed and Kathryn Belzer. They reassure me that Sandy would support our venture and would not have expected me to return. It is a solace but doesn't ease the loss. We fall onto the mattress on the floor of the dark ping-pong room in grief. I think of the words that Sandy sent to me recently, still pinned to my refrigerator at home.

> I believe …
> > that imagination
> is stronger than knowledge.
> > That myth
> is more potent than history.
> > That dreams
> are more powerful than facts.
> > That hope
> always triumphs over experience.
> > That laughter
> is the only cure for grief.
> > And I believe …
> That LOVE is stronger than death

How true these words are. Love is stronger than death. If only tonight I could tell Sandy now how much we love him. In the night, I am awakened by Maria, who is tugging at my arm, sitting bolt upright. I can't see a thing in the windowless room, but sense her anxiousness. "Look where we are, Mom," she announces before sinking into a deeper sleep. This little quote, in Maria's sleep, will become part of our pack lingo in the days to follow.

Alberta

August 10

Place: Lake Louise to Nelson, British Columbia (Drive day)
Distance hiked: 7 km
Wildlife: elk, birds, sparrows

(from Chris' diary)
Today is the beginning of my second full day with the fabulous Hike 2000 crew. It's great to be a part of this group of people I met a few weeks earlier while they were hiking the Rossburn Subdivision Trail in Manitoba. The ping-pong room in the Lake Louise hostel turns out to be quite comfortable for us. Eight mattresses laid out on the floor with all of our gear fill most of the floor space. After the last couple of nights in my small tent it is nice to have leg and head room. We eat our toast, croissants and eggs quietly as a result of last evening's sad news.

All crew members are in the van by quarter after ten. We take a short drive to the Chateau Lake Louise for a quick view of the lake and glacier. Today is a driving day as we have a stretch of highway to cover to get to Nelson, British Columbia. As we enter the large parking area to the chateau, we stop to ask a national park officer for directions to the lake. She points in the direction of the path. Since we need to get on the road, Kathy asks if there is a way to see it from the van. The park officer says we'd have to park the van and walk about ten seconds through some trees.

It occurs to us what this must look like to her. This large, blue van, full of people, with Hike 2000 boldly displayed on the side asking if we can see the lake from the van. If she only knew the places and distance this crew has traveled. After a few minutes and an exchange of cameras for photo opportunities with a German family, we are back on the road again, heading west toward the Alberta/British Columbia border.

Thanks to Billy's confident handling of the van and trailer, we make another quick stop at the border sign for British Columbia. This is an important stop, marking the end of our journey in Alberta and the beginning of our ten days in British Columbia. A short distance later, we stop for lunch at a provincial park rest stop. An attractive bird, blue and black in colour, catches a grape swept from the picnic table.

As we carry on our way, Nora reads us the story of Swift Runner from Outlaws of the Canadian West. It contains some horrific events, like the cannibalism that resulted from the disappearance of the prairie buffalo. A short while later, we descend into Revelstoke, where Kathy is able to get in touch with Phil Mason, who is assembling a train in the yard with the switcher. Kathy disappears while a crib game takes place with the rest outside the museum. She reappears in a large diesel locomotive, # 3034. We all run over to take photos and greet her. Certainly one of today's highlights.

I have been in touch with Phil Mason many times before our hike began. I am excited to finally meet him. He pulls me up over the front of the train to join him in the cab. I have never been in the cab of a train before. I am amazed at how close oncoming trains look and really are. Phil chats away as he shunts back and forth, picking up and dropping off cars. I can't get the grin off my face. I am so excited to finally be in a freight train. We drive up to the museum where Phil lets me out. This definitely is my best for the day.

(from Chris' diary)
A sugar binge from the local ice-cream and convenience store keep things lively in the van for a while as we continue our drive south along the Columbia River. The Columbia has several dams along it, creating lakes filling the lower basin of the valley. One of these is the Upper Arrow Lake, which we cross on a BC ferry. The half-hour crossing is a chance to see the views from the water level for a change. While we are waiting for the ferry we notice a dog has been crated in the back of an enclosed pick-up truck, full to the top with gear. There is no fresh air, and it being a hot day caused some concern among us. During the ferry crossing, Nora searches out the driver of the truck. This turns out to be a pleasant experience, as the driver says he forgot to open the back hatch and is grateful to be reminded. We all have the chance to meet this friendly animal.

Back on the road, we pass some attractive signs advertising hot springs. We keep driving. It is too hot anyway. By the time we reach Nelson, it is getting dark and we are tired. The toughest job is for Billy, who has to drive us around the streets of Nelson while we look for a suitable place. The Dancing Bear Hostel turns out to be the best location for the night. We cook some pasta and have a filling supper before bed. It is a quiet night, other than 'some people' complaining about some snoring, which turns out to be me, unfortunately. I had no idea I snored.

British Columbia

August 11 - August 21

Sporting our new "snake gators" at the British Columbia/Washington border. Nicholas, Nora, Heike, Kathy, Chris, Maria and Iain.

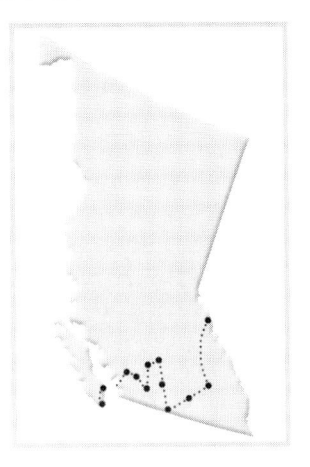

August 11

Nelson to South Slocan
Distance: 23 km
Wildlife: snake

After a very restless sleep, I am in the shower with plans for the day circling in my head. We are on our way to Castlegar, the former home of my brother-in-law, Roy Englund. We have heard a lot about this place and I am anxious to finally see it.

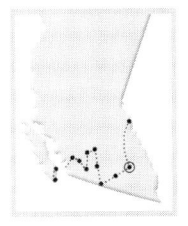

(from Heike's diary)
After a hot and stuffy night, I decide that a walk about town is just the thing to revive my spirits. There aren't many people around since it is fairly early, and I enjoy watching the town wake up. There are some people already working in some of the lush gardens of the Victorian houses on the slope on the other end of the town. I read an announcements for a "building with straw bales" workshop on the notice board outside the cinema. Maybe I should be wearing flowers in my hair...

On my way back to the hostel, I talk with Ritch, who is working on a garden on the uphill side of Baker Street. This garden is kept up by 'Earth Matters,' a local environmental group that utilizes unused public spaces, turning them into community gardens. Ritch points me in the direction of Cottonwood Falls Park, one of the projects located just around the corner from our hostel.

After checking with my traveling companions, I decide to nip over there before breakfast. It turns out to be an oasis tucked away between a brewery, a car dealership, a bakery and the embankment of Highway 3A. The waterfall after which the park is named makes this a very atmospheric place. The garden also features a small straw bale house, the first one of its kind in Nelson. I particularly like its Hundertwasseresk details. The concept of the garden is to display herbs and medicinal plants and to conserve water. After our decadently delicious breakfast at one of the town's many inviting eateries, we start our hike at this park.

Today is one of our more difficult and less straightforward trails. The staff at the local Valhalla Pure store help us find the best route. The trail from Glade, a small village only accessible by ferry, to Castlegar sounds enticing. But, since details on trail conditions are not known and due to some of our previous 'surprises,' we decide to hike out of Nelson along the old road with the van driving ahead. So, off we go uphill for many kilometres. What an unusual experience for us old railroaders. We have great views of the Kootenay River and there are many interesting and beautiful things to see along the way: houses, gardens, wooden barns, giant cedars and horses.

Since it is a very hot day, we all run out of water before the end of the hike. Katlin, a young boy tanking around on his moped, leads us to his house where we can get a refill. His mom, Debbie, is interested in our project and would come along for a bit if she weren't varnishing chairs. Another highlight is our visit at a riding club where we talk to some very exhausted riders and where I see my first American Bashkir Curly. We soon find that we have enough 'clicks' so we all pile into the van and drive to Castlegar via two of the dams on the Kootenay River. My day pretty much finishes here since I am knocked out by a severe bout of tiredness and so miss all the fun mixing with the locals around the campfire on the river.

The campground next to the river on the opposite bank to Castlegar is alive with activity. A bonfire is planned for tonight right in the lot next to ours. The locals are warming up for the activities next door as we cook our supper. Two young men drive golf balls from the campsite into the river as they wash back a few beers. Johnnie Cash tunes blare from the car stereo as the group builds a huge pyramid of logs for tonight's bonfire.

Nora and I begin dancing to their tunes on our campsite and are quickly joined by one of the revelers. He loves to dance and is quick to invite us over tonight to enjoy their hospitality. It is not like we could avoid the celebration if we wanted to, but we are happy to accept this invitation and promise to come over to their site after supper. With dishes washed up, we venture over to meet our new friends. The picnic table is full of beer bottles and they offer them around. Iain, Nora, Maria, Billy and I sit back for some entertainment. We learn that the Castlegar song that my brother-in-law Roy has been singing all these years actually does exist and has verses, not just that famous line…"Here we are in Castlegar, Nelson can't be very far."

With more beer, songs and stories, I begin to get some flack about why I would ever want to walk across Canada. One young man attacks me with accusations of stupidity, "Fuckin' think! They have planes, you know." Before the night is over, he is offering to pay my way to Vancouver and relieve me of my walking. It is a crazy night with the Castlegar gang, who leave several times to replenish the beer supply and restock the fire. We finally say our goodbyes and crawl into bed in the wee hours of the morning.

August 12

Castlegar, Paulson Bridge
Distance: 18 km
Wildlife: osprey

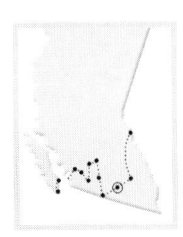

(from Nicholas' diary)
Mom makes some omelets for breakfast this morning. I have my usual chocolate feast. They partied all night with the campground owners and their friends by the bonfire. We go to the Doukhobor settlement and I wave my hand over the unseeing eyes of the paper maché girls, as a joke.

The Doukhobor 'spirit wrestlers' museum displays a replica of a typical home of the five thousand or more Russian immigrants who arrived in the area between 1908 and 1913, seeking a place where they could practice their religion. Believing in toil and a peaceful way of life, they lived off what they could make themselves.

We are told at the railway museum that there are two rail lines in Castlegar and that the one on the bridge rarely sees a train. We hike

Nicholas, Iain and Maria stroll along the boardwalk on the trail in Castlegar.

along looking down at the river and the green banks on the far side. Small watercraft buzz underneath us and private planes dip close to the wide expanse of the river. We walk to the other side, a walk my brother-in-law would have made many times as a boy, delivering papers. The path on the far side takes us to the large highway bridge that has a pedestrian walk. Perched in a sprawling nest on a pole by the trail is a large osprey. To our surprise, as we stroll across the second bridge spanning the river, a train is chugging its way across the railway bridge we have just crossed. It is our good omen to see at least one train a day at the most unexpected times. We finish the loop in Castlegar and drive on to the Paulson Bridge.

Paulson Bridge is located along the highway leading to Greenwood, where we will spend the night with Billy's brother, Doug, and his wife, Kate. There is a long trail, leading deep into the valley, which swings onto the old rail line that runs under this 81-foot-high structure. Our plan is to hike along this woods road, turn onto the abandoned rail line, follow it until we come to Paulson Bridge, then return on the same route. The road begins with a steep uphill climb, which slows our pace tremendously. We talk about the possibility of bears in this area. It certainly looks like bear territory to me. The trees bear witness to my suspicions with long claw marks—a trace of the hunt for ants in the bark. We hike close together, not giving the possible attack of a bear the benefit of a straggler. Soon, we come to a deserted cabin. A foreboding aura surrounds this dilapidated building and we hurry on, with a cold shiver on our backs.

It is a long way before we see the Paulson Bridge. It is almost dark in the deep canyon where the train tracks once ran. It is too late to retreat back to the van on that same road. We have been warned of the possibility of cougars on the cliffs that overhang the canyon. With darkness fast approaching, we decide to climb the steep embankment to the bridge.

British Columbia

(from Nicholas' diary)
We decide to clamber up the side of the cliff where all the rocks are piled. It is 81 meters to the top of the pile. Mom keeps calling me to wait even though I know I am the lightest one and the rocks are least likely to give way under me. It is probably the best part of the entire hike because we don't usually do any climbs—we're mostly on railway lines. With many thorns in our hands from the rosebushes, we get to the top of the bridge. We walk across the bridge to find a very surprised Billy, who expected us to come from the other direction. He wouldn't have seen us for a long time if we had come the other way. We drove to Doug and Kate's house in Greenwood, Canada's smallest city.

Greenwood is a small, cozy city with the feeling of the real old west. It was for this atmosphere that the movie, Snow Falling On Cedars, was filmed here. We wind our way through the narrow streets and pull up beside the house of Doug and Kate Redden. It is a two-storey home with its back lawn sloping down to a gurgling brook. Billy goes in to see if this is, in fact, the right house. When he returns, he crawls up on the seat of the van and gives himself a couple of slaps to regain his composure. It is the first time he has seen Doug since he had a stroke earlier this year and the sight of him in a wheelchair is a shock. Doug, who spent most of his life tromping through the wilderness prospecting for gold, is also disheartened by his condition. As we sit down to enjoy cold refreshments with them, Doug and Kate carry on in their usual good-humoured way. It isn't until later that we discuss the problems that come with Doug's inability to care for himself and the unhappy state this stroke has left him in. Kate has made sandwiches and we sit around their table sharing stories of our journey and reminiscing about the fun we had the last time they came to Nova Scotia. It was Doug who introduced us to polar bear swimming on one of his returns home in the seventies. We carried on the tradition for 12 years.

Doug Redden

Doug retires to bed early and Kate tells us we have to see the old bar in town. We walk out in the warm evening air. Walking into the bar is like walking into the set of a western movie. The long wooden cradle of the bar is reflected in the mirror, which serves as the backdrop for the many bottles of spirits. I can imagine a gunfight breaking out here and the huge wooden chairs being thrown against the glass.

The tall bar stools are lined with locals catching up on the day's activities and sharing mugs of frothy beer from the shiny golden taps. We pile around one of the more inconspicuous tables and order drinks. The waitress treats us in a friendly fashion and we joke and laugh around the table as Billy entertains us with stories of his navy days. As we are about to leave, Nora and Maria spy the juke box in the corner and drop in a few coins to play a tune. We congregate down on the dance floor at the back end of the bar. Soon, we are twisting and jiving the night away. Not a soul from the bar joins us. Instead, we have the floor to ourselves and make full use of this luxury. Suddenly, a group of young women, sparsely dressed in shimmering summer sheers, enters the bar and makes their way to their dancing area. They look disdainfully at our hiking garb and push their way between us. We get the message quickly and pick up our things to go.

Back at Doug and Kate's, we creep into the tents by the stream. The moon is bright in the sky, reflecting on the water that rushes by us in the brook. This is a perfect spot for Doug and Kate, I think. There is the feeling of the country, but the flair of a small town, too.

August 13

Greenwood to Midway
Distance: 23 km
Wildlife: grasshoppers, June bug

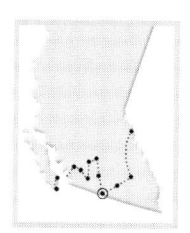

(from Nora's diary)
It seems like every day there are different obstacles to be paranoid about. Take this morning, for example. 'Anything we should be worried about on the trail today?' Mom asks. With a mischievous glint in his eye, Doug answers, 'Only hungry black bears, vicious cougars, rattlers, bull snakes and moose with really big antlers.' Funny! Especially since we heard about a cougar killing a lady on a horse this year not far away, not to mention local warnings about rattlesnakes on the trail. It makes for an unsettled walk…me skittering sideways at the slightest rustle among the dead dry shrubs along the trail. Of course, it is only those hundreds of locusts flying haphazardly

British Columbia

Nicholas on the hot, dusty trail from Greenwood to Midway, mile "0" of the Kettle Valley Railway.

into the plants making all the noise...right? Nonetheless, we don our new leather Manitoba snake boots or "snakers." Besides, before we can patent them, there should be a trial period, I guess.

Along the trail, there is a fence that holds a starving white stallion. The grass burned to the ground long ago in the summer heat and there is no sign of water in the field. Maria opens her pack and gives the horse her apple. He rubs his bony skull against her in appreciation. Where is its owner? We give more apples and vow to find someone to help this poor animal when we return tonight. The trail turns to a pipeline for about five kilometres. It is a ridge of rough earth with huge pipes providing obstacles to our crossing. It is on this section that we find a much-needed (though decrepit) outhouse. We decide to stop for lunch, choosing our seats on the big pipes that are piled on the trail. Chris, a world-class bagpiper, takes out his tin whistle and serenades us through the pipe. The sound reverberates in the still air to the farms below.

We walk on through tall weeds that brush our sides. Locusts hiss and snap out of the grass. We skitter sideways at the anticipation of the much-dreaded rattler.

Dry and dusty from our walk through the semi desert hills, we arrive in Midway at the Mile 0 train station. Formerly known as Boundary City, Midway had its first resident in 1884. The name was changed in 1994. When gold was discovered in Rock Creek, miners from the United States came swarming into this town. By the early 1900s, the town had five hotels, stores, a stagecoach company, a pharmacy and a sawmill. The first passenger train going east rolled through in 1915, fifteen years behind the establishment of the western terminus for the Columbia and Western Railway. The Kettle Valley Line, linking Midway and the west coast, began in 1910. The last passenger train to leave Midway through the Kettle Valley was on January 17, 1964.

Hiking the Dream

We hike five kilometres off the trail to the Washington/British Columbia border, where the guard tells us the hills we just came through are "crawlin' with rattlers."

(from Nora's diary)
On a spur of the moment, we decide to hike to the Canadian/United States border into Washington. The border security lady, strapped with guns, ammunition and all, is very friendly and open to all of our questions. As we drink our water, sitting on the steps of the customs house, a car pulls up and a perfectly groomed southern American, middle-aged couple gets out. Looking at us, they inquire where we are from. We tell them our story. The man looks at us skeptically and says in his southern drawl, 'Don't you sometimes wonder if you're all there?'

This has become the common reaction by the people we meet who can't fathom why we would choose to walk when we don't have to. It is a question that is hard to explain. Most people can't picture themselves spending four months on the trail, living in a tent and hiking in over 30°C temperatures all day. They become almost angry that we dare be so brazen. It is something we can't easily explain to people who think we are crazy. So, we usually don't bother trying to justify our motives. People walk away, shaking their heads as though they've just met a group of lunatics. Maybe they have, but we are having a lot of fun and are seeing part of a country they will never see from their cars on the highway.

Maria's passport gets stamped, then we hurry back to be admitted into Canada before the crossing gates close at 5:00 P.M. The Canadian guard is much more official, asking us all where we are from. He pauses, contemplating whether to let us in. We passed him only a few minutes before.

With all our attention to obstacles and dangers, we experience a new possibility today...forest fires! As we walk back to Midway to the grocery store, fire trucks whizz by, horns blaring. Midway and surrounding areas have already experienced two forest fires in the last four days and here is its third fire in less than a week. Fortunately, no real damage is done. There is a fire ban straight across British Columbia.

Billy picks up dirty us and drives us back to Greenwood. At the bottom of Doug and Kate's yard is a cool running stream, where we immediately immerse our feet. Chris, Iain and I walk across to the other side and quickly claim 'our island,' a small rock partially exposed from the water. We paint ourselves with a reddish slime made from scratching a wet stone on another rock. Mom makes supper over the barbecue, and afterwards we play music outside on the porch. After everyone else is in bed, mom and I work on the website.

August 14

Rhone to Coyote Creek to Beaverdell
Distance: 18 km
Wildlife: rabbit, ducks, fish, worms

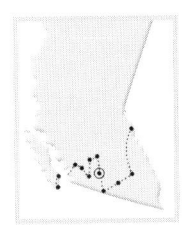

(from Maria's diary)
We pull ourselves out of our cocoon of warmth into the crisp morning air. Another beautiful day is unfolding before us. We eat a quick breakfast, then say goodbye to our hosts, Doug and Kate Redden. We drive to meet Paul Lautard, a Trans Canada Trail and train enthusiast. He has made a rest stop for travelers of the trail and brings cold water for anyone who rings the old sprinkler with the available hammer. The walls of the rest stop are covered with signatures from those who have stopped by, so we add our names and web address to a beam. Paul shows us the tricks his dog does, attacking a rock and pushing it around with his snout. It is quite impressive, with the rocks being very large.

Seventy-eight-year-old Paul grew up in a family of ten children, living with his mom and dad at the summit station of the Kettle Valley Railway. They were far from any neighbours and had to stay in an orphanage to attend school. Paul recalls trains coming through with car tops full of hobos. As little food as they had, his mother would give the hobos bread. Later, when Paul was around six years old, the family moved down to the little station at Rhone. Paul's father was the station master and the entire family lived in the station. He shows me where the kitchen, living room and girls' bedroom used to be. They also had an upstairs. He says there really wasn't room for all of them in the house at one time when they were awake and they would often eat in shifts. In the summer, they never wore shoes. When the train came by, they would all run out to see the train, ten little barefoot children, lining up

Paul Lautard fills us with stories about growing up next to the Kettle Valley Railway.

to watch the passengers going to places they might never see. Once, when the train came in the fall, a bundle was tossed from the train. It broke open at their feet to reveal…shoes! The children made a mad scramble to pick out a pair they liked. Mostly, they were too big or too small and Paul recalls his toes bending over so the shoes would fit on his feet. Those shoes did them until the snow fell, then they would wear boots. They only wore socks in winter.

As we stroll around the old foundation of the family home and station, Paul tells me about his life, growing up along the famous Kettle Valley Railway. As kids, Paul and his brothers and sisters would often ride the train. If his family had an emergency, his mother could get a train pass. Once, Paul's brother threw a butcher knife at Paul's head, striking him but just missing his temple. Luckily, it happened just before the train arrived and he and his mother boarded the train and he reached a doctor. He remembers wearing a turban covered in blood on his head. Paul is married to a woman 20 years younger than him. He tells me they are happy now, both with a better life. They have running water, electricity and a cozy home overlooking the Kettle Valley. I have to agree, it is a spot that many people only dream of owning. Paul is a fan of Scottish music and is delighted when Chris pulls his bagpipes from their case and warms them up to play a tune. The pipes ring out over the hills far below. It is a touching moment for all of us. Before we leave, Paul offers Nora a ride on his bulldozer. It is an unusual offer and Nora jumps at the chance.

(from Maria's diary)
Paul piles us all into the back of his truck and we set off down the trail. We drive to the Rhone Canyon where the rail bed clings to the rock wall on one side and is bordered by boulders that protect the rail bed on the other side. Beyond the boulders is the canyon, deep within two rock faces where water fills the crevasse. A small sand beach borders the water far below, looking much more inviting than a long day of hiking in the hot sun.

As we drive to the canyon, Paul tells me how the Chinese were hired to build the railway and how, the day before payday, one or two

July 31 - August 21

Western Canada

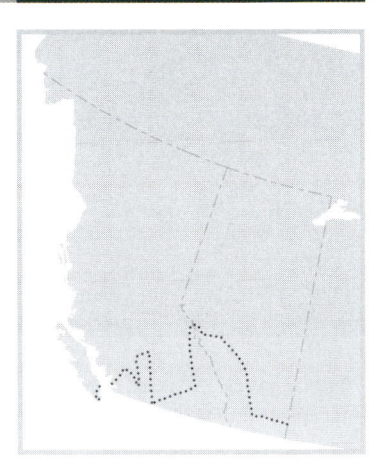

Alberta - Medicine Hat. The ground is dry and parched, with cacti pushing their way though the brown grass. The valley is lush and green. Buffalo were once forced off the cliffs here.

The amazing sunset at the Saskatchewan/Alberta border.

Hiking the Dream

Alberta - (Above) Teepees depict aboriginal art in Medicine Hat.

An abandoned rail line in Medicine Hat.

Prairie farmers opposed to the trail's dissection of their farmland, sometimes plant bulls to discourage trespassers.

Hiking the Dream

Alberta - We detour for a quick hike to Lake Louise, one of Canada's most photographed lakes.

(Left) Chris Milne steals a moment of reflection on the trail from Canmore to Banff. Salt outlines the shape of his pack on his back.

(Bottom) Nora and Maria on the trail from Canmore to Banff.

Hiking the Dream

Alberta - (Right) Canmore. It is the aprés-hike moments that we treasure the most: music, boots off, great chats and an "apple."

The trail to Banff becomes more narrow, with bear scat and claw marks constantly reminding us that we are in grizzly country.

Hiking the Dream

British Columbia - (Right) Nicholas at Rhone Creek on the trail to Beaverdell.

Looking across the Myra Canyon at the stretch of Trestle #4.

(Inset bottom) Iain, Maria, Nora, Nicholas and Heike take a rest on the Kettle Valley Railway at Myra Canyon.

Hiking the Dream

British Columbia - (Right) On the trail to Okanagan Falls.

Heike cools her feet in the stream at Beaverdell.

(Inset) Maria tends blisters on Chris' feet. This has become a daily ritual with all of us.

Hiking the Dream

British Columbia - Rhone Creek on the Kettle Valley Railway

(Inset) First Blood with the "Billy Miner Gang" holdup in the Othello tunnels. Iain, Maria, Heike, and Nora.

Hiking the Dream

British Columbia - (Right) Billy; our faithful driver, on that last day.

(Centre right) Chris serenades us as we walk into the Pacific Ocean.

(Centre left) No hiking boots, no sticks…we've done it. East to west. It is a perfect ending.

(Right) The time has come to sort our belongings and head home. Note the "full" sign at our campsite.

would be killed on the railway. He suspects the deaths weren't accidental—a way for the railway to save some money. The graves of the Chinese would be dug right along the line. I think how sad it must have been for the families of these men who would never learn the truth about the deaths of their loved ones. We part ways with Paul and walk along the old abandoned rail line. It is hot now and I wonder about forest fires in the area.

(from Maria's diary)
We are lucky to come across another swimming area later in our hike. We sneak off the trail on a small path to the gravel beach by the sparkling, cool water. The ripples of the creek pour over an open flat of stones into a deep pool of crisp water where we dip our already hot feet. The initial touch is shocking, but it is always warmer when you get in. The break is absolutely perfect as we swim around the rock cliffs, longing to jump off, if only once. However, we obey the rules and pull ourselves away from the creek before jeopardizing our necks.

Everyone is swimming but me. It looks very inviting, but I have just doctored my feet and have no Band-Aids to replace wet ones. I lie back on the warm stones, thinking about Billy's brother and my cousin, Doug. He told me last night he dreamed all night that he was walking…to the mother lode, he said. He has spent much of his life roaming the hills, looking for gold, like one of the old prospectors. It is so unlike him to be sitting in one spot, depending on someone to help him eat and crawl into bed. When I hugged him goodbye this morning, his strong arm held tight and he said tearfully, "I'm such a mess." I told him to think positively and that in a year we will wait for him in Caribou, his childhood home in Nova Scotia. God, I hope that is true. How sad it is that he is paralyzed. He should be here swimming with us. This morning he told me my eyes look like my father's. He remembers my father, also a prospector, quoting poems by Robert Service. I recite "Sam McGee" as tears of both laughter and sadness fill his eyes. He tells me he has no control of his emotions now. I tell him, I never did have control of mine.

I am jolted from my thoughts by a stone splashing in the water in front of me. Paul Lautard has returned to his old swimming hole and is standing high on the rocks above.

(from Maria's diary)
Back on the trail, the hiking seems much harder as we think about the sensation of swimming, and lug wet clothes and heavy feet. We are also tormented by the occasional huge, slow, bothersome mosquito.

We continue our walk along the old Kettle Valley Railway. The valley is tree sloped and large shadows pass over the forest from the floating clouds above. The rail line runs by the creek, not far from the road. We stop at the old "Taurus" station, where the octagonal water tower once stood. Long stalks of Mullin stand in the crumbling foundation. On the other side of the rail bed, a typical CNR red storage building stands vacant among the bushes.

(from Maria's diary)
Seeing the van is wonderful and we head for Beaverdell to get supper food and a find a camping spot. Thankfully, we find both. Our camping spot is beside a gurgling brook.

Maria and Iain are cooking supper. Heike is playing her flute next to the stream where Billy is fishing. Nicholas is practicing his 'hacks' with the volleyball and Nora and Chris are working on the website. We have placed some 'Wildcat' and 'Grasshopper' beer in the brook to cool. It is a nice night and we are alone in this camping area.

(from Maria's diary)
Billy catches a little fish in the brook. Iain and I are chefs tonight, creating both vegetarian and hearty Bolognese spaghetti with a side tossed salad with dressing à la Maria. Dinner isn't served until 11:00 P.M. then the dishes are taken to spend the night in the shower.

As I watch the sun sink below the mountains in the west, I think of how it feels like fall tonight. We have been together through such a range of temperatures, almost like the four seasons, from the late winter snows of Newfoundland to the dry heat of the prairies and now the hint of fall in the evening mountain air. Soon our little group will be parting ways. It is hard to think of us all living separately in real houses. I will always treasure these 'after hike' moments when everyone retreats to their own pastimes, then draws back together around the campfire for great conversation, songs and laughs.

August 15

Myra Canyon
Distance: 22 km
Wildlife: chipmunks, squirrels, rabbit

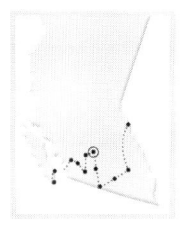

It is 3:00 A.M. and my senses have perked to the sound of padded footsteps in the brook, which lies between the tents and the deep forest. 'Maria …Maria…Listen!' No response. 'Maria …LISTEN!' Maria's head rises up and lies back down on her pillow. 'Maria, you are not trying to listen, you are trying to sleep.' Maria groans, 'Yes, Mom, you're right, I am trying to sleep.' I spend the rest of my night straining to hear the sound of what I believe to be a cougar in the brook. I swear that as a mother sleeping on the forest floor for this long I am gaining the instincts of a mother of any wild creature. The need to protect is innate in all of us, we just are not always put to the test or we fall into the comfort zone of always knowing there is help nearby. Now, in the deep night, lying next to a forest with the wild Rocky Mountains surrounding us, I feel vulnerable to whatever predator may be lurking nearby.

It is 6:30 A.M. 'Get up…it's flipping cold out here.' Billy's arms are wrapped tight across his chest as his breath puffs from his mouth. It is cold and the dark clouds forebode rain. Zack, the owner of the campground, gives us a rundown of today's journey to the Myra Canyon. I have a great idea to make scones on the griddle. The attempt is a failure and they end up resembling pancakes. This famous concoction has since been dubbed "Scancakes." Everyone eats them up with great compliments, despite my disappointment with them. Before leaving the campground, I run into a guy named Tex, who offers me his son's phone number in Kelowna. His son, Cash, promises to direct us to the trailhead today into the Myra Canyon.

We drive through rugged mountain terrain in a thunderstorm to Kelowna. Billy twists and turns the sacred Hike 2000 van around the hairpin serpentine road as the rest of us sit, silently pressing our own brake peddles to make sure we make every turn safely. Finally, we reach Kelowna, where we will meet Cash, the son of Tex. We appreciate his kindness in breaking from his work to escort us to the Myra Canyon. The drive from Kelowna is through ranchland and orchards, now hanging with fruit.

The Myra Canyon is spanned by a myriad of trestles and bridges, which must have presented a formidable challenge to trains in the past. The tracks follow the side hills of the mountains in a long curving route, with the canyon far below. In less than 12 kilometres, we cross 18 trestles and pass through two tunnels. Below us lie piles of rail ties and crossbeams from previous structures. In 1932, many of the trestles over the forks of the canyon were replaced with steel bridges. The passage through this part of the Kettle Valley railway must have been spectacular. I speak with a gentleman who traveled the line in the mid forties. He says in the winter, at night, it was majestic to see the cliffs hanging with ice and the moon glistening on the gorge far below the train. It was this same ice and snow that caused havoc with the rail line and eventually brought its closure. Avalanches and mudslides were a common occurrence and the cost to maintain this section of railway was just too great.

We hike along, stopping frequently for pictures. This time of year there are many bikers on the trail and we jump off their path as they approach. At one rest stop, Iain and Nicholas gain a friend in a little chipmunk who dares to eat trail mix from their hands. We expect that handouts are a common occurrence on this popular portion of the Kettle Valley Railway.

The sun is low on the horizon when we meet the van. We decide to spend the night in Kelowna, providing we can find a camping spot. After a prolonged grocery shop, I come out of the store into complete darkness. Where has this day gone? To our chagrin, the local camping areas are posting 'No Vacancy' signs. I try the hostel but with no luck. By now, it is very late and we haven't eaten in nine hours. Suddenly, Chris has an idea. He remembers as a boy traveling with his family to Kelowna to visit a university friend of his father. This is a long shot, but we have few options left. First, Chris has to remember their names, then check out the phone directory for a listing. Sure enough, Bob Jablonski and his wife, Margaret, are home and willing to let us camp on their lawn. The problem for us is to find them. We drive through Kelowna to the far end of the tracks. A fierce party is going on in the parking lot. Chris bounds from the van, his blonde hair

British Columbia

Eighteen trestles span the treacherous gorges of the Myra Canyon on the Kettle Valley Railway.

bouncing under the light of the street lamps. Billy, who is not amused by the situation, stares grimly out the window. Our reaction to this embarrassing situation is totally opposite to his as we try to squelch our laughter as we watch Chris politely knocking on doors looking for the right house.

Finally, Chris arrives back at the van but doesn't get in. We wonder what is wrong. In his deep, polite voice, Chris explains, "You could just drive on and I could hold the door shut, but I have got my thumb stuck in the door latch and it has closed on it." It is too much. We burst with laughter at this ridiculous situation. Chris is so calm about it and Billy is enraged. "This isn't funny," he reminds us, which makes it even funnier to us. Poor Billy. If there is a night that he doesn't want to remember on this trip, I am sure this is it.

We release Chris' thumb from the broken door latch and drive to the other end of town where we find the Jablonski's. We pull up beside the neatly trimmed hedge of Bob and Margaret's home, spewing our bins on the sidewalk. We truly are hobos tonight. We set up our tents under their fruit trees, which are laden with ripe peaches. What a temptation. We are starving. We call pizza delivery to our new home on this immaculate lawn in the rich district of Kelowna. The pizza arrives and disappears in seconds. We crawl into our sleeping bags. I can hardly believe this has all been one day.

August 16

Naramata
Distance: 17.5 km

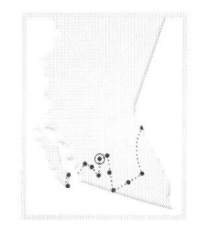

I am awake, lying in our tent on this neat lawn on this orderly street in Kelowna. I can hear motors starting with 'regular' people getting ready for work. Here we are, the transients, asleep on the lawn of this person we have never met, under these perfectly groomed peach trees. I emerge from the tent and slide open the door of their house, which has been left unlocked for us. I quietly turn the knob and creep into the bathroom, which is adjacent to the kitchen. Margaret is putting away the dishes, wearing her cool morning attire. I feel like such a street person, having slept in the same clothes that I wore hiking yesterday. Last night we were just too tired to even think about changing. We are grateful to have been given this refuge for the night, but now, I just want to get on the road. I start pulling the pegs to the tent even before I wake the others. Billy has gone down the street in search of coffee and by the time he returns, we are totally packed up.

(from Iain's diary)
This morning we wake to a very different sound than I've been used to—that of cars whizzing by. Although this isn't the most pleasant sound to wake up to, we are all glad for the hospitality we receive from the Jablonskis. Their yard has several peach trees that are flush with ripe fruit and I don't think I'm the only one getting hunger pangs from the sight of these. This hunger, and making sure we don't overstay our welcome, prompts us to pack up and move out as soon as we wake up. So, after thanking our hosts one last time, we drive to a bookstore so that Kathy can pick up a book on the Kettle Valley Railway that has been recommended to her. Kathy and Heike return with a treat of coffee and juice, which we have with the huge muffins that we bought the night before. On the road again, we weave through Okanagan roads surrounded by orchards of apples, peaches and apricots.

We find the Camp Along camping site and everything we could ask for: a pool, a volleyball court, a beautiful site on a plateau overlooking Okanagan Lake and even an apricot orchard. After setting up our tents, we drive to the first winery on our tour. The Nicoll Winery, the smallest winery in British Columbia, marks the start of our hike. We test only three wines here and, in my opinion, the Pinot Gris is the best. The second winery, the Red Rooster winery, has a much wider selection. The wine-tasting room is beautiful, with an adjoining restaurant. The servers are very professional, advising us in which order to try the wines. The Kettle Valley Winery is a small family winery with a tasting room attached to the owner's house, where pictures within pay tribute to the KVR from which it borrows its name. The Lake Breeze Winery is picturesque with a restaurant overlooking its vineyard. Here we find a wonderful selection of perfectly chilled wines, including

British Columbia

several dessert wines; we proceed to work down the list. They also have a beautiful (deaf) cat whose job it is to observe the tasters and make sure they don't get away without scratching her belly. At one point, the owners bring a small bowl of water which Kathy thinks is to cleanse her palate, but which turns out to be the cat's water bowl. The final winery, Langs, involves a very steep climb. Their signature wine is a maple wine available in both white and red. It is a wonderful dessert wine, which is fitting for our final tasting. On the way back to the campground, we stop in at a hemp shop, which sells just about every hemp product available. It is truly an eye opener. Back at our site, Kathy begins making soup while Chris, a loyal vegetarian, makes a lentil dish for us to try.

As if we didn't have enough wine for the day, we pull out the homemade wine that Russell Penny gave us before we left Newfoundland. We have been saving this wine for a special moment and what could be more special than sitting on this site, overlooking the Okanagan Valley after a wine tour in the Naramata. How ironic that we end our day with some good homemade wine from Russell in Newfoundland.

(from Iain's diary)
I end up going down to the lake for a swim as the pool is packed. The hills on the way back are certainly a lot harder to climb than they were on the way down. The dinner is fantastic and we are all a bit bushed but I still have laundry to do. Everyone went to bed after watching a beautiful moon rising, and I spend the next couple of hours waiting for clothes to dry.

August 17

Kaledon to Okanagan Falls
Distance: 25.5 km
Wildlife: deer

Billy has taken my request to be woken early seriously and calls me at 6:00 A.M. Today we will hike to the Okanagan Falls while Billy and Nicholas relax at the campsite and enjoy the swimming pool.

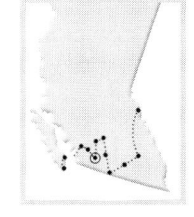

275

Fresh croissants and cinnamon buns are presented to us by the campground staff, a great start to the day.

The trail, which winds along the shore of the Okanagan Lake, is not accessible through the RV Park, so we must travel by the neighbourhood sidewalks. Water hoses hum and squirt, trying to keep alive the parched lawns in the summer heat. We walk down to an old abandoned winery with vines growing over the bare doorways. Private properties along the shore have posted signs forbidding access to the trail, which is part of the Kettle Valley Railway. It is a clear morning and every turn is a picture with the still blue lake on our left and the dry cliff, home to many birds, on our right.

The trail comes to an end in Okanagan Falls. We have visions of enjoying our lunch in the cool mist of the falls on some shady green bank. I enter Norma's Hair Salon to inquire about directions to the falls. The ladies, lined in the chairs, with their fresh new perms, laugh in unison. Another sucker has been caught. There are no falls. It is only a myth. I will have to learn the legend of the falls another time. I am too humiliated to ask these ladies with their perfect coifs. I go back outside to the waiting crew and lead them into the little tearoom to break the news. We sit in a ring with our ice cappuccinos, deciding on an alternate lunch spot.

Outside the shop, while waiting for Maria, Chris finds a tennis ball. The instinct to convert my carved Cuban hiking stick into a field hockey stick overcomes me. I turn the stick over, swatting the ball with the curved handle. This game of field hockey, which claimed my every moment for so many years, comes back to grab me and I lose all control. Chris bounds and leaps through the parking lot, retrieving balls that I smack with my stick. It is a wicked game with my hits getting wilder and Chris darting in front of oncoming cars and crawling under parked trailers, just to give me the ball once more. As Maria emerges from the teashop, oblivious to the scene, one final smack sends my hiking stick flying in pieces across the parking lot. By now, Iain is on his hands and knees on the pavement, laughing at this ridiculous display and Maria, laughing, falls straight backwards into a planter of rosebushes. It is so unlike our peaceful Chris to be this boisterous and as for me, I have totally smashed my precious stick. It is an insane moment. As Nora says, "The only time I saw Iain laugh harder was the night we had no place to sleep in Kelowna and Chris got his thumb caught in the door of the van and was too polite to say anything." We sit by the beach under a shady tree to 'eat our banquets' (pack lingo picked up in Cape Breton). Iain and Nora go out to the volleyball court to entertain us with a game using that same tennis ball. It is too hot and they retreat to the shade of the tree with the rest of us.

The walk back to Kaledon is desperately hot. There are a number of strollers on the trail and a few people fishing off the shore of the lake. The afternoon sun radiates its heat in a blur on the horizon and crickets chirp. This time we defiantly walk on the trail straight through the park. 'Beware of Bears' signs are posted to deter us. We have our doubts about bears in this residential area and continue through the park and up the steep hill to our campground. Nicholas and Heike jump into the pool for some fun while the rest of us shower and prepare to leave. It is a perfect camping spot and we hate to leave it. It definitely gets a ten from us!

We drive on to Princeton to be closer to our trailhead tomorrow. Billy winds the van through the mountain roads as we search for the Princeton Castle Resort. An old castle-like structure is said to be the hiding place of the notorious train robber, Billy Miner. Billy Miner, dubbed the 'Gentleman Bandit' because of his politeness while robbing trains, was well known in this area in the late 1800s. He apparently lived two lives, one as an elderly ladies' man, known for his generosity to those in need, and the other as a stagecoach and CPR robber. He was well liked and people in the area often hid him from the law. This spot in Princeton would be the perfect hideout. The old cement plant, built in 1910, cost hundreds of thousands of dollars and many lives in its construction. It was only operating nine months when it closed down. Billy Miner's hideout was on the hillside, near the Princeton Castle.

The Kettle Valley Railway runs right through the property on the ridge overlooking the horse paddock and stream below. The old building looks as though it could tell a tale about the grand days

A Billy Miner look-alike greets us at Princeton Castle Resort.

of the stagecoach and this infamous individual. Our campground host, a Billy Miner look-alike, is named for this bandit of the 1800s. He is kind to us, as the real Billy Miner would have been, bringing us free firewood despite the fire ban. He stands by our campfire relating stories, his eyes twinkling with mischief. We have chosen a site overlooking the creek and the horse stables. Heike, Iain, Maria and Nicholas go down to check out the possibility of trail rides while Nora and Chris struggle with the web pages. There is a hint of rain in the air as we pack our food away. Tonight the threat is of cougars. Not a comforting thought as we zip up our tent flaps.

August 18

Coalmont to Tulameen
Distance: 11 km

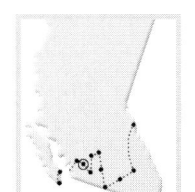

(from Heike's diary)
Finally, this long adventure is coming to an end. I feel cheated in a way, it all happened so quickly, and I don't feel ready for 'life after the trail' yet. These last few days are so busy that there isn't much time for journal writing.

I awake to a gray morning at the Castle Campground. Just as I get my sketchbook out to add some final sketches of my rendition of Chris serenading a Clydesdale horse with his bagpipes, it starts to rain. This means that we break a rather wet camp this morning. Kathy has an appointment with 'Billy Miner,' and I go and explore the Trans Canada Trail, which runs just behind our camp.

Billy Miner is waiting for me as I stroll over from our campsite. He has prepared some very strong coffee and we sit in his open-doored trailer listening to the rain pouring on the metal roof. The big overhanging trees provide some relief for the campsites and we remark how the rain is needed at this time with such a risk of forest fires. We stop long enough for photos at the old castle before leaving.

The drive to Coalmont is along a precarious mountain road, which is completely closed in winter due to avalanches. Large stones lay at

British Columbia

the base of the cliff on our right. The raging river runs far below the broken pavement that wraps around the mountainside. Seven pairs of eyes help Billy guide the van around the hairpin turns as we crawl farther into the wilderness of the old mining area of Coalmont. The Coalmont Hotel stands bold in the centre of the town, where most houses are locked and windows are covered in blinds. Old car bodies line the streets as if the people all left in a hurry. We pose by the old West style hotel, then pull on our hiking boots for the trek into Tulameen, another mining town.

As I am tying up my boots, a fifties model car drives up beside the van. Two 'cow poke' characters, wearing dusty, bent cowboy hats and with less than a full mouth of teeth between them, lean out the window. I ask them about grizzly bears. They tell me this is where they airlift the trouble-making grizzlies from the more inhabited parts. "What about cougars?" I ask. "Yep, lots of 'em," they reply. "This is the Rockies, lady, what do you expect?"

So, with bear bells dangling and bear spray on my belt, we head to Tulameen. The rain returns and we don our beloved Valhalla rain gear. The creek runs on our left through the tall, dry grasses of the deserted fields. We have the unnerving sense that there is another presence with us today. Perhaps it is the ghosts of the community that was once alive here, with horse and buggies carrying families to their homesteads or wagons full of miners returning from a day's work in the nearby mine. Whatever it is, it sends a bit of a chill through us as we

---

We sit on the steps of the Coalmont Hotel in this near ghost town before walking on to Tulameen.

walk the deserted rail line to Tulameen. Small piles of stones line the overgrown trail, another reminder of the backbreaking work of the early rail workers. Heike picks up some more railway spikes to add to her 'juggables' as we walk along in unsettled silence.

We arrive at a small rock dump where a man is digging with a piece of heavy machinery. Nora and I scramble over the rocks to ask him how far we are from Tulameen. "Where am I?" I shout, over the grinding of the machine. He corrects me. "Where are you at?…Tulameen." So, this is it. Tulameen. We walk on for another two kilometres to the village centre where Billy is waiting. We are starving and spread out our usual bread and cheese. I scour the Kettle Valley book to make a plan. Will we stay at the Coalmont Hotel all night? Will we continue on to Hope? We are wet from the rain and the decision to drive to Hope is unanimous.

(from Heike's diary)
After our hike, we have a long drive to Hope, a place name I just love. "Last gas station east of Hope." Our drive is broken up by our visit to a farm market, and, thanks to an urgent call from Nora's bladder, a very pleasurable stroll through an old-growth cedar grove in Manning Park. The spot is hidden from the main road, so we were lucky to discover it.

When we arrive in Hope, we find that we don't care much for pitching our tents and being cold and miserable all night, so we splash out on two rooms at the Flamingo. This motel has self-catering units, so Chris and I are able to treat our co-travelers to a feast of stuffed green peppers and pasta and sauce, which go down well, once it is ready. Cooking with Chris is a lot of fun and makes my last supper duty a very satisfactory one.

August 19

Hope
Distance: 17.5 km
Wildlife: mad dogs

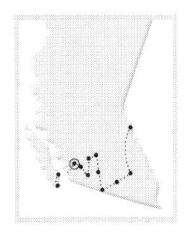

It is strange waking up in a bed. For so many mornings, my focus has been on the blue ceiling of our tent. Maria scrambles up some eggs as I do up a batch of toast. Today's hike will be in the Quintet Tunnels, also known as the Othello Tunnels, overlooking the Coquihalla Canyon. This section of the Kettle Valley Railway cost $85,000/kilometre to construct with avalanches and mud slides wiping out large sections every year. Andrew McCulloch, an experienced railway engineer, devised the plan for the four tunnels and two bridges that pierce the canyon to be opened in 1914. These tunnels were part of the setting for the movie *First Blood*, starring Sylvester Stallone as Rambo. We decide to stage our own version of this movie in these famous tunnels. I dig out headbands for everyone and we dress in our gang clothes with sunglasses, black shirts and face paint. I tuck into my belt the toy gun that we found on the trail in another province. Angus MacKinnon, owner of the Pink Flamingo, escorts us to where the hike will begin. Seven kilometres from the Othello Tunnels we are dropped off by Billy and Angus. Billy will wait for us back at the hotel. It is a cool day after the rain, with a dark, threatening sky. With the bear spray and gun slipped onto my belt, bear bells jingling on our packs, we set out along the dirt road that leads to the tunnels.

As we walk along the lonely road, we notice an old building surrounded by an overgrowth of alders. In the cobwebbed window are rows of telegraph insulators. It has been my quest since the beginning of our venture to find an old insulator on the trail. Despite finding many other railway artifacts, I have not spotted an insulator until this moment. As we move closer to the building, we notice that a high fence topped with barbwire surrounds the entire property. The gate is secure with a thick chain and padlock. A bold sign reading 'Private Property' warns us to keep away. Failing to see the 'Trespassers will be Shot' sign, the temptation to secure an insulator overcomes me and I approach the fence. There is not a hint of life on the property, so I scale the fence and drop into the forbidden territory. To my delight, there is a pile of coloured insulators lying next to the building. Surely, they won't miss just one. After all, these are stolen goods from the CPR. How can you report that someone has stolen your stolen goods? I weakly convince myself. With my scary Rambo outfit on, who would dare to confront me?

So, nabbing a nice green insulator, I make a run for the gate. Too late. Lights in an old pick up truck that is parked by the dilapidated

"Rambi" scales the rock face with the stolen goods in tow.

trailer come on. The truck edges toward the shed as I scramble over the gate. Frantically, I ask Chris, who has been waiting on guard, to help me to conceal my goods. There is no time, so he drops the insulator into his open camera case. An irate, weasel-like woman springs from the truck. Strangled hair flows around her face as she screams hysterically at me. "This is private property, you know, who do you think you are? This is none of your business here"…and on and on.

Like a dog with his tail between his legs, I tell her that I am sorry and that we are only taking pictures. This doesn't do. She screams louder, and then begins searching for what might be missing. She is enraged and on the verge of hysteria. We hustle away, hair standing up on the back of our necks. With a constant glance over our shoulders for the truck to start advancing on us and the woman to start shooting, we are now pounding down the road. Guard dogs, now awake, bark and froth behind the wire fence. "What are they hiding?" we wonder as we hurry along in giddy fear. So Rambo, who began the day in strong toughness, is dubbed 'Rambi,' a fearful cowardice.

When we are at a safe distance, we begin our movie plans. Maria rubs paint from the rocks onto our cheeks. An interested tourist wanting to be in on the fun asks to be painted, too. We tell her she can be an extra in our movie. Our first pictures are down by the river where large boulders and driftwood provide the backdrop. We hang from the stones and suspend ourselves from the large logs. We enter the first tunnel where headbands are converted to face masks for the 'Billy Miner' train hold-up. The water roars below us in the Coquihalla Canyon. Many years ago, Andrew McCulloch, the railway engineer, had been lowered over these same slippery walls of rock in a basket to survey this spot. He was to decide if a train bridge could actually be built here. It is hard to believe that he actually decided in the positive. Moss now grows over the tunnel walls where once trains ran twice a

Michael, Darlene and Sydney Worthylake in Chilliwack.

day. I am told that the trains only ran in the dark so that passengers couldn't see the drop below and wouldn't be so afraid.

We exit the tunnel into the sprinkling rain. The path leading back to Hope is canopied with tall cedars and huge maples. Billy is waiting for us at the Flamingo, where we are offered another night's accommodation. We appreciate this generous offer, but we have plans to stay with Billy's sister Sue and her husband, Byron Worthylake, in Chilliwack.

Sue and Byron are waiting when we arrive. Their ranch-style home is set in a garden of tall flowers and ornamental trees with a backdrop of mountains in the distance. Inside, the table is laden with food for us: corn, potato salad, barbecued salmon, and blueberry pie. It is a feast. Sue's fresh homemade rolls taste like those Aunt Erma, her mom, would make. The couple is happy to reunite with Billy. Sue and Byron's sons, Michael and David, and their wives Darlene and Cindy, arrive to greet us. We retire to the big comfortable living room to chat and sing. Nora entertains on her fiddle and Maria and Heike join her for some songs. To their delight, Chris warms up the bagpipes for some Scottish tunes. Neighbours drop by to wish us well. We feel comfortable here in the home of our relatives. Tonight we will sleep in real beds, mine with cool silk covers. How luxurious it is in this big bed in a room to myself.

August 20

Victoria
Distance: 19 km
Wildlife: geese, rabbits, ducks, blackberries

(from Nora's diary)
We are leaving Sue and Byron's house in Sardis, where we were treated to decadent meals, warm beds and stories.

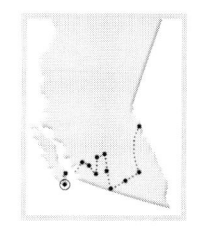

These are some of the nicest people I have ever met. They are so down to earth. Michael and his daughter Sydney arrive to say goodbye, as does Richard, the next-door neighbour. David decides to drive with Sue to the ferry to see us off to Vancouver Island. On the ferry, I listen intently to David as he tells us about his job as a security guard in a prison. On the island, we say goodbye to Sue and David, after trying to kidnap them and take them with us.

Once we reach our campground in Victoria, we go on a search for the Galloping Goose Trail. We stroll along a path by the harbour where geese are floating in the still water. Sweet, ripe blackberries fall onto our path and we stop and consume the irresistible fruit. We eventually find the Galloping Goose Trail, which is a paved rollerblading, biking path that runs through the forest to Victoria. Blackberries droop over the high stone walls and we stop frequently, with Iain even filling his water bottle with the luscious berries.

Back at the campsite, we approach to the sound of Nicholas and Billy laughing. They are in the midst of a crib game, Nicholas with his hot chocolate and Billy with his Kokanee beer.

I put chicken, potatoes and carrots and Sue's green beans on the camp stove to cook as we sample some Chilean wine. The wine sampling leads our attention to some extended trail talk and away from the burning pots. Supper consists of chicken, green beans, potatoes and some wonderful caramelized carrots.

(from Nora's diary)
Today is our second last hiking day. It is kind of hard to comprehend. For the last few days I have been feeling excited about going home, getting my bedroom decorated, buying food and putting it into a fridge…even studying. This morning, however, I woke up to pee and got a terrible twinge of sadness. It came to me all at once, this weight, and it hasn't left me since. It just doesn't feel right to end yet. When will I ever hear Billy calling out into the tent, "Is anybody up in there?" again, or double over with laughter at supper because Heike cracked a joke, or have Iain running around making drinks and giving us special 'Valley Boy' treats, or hear Chris' bagpipes, or Mom and Billy's 'All Aboard!!' or have that constant 'thump, thump, thump' of Nicholas trying to break his record hacks with the soccer ball, or Maria massaging feet in the van…and all the people who joined us or who we met. They all offered something so totally individual and special. Maybe I will have this all again. But, it will never be the same feeling. It could never have

Sue Worthylake and her son David accompany us to Victoria.

the same meaning. This is a once-in-a-lifetime thing, and how lucky I am to be a part of it.

And how fortunate I am that I have a mother who gets these crazy dreams, which are to most, including myself, so unbelievably outrageous that they seem impossible. Yet, she does them. She just says, 'alright, I'm going to do it' and it gets done. We all put our total trust in her abilities. Every day, I just jump into 'my seat' (how protective I have become of my spot) in the Hike 2000 van, and trust that mom will know where to go and that Billy will get us there safely. None of us would be here were it not for her persistence and dedication. Even someone on the trail that we've never met before quit his job and joined the bandwagon, not knowing what was in store for him. What an influence! I just hope that some of whatever she has is genetic.

August 21

Victoria
Wildlife: rabbits, blue herons, Canada geese

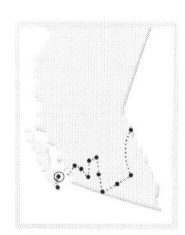

I look around me in the early hours of the morning. The sleeping bodies are next to me, legs twisted out of their sleeping bags in the warmth. On the far side, on her self-inflating mattress, is Heike. Her blue scarf is wrapped around her trail pals, which lie close to her pillow. I am so glad she stayed with us to the end. Next to her is Nora, her long, curly, brown hair spread around her face as she sleeps. She has worked so faithfully on the website, in such diverse conditions without complaint. Without her, I would never have been able to maintain the web pages that keep everyone informed of our whereabouts. She senses my concerns and, with her arm over my shoulder, gives me the strength to keep going. By my side is Maria. She has suffered with a knee problem since the beginning but has walked on cheerful and without complaint, faithful to the finish. She is cuddled against Nora's back now, as they did when they were very little girls. In the other tent is Nicholas, that witty little boy who has grown higher than my head in these few months. I think how lucky I am to have children who support me and make my cause their own. We have had moments on the trail when we can no longer walk because of hilarious laughter. We have shared times of grief and held people we have met for the first time as close as family as they poured out their stories to us. The emotions that we have shared are strong and come straight from our souls. They have spilled over onto those in our path. We have been blessed with a warmth from total strangers who have cared for our needs as we make our way across the country.

I slowly crawl from the tent. Billy is perking the morning coffee over the fire. I try not to reveal the emotion that is sweeping through me as I brace myself for this, our last day to hike. There are certain ingredients that will make this day complete. We need a hike long enough to reach our goal of 2000 kilometres and a beach where we can walk into the Pacific Ocean. Island View Camping is located near the Galloping Goose Trail and has a long stretch of beach. It will be perfect.

I walk over to the tourist information of this campground and check my email on their computer. I read the ton of email we have received congratulating us on reaching the end of our journey. As I sit with my back to the tourists milling around me, tears run down my cheeks. It is so heartwarming to have all these people who we only met for a day, and many we have never met, send us their wishes. I feel overwhelmed with this outpouring from people who have been following us on the web pages across the country.

"We, the members of the Lions Club at Elphinstone have been following you right to the end. This was a tremendous achievement. Once again, you have to be commended on your fortitude, your courage, your endurance….what else can I say. Congratulations to you and the whole group."
Walter Kiliwnik, Elphinstone, Manitoba

"I just finished reading your last journal entries, and I can hardly make out the letters on the keyboard for the tears in my eyes. It was so thrilling to know that you made it all the way, and so sad to know that it is over. You all deserve hearty pats

on the back for your commitment and strength of will, not to mention the great personalities that kept you all so close to one another all along the way."
Charlotte Allen, Ottawa, Ontario

"Congratulations on completing your cross-Canada tour. I have really enjoyed your diary entries and looking at the photos on your website. It was almost as good as knocking around with you."
Bob Diamond, Steady Brook, Newfoundland

"Congratulations. That was an amazing feat! I have been following your journals for the past months and I am sure this has taken much determination and hard work, not only in the travel, but also the planning and navigating. Your adventures are motivational and inspiring."
Kelly Hryhorchuk, Red River North, Manitoba

" Way to go! I'm sure these final days have been full of emotional events as you marvel/delight/dread/ saying goodbye to this adventure and head back to the real world. I bet you wondered at times if this day would ever arrive. You made it and by the sounds of things, in fine form. Cheers! And remember, beautiful Nova Scotia awaits you!"
Jan and Eric Boutlier, Nova Scotia

"I am so impressed. Even through the heat and cold and rain and lightening, I am really envious of you; not to mention awestruck at the magnitude of your trek. What an amazing journey you've had!
Rob Lutz, Nova Scotia

We pack up and head out to Island View Camping. One last time, Billy yells out, "Everyone got their bins ready?" We pile into the van and drive up the coast to our new camping spot. Then slowly, very slowly we begin to pull on our boots. We linger, prolonging the end. The road leads up from the Island View Campground past long farm fields. We join the old rail line, which cuts through acres of fresh produce. Harvesters, wearing large-brimmed sun hats, are busy in the fields, carrying baskets of carrots and greens. We stop for lunch on the edge of one of the fields and pass around our ritualistic bread and cheese. This time, we have chosen Edam.

The trail then takes us into a residential area where the perfectly

Hiking the Dream

groomed lawns border our path. For long sections we stroll through wooded areas where trees arch high above our heads, giving us shade from the hot sun. We stop at a little ice cream shop for a treat and continue on until we spy our precious van. Billy is waiting for us with outstretched arms. He has had to find a detour today as the bridge is out on the trail. Billy gives us each a big hug before we get into the van. We still have three kilometres to go before we reach our goal but we have saved them for the beach. We stop to pick up supper food on the way to the campground then go directly to the beach.

It is time to make these final steps. I had never dreamed it would be this emotional. So quietly we walk. We are so solemn as we make our way up the beach that is strewn with driftwood. Other vacationers are sitting in the sun or strolling along the sand. None of them are aware of the significance of these steps for us. Nora and I need to make a pit stop. We rush ahead, telling the others to wait. At the far end of the beach is another campground. As we frantically look for a washroom, two campers begin talking to us. We explain to them about our journey and they pump us with questions. We edge away from them and rush to the 'Johnny on the Spots' that are lined by the campground entrance. We each choose one, side by side. In seconds, I hear the high-pitched warning beep of a truck backing up. The sound gets closer and closer. My worst fears are realized. They have come to pick up the toilets and take them away. 'Nora, Nora, hurry,' I warn. Some things you just can't rush and I watch them begin loading the portable toilets, starting—thankfully—at the other end. We can't believe our luck. I can hear Nora laughing from within her cubicle as I think of ways that I can deter the work crew. In time, Nora appears and we retreat to find the others who have been waiting patiently for us.

Back across the warm sand, we begin our ceremonial walk up the beach. It is so moving. We join hands and begin to repeat the words to "Last Mile of the Way," which we have sung so many times over the past months. This is our last mile and as we near the water, we can see Billy waiting for us. This has been a monumental journey for him too and now he shares our anguish, knowing that these few steps mark the end to our great trek together.

Our boots, hiking sticks and packs are piled together on the sand as our scrawny bare feet, white from four months of being boot clad, make their way to the water. Chris has brought his bagpipes to the

> We stroll along the canopied trail, treasuring these last moments together.

beach and he warms them up preparing for this final serenade. We enter the Pacific, the cold water sending pains to our knees. With ceremonial pictures taken by Iain, we come back up on the sand and sit together on the driftwood. It is as though we want to hang on to these precious moments together and as soon as one of us gets up to leave, it will mark the end. The setting sun warms our faces and we think how perfect this has been. We have done it, from beginning to end, and here we are now, with no boots on, no 'clicker,' and no hiking sticks. It has been such a moving journey for us. We have shared so much laughter, talk, song, tears and jokes. It is a sentiment that no one else can share. The bonds that have grown between all of us, we will never forget. It is truly a perfect ending.

I remain on the beach watching the pale blue Pacific waters roll and retreat from the shore. Chris is playing his bagpipes far down the beach now, standing among the mounds of bleached driftwood. Soon the sun sinks below the horizon sending a pink glow over the water. Billy builds a big fire and evening birds make their way up the beach. A large flock of Canada geese, making their way south, flies overhead. Their voices fill the air. I think how they too are flying home. I make my way back to the campsite, carrying my hiking boots in my hand.

Changed into some warmer clothes now, I return to the beach. Nora is playing her fiddle, with the sun long gone from the sky. Silhouettes of campers dancing to her waltzes can be seen on the water's edge. They don't venture near and have no idea who we are or why we are here. Some watched us walk into the ocean to the sounds of the bagpipe, but no one questioned our ceremony. Iain and Maria arrive on the beach with a platter of hors d'oeuvres. They are baking a stuffed salmon on the fire. They return with corn and potatoes wrapped in tinfoil and a special shrimp salad. In the darkness, with flashlights tucked under their chins, crossing obstacles of driftwood, they return time after time to the beach, serving us appetizers and main course dishes. As a grand finale, our dessert appears from the coals on the fire. Cake cooked inside complete orange peels has been hiding for our surprise. It is delicious. I can't believe their persistence with this meal.

During this procedure, we have been treating ourselves to some good wine and spirits. Billy, who has been saving a little cache of rum for a special occasion, has brought it to the beach. He stands up and shakes my hand. 'I never thought we'd make it,' he says "But, now, I'm going to shake your hand." To top off this perfect evening together on the beach, a large orange moon appears on the horizon of the water, sending its glow in a stream of light to us. It is our moon, our night, and these are our final moments together.

Nora, Heike, Maria, Iain and Chris decide to spend the night on the beach and go to fetch their sleeping bags. I feel my way back over the driftwood in the darkness to our campsite. As I crawl through the flap in the tent, for the last time, I can hear a train in the distance. It is my good luck train. I drift asleep alone in the tent. It has been an unbelievable day, an incredible journey.

Our final steps on this long trek are into the Pacific Ocean.

Interviews:

Garnet Buell, Murray River, PE, May 28, 2000; Robert Burfoot, Winnipeg, MN, July 12, 2000; Violet and John Cameron, Railway History. Tape, July 23, 2000; Erwin Canam. Upper Kent, NB, June 14, 2000; Kaye Carter, Port aux Basques, NF, September 2000; Ira Corkum, Guysborough, NS, May 23, 2000; David Davis, Port aux Basques, NF, May 16, 2000; Walter DeLong, Fredericton, NB, June 12, 2000; Iain Dunlop, Upper Kent, NB, June 13, 2000; Julie Easley, Fredericton, NB, June 10, 2000; Tom Easley, Fredericton, NB, June 10, 2000; John Gosse, Whitbourne, NF, May 7, 2000; Brian Griffin, Elmira, PE, May 31, 2000; Ron Kelly, Howley, NF, May 8, 2000; Lawrence Kosedy, Melville, SK, July 23, 2000; Paul Lautard, Rhone Creek, BC, August 14, 2000; James LeFresne, Tatamagouche, NS, May 26, 2000; Mark Lockholzer, Melville, SK, July 23, 2000; Glen MacLean, Melville, SK, July 23, 2000; John MacLean, PE, June 6, 2000 ; Steven McCrum, Buffalo Pound, SK, July 28, 2000; Myles Meed, Bristol, NB, June 14, 2000; James Morrison, Boisedale, NS, May 19, 2000; Helen Murphy, Elmira, PE, May 31, 2000; Curtis Payment, Melville, SK, July 23, 2000; Ed Shanks, Melville, SK, July 23, 2000; Nick Slobojan, Melville, SK, July 23, 2000; Earl Symonds, Sandy Lake, MN, July 18, 2000; Walter Syslak, Clanwilliam, MN, July 16, 2000; Trevor Townsend, Fox Harbour, NS, May 24, 2000; Perry Young, Howley, NF, May 9, 2000

Bibliography

Fulford, Hazel. *When Trains Stopped In Dinorwic*. Thunder Bay, ON: Singing Shield Productions, 1990.
Halliday, Hugh A. *Wreck! Canada's Worst Railway Accidents*. Toronto, ON: Robin Brass Studio, 1997.
Johnson, Brian D. *Railway Country*. Toronto, ON. Key Porter Books Ltd, 1985.
Kearley, Wade. *The People's Road*. St. John's , Newfoundland, Harry Cuff Publications Ltd, 1995.
Langford, Dan & Sandra. *Cycling the Kettle Valley Railway*. Calgary, AB. Rocky Mountain Books, 1994.
Liddell, Ken. *I'll Take the Train*. Saskatoon, SK. Western producer Prairie Books, 1966.
Lingard, Mont. *Next Stop: Gaff Topsail*. Grand Forks-Windsor, NF. Mont Lingard Publishing, 1996.
Lingard, Mont. *Next Stop: St. John's*. Grand Forks-Windsor, NF. Mont Lingard Publishing, 1999.
Lingard, Mont. *Next Stop: Wreckhouse*. Grand Forks-Windsor, NF: Mont Lingard Publishing, 1997.
Richard, Serge and Phil Latulippe. *L'homme qui est allé au bout des routes*. Ottawa, ON: Arion, 1995.
Turcott, Agnes W. *Land of the Big Goose*. Wawa, ON: Alec Wilson Publications, 1962.
Turner, Robert D. *Steam on the Kettle Valley*. Victoria, BC: Sono Nis Press, 1995.
Woods, Shirley E. *Cinders & Saltwater*. Halifax, NS: Nimbus Publishing Ltd, 1992.

British Columbia

List of Contributors to the Hike 2000 Auction

Betty Belmore
Brier Island Whale Watch
Canadian Tire
Captain Cox Whale Watch
Chilkoot Pass
Citadel Inn
Courthouse Hill Farms
Coyote Hill Golf
Dalplex
Dave Whitney's Antiques
John Didkowsky
Discovery Centre
Foley House Inn
The Great Maritime Scallop Trading Co.
Thomas and Beverly Grove
Horne's Auto
Hot Toddy
Indoor Adrenalin
Barbie Jollota
Just Us
Kennetcook Home Hardware
The Left Bank
Loomis & Tole's
Mahon's Warehouse
Mersey River Chalets
Kevin Neil
New World Marble

Northumberland College
Nova Scotia Crystal
Personal Image
P'lovers
The Press Gang
Bonnie Price
Rainbow Farms
Riverview Herbs
ROW
Sackville Veterinary
Saint Mary's University
Sam the Record Man
Schooner Books
Scotia Paddle and Scull
Shubenacadie River Runners
Ski Wentworth
Stern's Mansion Inn
The Sun Room
Susanne's Weavery
Sykea Hair
TAZ Music Store
Terranita B&B
Thumpers
Top Cuts
Woozles Books
Zwickers Gallery